Schemas in the Early Years

Evolved through conversations with key early childhood education experts, *Schemas in the Early Years* focuses on the value of 'repeated patterns' of action or 'schemas' in young children's play. It stimulates readers to ask questions of themselves, to watch children closely, and to create a dialogue with parents and other educators as well.

Contributors to this fascinating book discuss their observation of children in naturalistic situations when they are deeply involved in play and identify topics or themes that can be linked to and inspire professional development opportunities. This book provides an antidote to beginning with the curriculum rather than the child and really considers children as learners. Each chapter focuses on young children and schemas, considering a wide age range from babies to children attending statutory schooling.

Schemas in the Early Years is an accessible and inspiring text and serves as essential reading for educators wanting to think further and in more depth about schemas. Newcomers to schema theory or anyone currently using schema theory to understand children will also find these enquiries useful.

Cath Arnold is an early years consultant associated with the Pen Green Research Base, Corby, UK.

Schemas in the Early Years

Exploring Beneath the Surface Through Observation and Dialogue

The Pen Green Schema Group, Edited by Cath Arnold

Routledge
Taylor & Francis Group

LONDON AND NEW YORK

Cover image: © Jan White, with kind permission from Childspace Early Learning Centres

First published 2023
by Routledge
4 Park Square, Milton Park, Abingdon, Oxon OX14 4RN

and by Routledge
605 Third Avenue, New York, NY 10158

Routledge is an imprint of the Taylor & Francis Group, an informa business

British Library Cataloguing-in-Publication Data
A catalogue record for this book is available from the British Library

Library of Congress Cataloging-in-Publication Data
A catalog record has been requested for this book

ISBN: 9781032123950 (hbk)
ISBN: 9781032123967 (pbk)
ISBN: 9781003224341 (ebk)

DOI: 10.4324/9781003224341

Typeset in Bembo
by Apex CoVantage, LLC

This book is dedicated to Chris Athey, who inspired us to set up our group

Contents

Acknowledgements

Thanks to all of the children, families and educators who have contributed so much rich information to this book.

A special thanks goes to Kerry McNulty and Tracy Studders for their contributions to Chapter 5.

With great thanks to the people and settings from New Zealand, Denmark, Switzerland and the UK whose photographs so richly illuminate the text of Chapter 8.

I would like to acknowledge the contributions of Zoe Austin and Antonio Griffiths-Murru who brought children firmly into the centre of my chapter (10) with insight, knowledge and respect. I would like to thank the children, families and staff team at Kingsley Special Academy, Kettering for all their continuing support, guidance and inspiration.

Thanks to the Pen Green Research Base for hosting our meetings prior to Covid restrictions and to Menna Godfrey and Christina Macrae for hosting zoom meetings for the group.

Introduction

Cath Arnold

This book has come about as a result of a group of professionals wanting to understand more about young children's development, learning, thinking and emotions, particularly in relation to 'schemas' or 'repeated patterns of action'. A chance conversation between Jan White and I at a European Conference in 2016 resulted in us arranging to meet up at Pen Green twice a year from then on and inviting other people interested in 'schemas'. Our focus during those meetings was learning from video observations of young children with what we knew about 'schemas' in mind (Athey, 2007). I described to Jan, on that occasion, how useful our sessions with Chris Athey had been in terms of professional development and understanding each child's development and learning. Chris would travel up to Pen Green for one or two days, and a group of practitioners would meet with her. We would each bring a five-minute video clip of a child deeply involved in self-chosen play (Laevers, 1997). There would usually be six or seven people who were pedagogical leads or senior staff. We would watch each clip and Chris would make notes in her tiny handwriting. A discussion would follow and everyone's views were listened to. We would spend a whole day watching and discussing four or five clips. Sadly, Chris Athey died in 2011, so this book is a homage to her and the study that she and Tina Bruce were involved in during the early 1970s, The Froebel Early Education Project, and which resulted in the seminal text *Extending Thought in Young Children: A Parent-Teacher Partnership*.

Times have changed in relation to publications about schemas! Chris Athey told me that schemas were not a popular topic at the time of their study and that she was not allowed to use the term 'schemas' in the title of her seminal text *Extending Thought in Young Children: A Parent-Teacher Partnership* (1990). When Sage published *Understanding Schemas and Emotion in Early Childhood* by Arnold and the Pen Green Team in 2010, Chris congratulated me on getting schemas into the title of the book. Although times have changed, as the inclusion of the word schemas in titles testifies, to many people schemas are still not in common currency. Some practitioners seem to attribute negative connotations to schemas, and, even in deciding on a name for this book and interpretations/definitions of schemas within these authors, there are differences in interpretation and concerns about alienating readers.

DOI: 10.4324/9781003224341-1

As a teacher and researcher, Chris Athey was interested in what young children 'can do' so there was no deficit thinking in her world. Chris Athey became a personal friend to me, and I was honoured to write an article for the *Nursery World (NW)* about Chris, as a pioneer in early education, with her co-operation, in 2005. I was also invited to speak at her funeral, which again, was a great honour. To quote from the *NW* article: 'Chris has an amazing way of working combining rigour, enthusiasm and genuine curiosity. She has a way of communicating that never diminishes the learner's knowledge' (Arnold, 2005).

So, as a result of Jan's conversation with me, we formed the Pen Green Schema Group. Our focus is very much learning from each other and from the children we view on film and discuss. Pen Green staff's experience of working with Chris Athey engendered a spirit of openness and curiosity that we have tried to retain and build on. A range of interested people with experiences of the early years and an interest in schemas have attended, and discussions have been lively. This group is ongoing and evolving over time. Our thinking is that the children's learning and our own learning is 'imminent', that is, never static and always emerging – constantly becoming. Learning is not something that can be pinned down or ticked off.

During 'lockdown', we could only meet online, so we decided to produce a book based on many of our conversations. Group members are finding it important to collectively share thinking that appreciates and encourages different viewpoints without collapsing into an orthodoxy. The group is about affirming common interests, but at the same time offering a space where different perspectives can be shared. Not everyone was available to write a chapter, so we are grateful to all of the people, who have attended the group seminars, and especially those who have become involved in this book.

Most of the group involved in writing this book currently work with adults, and we are, therefore, familiar with the type of questions adults ask when learning about young children's *development and learning*, especially with regard to schemas. So, in this book, we seek to explore some of the topics we, and some of the adult learners we work with, are curious about.

Athey's seminal text was first published in 1990, and although still relevant and influential, there are some aspects we might talk about differently 50 years after the study. For example, I no longer talk about the 'levels' at which schemas are explored. Athey (2007: 117–119) describes 'motor level' (learning through actions); 'symbolic representation level' (when one thing stands for another); 'functional dependency relationship' (the outcome being dependent on the action, a little like cause and effect); 'thought level' (when children can talk about something 'in the absence of concrete reminders'). I recognise these ways of schemas being explored but no longer believe that learning is linear or that expressing the ways as a kind of 'hierarchy' is helpful. Additionally, Chris very much focused on the cognitive development of the children in the study rather than their emotional development, although some of her examples could lend themselves to an insight into emotional development, for example, Lois, 'who drew her brother, Jock, in his cot . . . covered her drawing with a blanket (sticky paper) and said "And I'll put the cot in a cupboard [pause] and I'll put the cupboard in a cave"' (1990: 151). We could deduce that Lois may have been expressing an unconscious desire to get rid of her brother. It was not that Chris did not see those connections, but she chose not to comment on them, instead noticing how frequently Lois was 'enveloping' with different content in her play. Chris Athey was, however, an adviser to me when I studied 'schemas and emotions' for my PhD and she read the resulting book and commented on it:

> I loved everything about it . . . the repetition of 'cognition' and then 'affect' meant that the reader was able to concentrate on the individual content of separate examples. . . . Many of your examples are quite wonderful. There is sufficient untapped data to do an analysis of children's language and the thought it represents. For instance on p. 114 'Sharks are "at" Scotland' rather than 'in' . . .
>
> 'At' being at the end of a trajectory and 'in' to do with containment . . .
>
> I love the way in which you opened the door for future books . . . 'action schemas and metaphor'.
>
> (Athey, 2010, personal correspondence)

I am sure Chris would have loved this project, and I am proud to be taking forward the work on 'Schemas and Metaphor' as well as other aspects.

Each chapter begins with a short account of how the author(s) first came across 'schemas' as we think of them now. After much debate, we decided to refer to all early years workers as 'educators' unless, like Pen Green Nursery, they used a particular title that was important to the staff. For example, at Pen Green, teachers and nursery nurses in the nursery spaces are referred to as family workers, in order to emphasise equality and also the work with children and their families.

Chapter 1 is written by Julie Brierley and Julie focuses on 'treasure basket play', analyzing a set of observations with schemas in mind. Julie has become very interested in the youngest children and demonstrates, as Athey did with 2–5-year-olds, what these very young children 'can do and understand'.

Chapter 2 is the study of one child's play from 19–22 months. The author, Colette Tait, is Ezra's grandmother and shows the insights gained from observing her very precious grandson during the time she spent with him, as well as drawing on his own parents' reflections and his nursery educators' observations. Ezra is my great-grandson and I, too, draw on some nursery observations of Ezra in Chapter 5 when thinking about 'schemas and metaphor'.

In Chapter 3, Amanda Thomas presents observations of one boy with a dominant rotating schema and shows how that became important when planning for supporting his learning. Amanda also shares important information on introducing schemas to educators for the first time.

Chapter 4 is written by Emma Hewitt. Her focus is 'schemas and language'. Emma explores the idea of 'schematic pedagogy' first coined by Atherton and Nutbrown. Emma and the educators involved focus on 'tuning in' to children's conceptual concerns. Emma presents four case studies and makes emotional as well as cognitive links.

The topic explored in Chapter 5, by Cath Arnold and Sue Gascoyne, is 'schemas as emotional metaphors'. As well as considering the embodied nature of learning, they give a short account of the literature on metaphor. Cath and Sue offer examples of children's play that give clues about what children may be feeling and how they express those feelings through metaphor.

In Chapter 6, Kate Barker writes about 'schemas and gender', a topic that has fascinated many educators and parents over the years. Over a decade ago, Kate observed the play of four boys over a period of 3 months and engaged in discussions with their parents and educators. Kate brings this topic up to date with recent thinking about gender and schema.

Tamsin Grimmer and Sue Gascoyne write about 'schemas and autism' in Chapter 7. Rather than viewing schematic play as an indication of autism, they consider how the play is benefitting children on the autistic spectrum. Tamsin and Sue regard all behaviour as communication, and the play of a small number of children on the spectrum is analysed to try to ascertain what they might be communicating and the adult's role in noticing and supporting these needs.

The final three chapters go further in challenging our thinking and understanding. In Chapter 8, Jan White considers how landscape and embodiment perspectives add to understandings about 'schemas' by exploring the intriguing correlation between several commonly seen schematic behaviours and basic landscape elements. Jan suggests that common schematic behaviours might be building brain/body architecture for organising sensory information generated by movement and action in the environment so that they may comfortably exist, think and operate in the world.

Chapter 9, authored by Christina Macrae, challenges the reader to consider schema-play from a Froebelian and post-human perspective, considering the role of play materials in attracting children to engage with them. Christina's chapter will make the case that when children engage in schema-play, this is a world-making rather than a world-discovering form of action.

Christine Parker, in Chapter 10, opens up the dialogue about the relevance of schema theory when working with children further up the education system. Christine, alongside teacher colleagues, explores the relevance of an understanding of schema theory for working with older children. This is achieved by sharing narrative observations through focus group discussion.

In the Concluding Thoughts chapter, Cath Arnold and Jan White draw together common threads across the chapters and emphasise the importance of being open to new learning and ways of thinking. This topic holds a fascination for all of the authors of this book. Most of us are left with questions and reflections after observing each child with whom we come into contact. This book is our attempt to be open to young children's behaviours, particularly when they are repeated, and it is by continuing to be curious that we hope to be able to better understand and enable young children's play, learning and emotional wellbeing. What we all share is a recognition that there is something important about children's patterns of repeated behaviour that demands that we, as adults, pay attention to the children's actions and representations.

1 Treasure basket play – learning to move or moving to learn?

Julie Brierley

Discovering schemas

As a mother, a nursery owner and a researcher, my intrigue, excitement and fascination with young children's movement and learning continue to develop.

My University lecturer introduced me to the concept and theory of schema over thirty years ago. As a primary school teacher, I trusted and relied on schema theory. It steered my practice, my understanding and my beliefs around young children's learning. More recently, the experiences gained working with babies and toddlers in a private day nursery reignited my schema passion. Schema theory continues to provide a lens, my window to observe, reflect, question and ponder young children's ongoing fascinations and persistence.

In contrast, I discovered the complex and fascinating concepts of developmental movement patterns more recently due to my own young son's needs. My journey to understanding the importance and complexities of physical development evolved more slowly through my own first-hand experiences as a mother.

Neuroscience confirms bodily movement is central to the building of neurological pathways throughout the body. A rapidly growing bank of evidence reveals the links between physicality, movement and brain development. Yet within our education culture, there remains a belief that intellect is developed through the mind and exists separately from the body. As professionals working with young children, we must be aware of and understand the role 'the body' plays in learning and development. Within paediatric science and other health professionals, such knowledge seems more established. Yet, it appears that within the EYFS framework, the fundamental importance of physical development continues to be underestimated and frequently overlooked.

I am not an expert, just a keen observer who continues to be captivated by young children's thinking and learning. Within this chapter, I want to

---

DOI: 10.4324/9781003224341-2

both highlight and ponder the interdependency between movement and learning. The chapter is based on my observations of Peter, as he eagerly engages in treasure basket play. The observations are followed by my reflective ponderings, that is, my thinking and reflections, as I try to unravel and make sense of Peter's exploits. My intention is to start a conversation, to recognise and question the interdependency between movement and learning.

Treasure basket play

Elinor Goldschmied first conceived the idea of treasure basket play, suggesting that during the few months of a baby's life, when they can sit independently but are not yet mobile, it provides babies with a taste of freedom and independence (Goldschmied and Jackson, 2004).

Filled with everyday household objects made from natural materials with differing textures, temperatures, weight, shape, sounds and tastes, the treasure basket affords a rich sensory play experience. Young babies can investigate the objects at their own pace using the sense of touch, smell, taste (mouthing), sound and movement (shaking, dropping and bashing). Being free to rummage, select and discard objects at will. Whilst needing to be present, the adult should sit quietly and not interfere with the baby's exploration.

Figure 1.1 Peter and his treasure basket

Introducing Peter and the treasure basket

Peter lives at home with his Mum and Dad. He attended nursery for two full days each week. He is brought and collected from nursery each day by his Mum. Once Peter could sit independently, his nursery key worker introduced him to treasure-basket play. The following two observations were recorded 12 days apart by myself, who was the nursery owner.

Observation one: recognising schema

Peter settled quickly; his focus and concentration on the objects within the basket were evident. Peter used both hands to rapidly select and discard objects from the treasure basket; it almost looked like he searched for a particular object. After several minutes he appeared to become distracted. His gaze turned to his key worker; he watched as she welcomed a parent and child into the nursery room.

It was several minutes before his concentration seemed to return to the treasure basket. This time his interest seemed to be with the objects scattered on the floor around the treasure basket. He seemed to gaze at the scattered objects; he then selected a small sphere-shaped shell; holding it in his right hand, he swivelled on his bottom, turning his entire body 180 degrees around from the treasure basket. Selecting a small wicker basket that lay beside him, he appeared to carefully place the shell into the centre of the basket.

Peter then began to select a range of other objects that he had previously discarded from the treasure basket, placing one object at a time into the wicker basket alongside the shell. Peter continued to repeatedly put objects in and then take them out of the basket. Peter's left hand was stretched across the midline of his body, holding the basket, while his right hand selected and controlled the movement of the selected object (Figure 1.2). His care in selecting and placing the objects individually into the basket was evident. His intense concentration on this task lasted for over 12 minutes. As he put an object into the basket, he appeared to smile; as he removed the object, he vocalised with an unrecognisable sound.

Peter eventually indicated his investigations were complete, raising his arms to his key worker as if asking to be picked up. The final collection of objects placed within the basket consisted of the shell, a glass ball, a stone and a sponge.

My reflective ponderings . . .

Sensory play and brain development

We are aware that babies' brains are growing faster than at any other time in their lives and that the baby's brain develops in response to sensory input. As Peter interacts with the treasure basket resources, his brain captures information collected through his senses (touch, smell, taste, hearing, sight and bodily movement). Revisiting and consolidating ideas about this process is essential. It is imperative we fully understand how Peter's sensory experiences with the treasure basket enable him to construct an understanding of the world and his body.

At 10 months old, Peter's brain is only slightly organised; he has billions of neurons present but not yet connected. In simplistic terms, every sensory experience provides an opportunity for the neurons in Peter's brain to connect.

Figure 1.2 Filling the basket

The sensory stimulus provided by his exploration of the treasure basket continues to initiate the neurons in his brain, to connect to other neurons, forming neural pathways. Peter's body (his eyes, ears, taste buds, nose and skin) act as a fine-tuned sensory receptor collecting information from his environment.

Each and every sensory experience provides Peter with a learning opportunity. His whole body behaves as a sensory receptor, providing a sophisticated system for receiving and decoding information from the environment. When he touches an object, he does not touch one thing but two things: the object and his body. Peter's emerging knowledge, thoughts and understanding of the world he lives in are a direct result of the sensory experiences gained through his whole body (Payne and Isaacs, 2008; Hannaford, 2005).

Peter's continued experiences with the treasure basket will strengthen and thicken the neural connections and pathways in his brain. In fact, the richer the sensory environment Peter inhabits, the more intricate his neural networks and patterns of learning will become.

The sensory experiences Peter gains through his whole body initiate thoughts that are his ability to construct a unique understanding of the resources contained within the treasure basket. The process of nerve cells connecting in the brain is, in reality, learning, meaning Peter's active exploits with the treasure basket result in his ability to form thoughts.

As educators, do we recognise this essential early learning? The smiles and squeals of delight, the joy, the ponderings and the excitement as new discoveries are made. This is Peter's way of sharing and narrating his thoughts. How well do we listen?

Forms of thought, recognising schema

Schema theory provides a lens, a window through which to observe, listen, reflect, question and ponder Peter's thoughts and fascinations. Piaget (1936/1953) explained that as babies play, they experience movement, sound, texture, light, pattern, smell and taste. These sensory-motor experiences become mental operations called schemas. Schemas become more complex as babies assimilate further experiences into their existing schema and adjust their current schema to accommodate new experiences. Bruce (2005) explains that schemas are patterns of brain behaviour, which become more complex with development. Both Athey (2007) and Nutbrown (2011) advocate that schemas can be observed in children's play patterns and that children notice elements from their surroundings dependent upon their interests at the time. Identified and nurtured, children's schemas provide intrinsic motivation and continuity for present and future learning opportunities.

Observing and analysing Peter's activities through a schematic lens provides the possibility to make the 'familiar strange', to question and reflect upon his physical actions rather than simply focusing on the *content*. Providing an opportunity to identify possible *forms of thought* revealed through Peter's actions. Some adults may find it difficult to believe that at only 10 months of age, Peter can consciously select resources to meet his interest, his *form of thought*. Yet as Athey (2007), Nutbrown (2011) and Bruce (2005) all pointed out, a child's schema provides an additional awareness to the availability and properties of objects in the environment.

In Peter's case, his interest in placing objects in and out of the basket could be considered as a containing interest. Through his fascination with containing, Peter has become 'sensitised' to the environment, perhaps now even able to discriminate and recognise objects that will feed this form of thought (Atherton and Nutbrown, 2013: 50). It seems appropriate to suggest Peter's ongoing explorations and actions with the treasure basket objects provide evidence of his ability to select appropriate resources to nurture his current interest in containing (Figure 1.3).

It is important to note that to identify a child's schematic interest, the actions and interests would need to be observed in various situations. In this instance, further evidence of Peter's forms of thought (containing interest) were gained through conversations with parents and nursery staff. Figures 1.3 & 1.4 provide evidence of Peter's further containing exploits.

Atherton and Nutbrown (2013: 26) reminds us that looking closely at what children are doing can provide 'insightful views of the subtle, complex details of children's schematic behaviour'. Suggesting it is only through careful observation that we can start to piece together young children's interests and possible thinking.

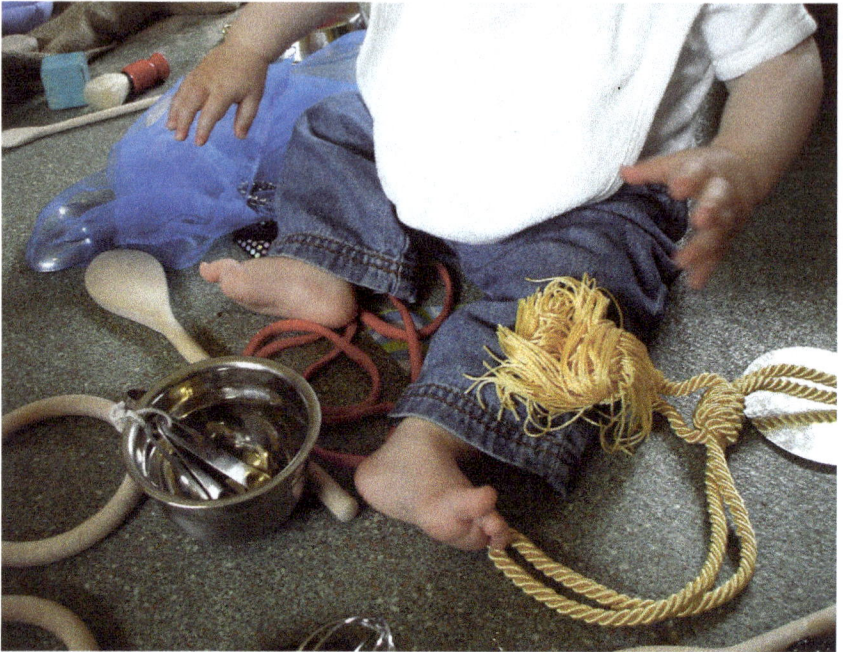

Figure 1.3 Further example of Peter's exploration of containing

Containing and enveloping schemas are believed (Athey, 2007) to assist in developing knowledge of insideness, going through and size. Observing Peter's actions through a schematic lens provides a window to reflect, question and ponder.

We do not know Peter's thoughts, but it seems probable to suggest that such practical endeavours form the foundation of future knowledge and provide an opportunity to 'germinate' (Atherton and Nutbrown, 2013: 49) future understanding of concepts, such as size, width, height, volume, perimeter, distance and circumference. Nutbrown (2011) describes schemas as being at the 'core' of such development when considering young children's cognitive development. Suggesting schemas provide the 'fundamental elements . . . for the process of learning' (46). Could Peter's interest and fascination be connected to the 'insideness' of the basket, the shape and space the object takes when placed inside the basket?

Dexterity and strength . . .

As children grow and develop, the sensory feedback gained through their hands helps shape their cognitive development. This, in turn, promotes the development of neural pathways making the hand and finger movements more regular and controlled (Hannaford, 2005).

Figure 1.4 Peter exploring his containing interest

Following his schematic interest, Peter is intrinsically motivated to explore placing objects in and out of containers. Peter's hands have a high number of sensory receptors, meaning the sensory feedback from this play encourages Peter to practise causing the repeated actions to continue developing muscular strength and control down his arms and eventually reaching the fingertips. The development of muscle control from the centre of the body outwards is described by Maude (2001) and Goddard Blythe (2005) as proximo–distal development.

It is plausible to suggest Peter's schematic interest in containing objects is responsible for reinforcing the neurological development of his hands and fingers and so increases his dexterity and control further. Peter's play requires him to be both 'physically' and 'mentally active' (Atherton and Nutbrown, 2013: 67).

How frequently do we recognise the connections between physical and mental activity?

Observation two: pushing the physical boundaries

Peter was already deeply engaged with his treasure basket play when I arrived. His interest seemed to focus on a small metal bowl; unfortunately, his previous explorations of containing objects into the bowl had inadvertently caused the metal bowl to slide across

Figure 1.5 Reaching out

the carpet away from him. The bowl was now situated out of his reach; however, Peter displayed no hesitation in his industrious endeavours, attempting to stretch out his arms and hands to reach the bowl. Initially, his attempts were unsuccessful; the bowl remained out of his reach and a little distance from him.

Peter showed no outward signs of distress and appeared undeterred by his initial failure in reaching the bowl.

If anything, he seemed to demonstrate an even greater determination and perseverance. He began to gently rock his upper body backwards and forwards, seeming to understand that the forward's movement allowed his outstretched arm to move closer to the bowl. Peter's motivation to reach the bowl was obvious; as he continued to rock his upper body forwards and backwards, he began to twist his upper body further forwards. After a few more attempts, he was able to lean his upper body over his lower limbs. Almost simultaneously, he placed his right hand on the floor as he stretched his left hand towards the bowl. After a couple more attempts, Peter could balance his upper body using his right hand and stretch out his left arm far enough to allow his fingers to make contact with the bowl (Figure 1.5). Peter repeated this movement several times. The excited look on Peter's face and the vocalised squeals suggested that he was very enthusiastic about this new discovery. Peter was able once again to resume his exploration of his containing interest.

My reflective ponderings . . .

Brain and body together

What struck me in this observation is Peter's apparent self-assurance, composure, deep pleasure and persistence. Seemingly Peter's containing schema afforded him the purpose, confidence and motivation to generate new movement possibilities within his body.

Almost through a process of trial and error, I witnessed Peter practising, mastering and integrating the process of embodied learning, the interweaving of his body and his brain. Peter's substantial physical and mental effort to move and balance his upper body highlights the importance of embodied learning. Such essential development must be recognised and valued as a critical part of the learning process (Duncombe and Preedy, 2020). Are we aware of the significance of such early movement opportunities and the importance of not splitting the mind and body into separate entities?

Successful movement requires secure balance, which is dependent on optimal muscle control. Our kinaesthetic sense, the feeling of bodily movement, is maintained through an internal sensory system consisting of the **vestibular system and proprioceptive receptors.**

The **vestibular system** ensures the brain is receptive to incoming sensory stimulus responsible for body orientation and the control of body movement and balance relative to gravity. Connected to every muscle, the function of the proprioceptive receptors is to sense the degree of stretch in a muscle and ensure corrective adjustments maintain balance and equilibrium. As Peter experiences the sensation of touch, the proprioceptors determine the position of his muscles in his body and inform his brain about the body's sense of place in space. In young children, touch to the hands, arms, feet, and face stimulates the growth of sensory nerve endings (Payne and Isaacs, 2008; Hannaford, 2005), helping Peter to grow and connect with his body. Signifying that movement is the result of both physical and mental activity.

Greenland (2000) uses the metaphor of a roadway to help visualise how the neural wiring system is constructed between body and brain. Stressing how the roadway can only be built in response to sensory stimulation and repetitive movement patterns experienced via the body and processed by the brain.

To reach and touch the bowl, Peter's vestibular and proprioceptive senses relayed information to his brain about gravity, motion and his body's muscular movements and position in space. Peter is starting to build a sense of self as his brain and body become interwoven and connected.

As I observed Peter's persistence and determination to reach out for the metal bowl, it felt special, a moment to be celebrated, a moment not to be rushed. Educators must appreciate the importance of integrated brain and body development. Movement stimulates the vestibular system, ensuring that the brain is receptive to an incoming sensory stimulus. If we do not move, the vestibular system is not active, meaning information is not collected (Payne and

Isaacs, 2008; Hannaford, 2005). Neuroscience continues to confirm that brain function and sense of self are one and the same.

Constructing a felt sense of self and body is complex and time-consuming (Goddard Blythe, 2005; Hartley, 2005); we must ask ourselves if *we* give children the required opportunity and time? Or are we guilty of rushing young children and constantly moving them on . . . to crawling, to walking? Critically we must consider if, in fact, we concentrate on the becoming and not the being?

Crucially we must recognise and understand that the neural connections process will be hindered if young children's early bodily movement is not supported or allowed to happen. Underestimating the importance of early movement could result in potential gaps in learning and development for our youngest children.

Repetition and practice . . .

White (2015: 36) suggests that 'movement lies at the heart of learning'. I consider for our youngest children that movement forms the foundation for learning and, importantly, their future school attainment. If children are to get the best start in life and achieve their potential, educators must acknowledge the role early movement has in bringing about the release of **primitive reflexes** and stimulating the emergence of **postural reflexes** (Goddard Blythe, 2005).

Babies have a series of **primitive reflexes** that emerge during life in the womb and equip them to survive following the birthing process. Primitive reflexes should have a limited life span; as the baby's brain function increases, primitive reflexes should withdraw. Movement experiences promote the development of a sophisticated neural pathway inhibiting primitive reflexes. And allowing the emergence of **postural reflexes**, which, together with increased muscular strength, allows the baby to gain greater bodily control (Goddard Blythe, 2005).

The effect of gravity introduces a whole range of challenges when it comes to mastering balance. The Tonic Labyrinthine reflex provides babies with a reflex response to gravity; head movement causes the body to flex or extend. Peter's exploits in stretching and reaching the bowl demonstrate his developing gravitational security, his ability to balance and control his upper body and head position. Postural reflexes are concerned with posture, complex movement and stability. I am not an expert but would suggest Peter's gradual control of placing and holding his head and body in specific positions implies developing a more sophisticated neural structure allowing greater voluntary control to develop.

Tipping his upper body forwards allowed Peter's fingers to touch the metal bowl. Moving his body backwards meant he lost contact with the bowl. In those moments, Peter seemed to be both physically and mentally active. Using his whole body as a sensory receptor to build a sense of balance, a sense of space and a sense of depth, a complex 'felt' sense of the experience (Figure 1.6).

The importance and significance of primitive and postural reflexes should not be underestimated. Recent studies suggest links between retained primitive reflexes and low attainment in reading, writing and spelling in school-aged children. Causing me to ask how much *do we* know about developmental movement patterns?

Figure 1.6 Peter and his ponderings

Reflections and questions

It is essential to acknowledge that pondering and reflecting on children's actions is a fundamental part of practice for all educators. Spending time reflecting and pondering allows an opportunity to think critically and creatively, to interpret and respond to children's actions and voices.

It seems evident that children's individual schematic threads reveal themselves as intrinsic motivation. Peter's schema provided him with the interest and threads of thoughts to motivate his continuous and ongoing explorations and investigations of the treasure basket. As Neisser (1976: 56) concluded, 'schema is not only the plan but also the executor of the plan. It is a pattern *of* action as well as a pattern *for* action'.

To continue his schematic explorations, Peter uses his whole body as a sensory receptor (Hannaford, 2005). Using body movement to explore his schematic interest, Peter opens up his senses, allowing a greater collection of sensory input; his brain and body are becoming interwoven. Allowing him to build a more complex felt sense of self and experiences

(Greenland, 2000; White, 2015). Through the joint action of body movement and thinking, Peter can control his body to balance his upper body and reach out to touch the bowl. It seems Peter's schematic interest is unlocking new opportunities for the collection of sensory input, but without *movement*, Peter's learning potential would be significantly reduced.

For several years, I have held the belief that our society deems children's physicality and movement to be less important than language or mathematical success. I often hear parents telling young children to 'Walk properly! You are big now! You do not need to crawl!' Parents consistently appear pleased when their child has mastered the technique of writing their name but much less impressed when children spend large amounts of time working co-operatively to design and practice a dance or movement routine.

Yet if movement provides the stimulus for new learning, why, as a society, do we not respect, acknowledge and accept the importance of movement in young children's learning?

In an ever-changing world, educators must continue to further their skills and knowledge to meet the needs of the children and families they work alongside. Treasure basket play offers vast potential for nurturing young minds and bodies, providing relevant open-ended activities that involve children creating and seeking their own learning opportunities. Reading about theory and child development is essential for developing knowledge, but done in isolation, it can be a mechanical approach to knowledge development. Without reflection and the opportunity to ponder, our understanding of the interwoven connections between movement and learning will remain difficult, if not impossible, to refine and share.

Recommended reading

Books

Duncombe, R. (2019) *The Physical Development Needs of Young Children*. London: Routledge.

Gascoyne, S. (2012) *Treasure Baskets and Beyond Realizing the Potential of Sensory-rich Play*. Berkshire: Open University Press.

Van Wijk, N. (n.d.) *Getting Started with Schemas Revealing the Wonder-full World of Children's Play*. Christchurch: New Zealand Playcentre Federation.

Websites

Jabadao – National Centre for Movement play. www.jabadao.org/

The Institute for Neuro Physiological Psychology (INPP). www.inpp.org.uk/about-us/

The Pikler approach. www.pikler.co.uk/about

2 Lines and connections everywhere

A possible insight into Ezra Moores' conceptualisation of the world

Colette Tait

Discovering schemas

I first came across schemas when my daughter, Georgia, was in nursery. At the time, Georgia was enjoying a lot of pram pushing and baby games. I'd had my son, Harry, a few months earlier and was myself doing a lot of pram pushing and baby games, which, of course, Georgia was witness to. When the nursery practitioner said to me that Georgia had a transporting and enveloping schema, I think I smiled and nodded and secretly thought, '*no, she hasn't – she's copying me*'. I was a real sceptic to begin with. However, over time, and with lots more examples from nursery that evidenced Georgia's repeated actions of enveloping and transporting with things that she was not doing or seeing at home, I began to change my mind.

Ezra

In this chapter, I hope to convey the utter joy, fascination and delight I experience in Ezra's company, a true companionship in Trevarthen's words (2002). Ezra is currently 24 months old and I am his grandmother, known to Ezra as 'Coco' (far too young to be called anything else). Ezra lives with his mum, Georgia, dad, John and cat, Lola. He also has a close relationship with his grandad, 'Papa'. Within his household, rules are sparse but boundaries are consistent and often pushed by Ezra, as is a toddler's wont! One of his mum's latest Instagram posts was the following, which really sums Ezra up:

> I told Ezra we couldn't go out and jump in the puddles because it was nearly his bedtime, so he went and got mouthfuls of water . . . and made his own puddles to jump in.

DOI: 10.4324/9781003224341-3

Ezra's parents describe him as 'determined, humorous and quietly confident'. They report that he loves a 'social gathering . . . just having everyone around', and that he 'challenges himself . . . he assesses the situation and then attempts things', taking appropriate risks. Georgia said she thinks he is 'quite reflec-tive . . . he always wants to re-visit things', and then considered that perhaps that is because of how we all talk to him. Georgia thinks reflection is impor-tant 'in the context of wanting him to be able to talk about something that's happened, if he wants to'. Ezra is currently exploring a cluster of schemas, including trajectory, connecting, transporting, containing and going through (Athey, 2007).

Schemas are the underpinning to conceptual understanding, and I believe that once this is understood by adults, then the supporting of them becomes much more important and relevant. Athey (2007) tells us that schemas are partial concepts, and I am going to hypothesise and try to illustrate how Ezra's schematic play, which can be seen in his actions, may be creating internalised images in his mind which are supporting him to develop understanding in relation to abstract concepts. Athey (1990: 189) refers to children developing 'mental maps' as a result of their trajectory behaviour. What I am proposing is more akin to Bowlby's notion (1998: 82) of an internal working model, in that children can apply their internalised images to situations and events in other domains. An internalised image is not identical to what has already happened but gives us a propensity to re-experience events and recognise con-ceptual similarities. I propose that these conceptual similarities may be in dif-ferent domains, i.e. intellectual, emotional or relational. As adults, we often use 'metaphor' to illustrate points we wish to make or to explain an abstract concept to one another. Carofiglio (2020) says that 'Metaphor is a form of thinking; it represents the way our mind works in that moment of attempting to extend the realm of knowledge. We use what is known in order to define what we don't yet know and to communicate new discoveries'. In schematic play, children use what they know to extend their 'realm of knowledge'; they repeat actions with different resources in order to find out what happens, assimilating their new knowledge into their existing and 'developing cognitive structures' (Athey, 1990: 33). Between action and partial concept, I am trying to work out what may be going on for Ezra. This is my 'train of thought', a metaphor which has, I hope, given you an image of what I hope to explore in *your* own mind.

This chapter will consider:

- Ezra's cluster of schemas and significant events outside the observation period
- Three observations of Ezra, giving consideration to what he may be learn-ing in the cognitive domain, from his repeated actions
- A conceptually focussed pedagogy
- A line in Ezra's mind.

Ezra's cluster of schemas

Ezra demonstrated a cluster of schemas during this three-month period, and whilst I am going to concentrate on what an understanding of trajectory, line and connection may have contributed to Ezra's development in different domains, I will share other examples that offer further clarity to my thinking and explanation. Similarly to Arnold (2015b) when studying her granddaughter, Gabriella, we were led by Ezra and whatever he wanted to do at the time. We tried to support and offer content and language that we hoped tuned in to his conceptual thinking (Athey, 2007).

Significant things that occurred prior to the observation period . . .

The very first actual story Ezra loved at five months of age was *Going on a Bear Hunt* (Rosen and Oxenbury, 1989); he would lie on the floor on his back, with me next to him lying down and reading the book to him, holding the book above us both.

I assumed it was the rhythmic sound of the narrative that he loved; I didn't consider the aspect of a line of people making a journey and returning, but now I wonder if that was an aspect of his interest. After having this story read repeatedly, every time I saw him – which was most days, Ezra then lost interest in it.

I then became puzzled by two particular pages in books Ezra liked. At around the same time, he liked a page in *Dear Zoo* (Campbell, 2010) and a page in *Guess How Much I Love You?* (McBratney and Jeram, 2007) He would insist on remaining on each page for longer than any other pages in the respective books and would often want to return to them. It took me some time to realise the similarity – which Ezra had seen immediately. The page in *Dear Zoo* was the 'Lion in a cage' page, and the page in *Guess How Much I Love You?* was a page with a fence; both had vertical lines and this was what Ezra was concentrating on – the form – in both instances vertical lines, in what Athey (1990) refers to as figurative form. This was perhaps a time when Ezra's environment provided a match with his 'inner patterns' (Athey, 1990: 35).

Waiting . . .

Another event that has stuck in my mind is when Ezra was 13 months and 2 days old. Georgia, Ezra and I had been out for lunch, and when we came out of the restaurant he wanted to walk (he had first walked at 10 months and 15 days old). It was one of those situations where we had to walk across a very busy car park and so needed Ezra to be in his buggy. He was not keen on our point of view, and so we negotiated with him. If he sat in the buggy, he could have some chocolate (I know that is sometimes referred to as bribery, but I am keen to consider it 'negotiation', in order to feel a 'better' grandparent). Ezra readily got into his buggy in exchange for the chocolate he wanted. We did not *actually* have the chocolate at

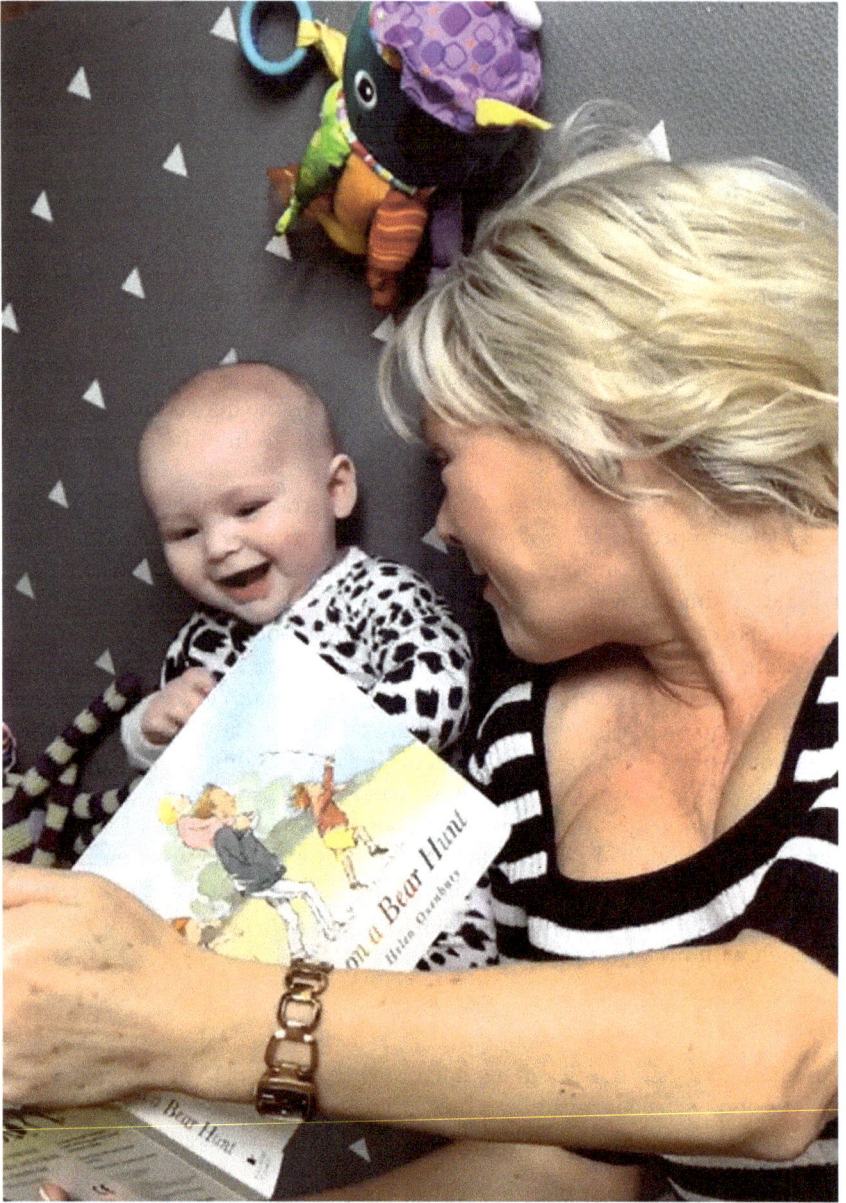

Figure 2.1 Ezra enjoying '*Going on a Bear Hunt*' at 5 months and 12 days

this stage and had to go and buy some. What surprised me was that Ezra was able to tolerate the wait of several minutes for the chocolate. We had to walk across the car park, go into the shop and buy the chocolate before he could have any. On the way, he pointed at himself and said, 'En' which is how he refers to himself, and I responded, 'yes, we are just going to buy you some chocolate Ezra', and he quietened again. I wondered what it was in his experience that enabled him to wait . . . at such a young age. This is something I will return to later in the chapter.

In the intervening months what did Ezra gain expertise in . . .

In relation to the dynamic line or trajectory, Ezra became adept at throwing. He had various different sizes and shapes of balls and spent lots of time throwing them. He could throw with both hands in a strong overarm movement, throwing quite some distance. At 17 months and 2 days, he launched his plastic lion from one side of the living room towards the television. The force with which he launched it caused the television to crack! Athey (1990) might say that the smashing of the television screen was functionally dependent on the direction and force with which Ezra threw the lion. A small compensation for his parents.

By 18 months of age, he often tried to pick up two balls in one hand and throw them, quite an achievement with such small hands. Most days in the garden, Ezra and I would play throwing objects into a bucket. Ezra chose the objects, sometimes balls, skittles, stones – whatever he had to hand, and we had to try to throw them into the bucket from varying distances. Lots of cheering would ensue if either of us got the objects in the bucket, and each time we failed, we tried again. Failing was as much fun as achieving and was accompanied by shouts of 'ooooohhhh' which conveyed – 'oh that was so near – let's try again'. Ezra showed a persistence and determination (Laevers, 1997) in the games we played and was praised for the effort he made, as well as the achievements (Dweck, 1999). Being disequilibrated (Athey, 1990) delights Ezra and often prompts him to carry his investigations further, sharing his delight with those around him. The occasion he threw a wet flannel at the bathroom wall and it temporarily stuck before sliding slowly down the tiles was joyous. A couple of days later, he took some tissues out of my bag and wet them in his mud kitchen and spent a long time throwing them at the wooden fence, this time with them often sticking to the fence and remaining there. This caused squeals of laughter and pointing.

What will follow are three observations that are indicative of Ezra's play during this period. Each is considered in relation to cognition.

Observation one

19 months and 4 days

In this sequence, Ezra is dropping various things into his bucket, which has some water in it. Firstly, he drops his lion into the water, and it sinks quickly to the bottom. He lifts it out and drops it again. He does this several times, always using his right hand, watching intently each time.

Figure 2.2

Figure 2.3

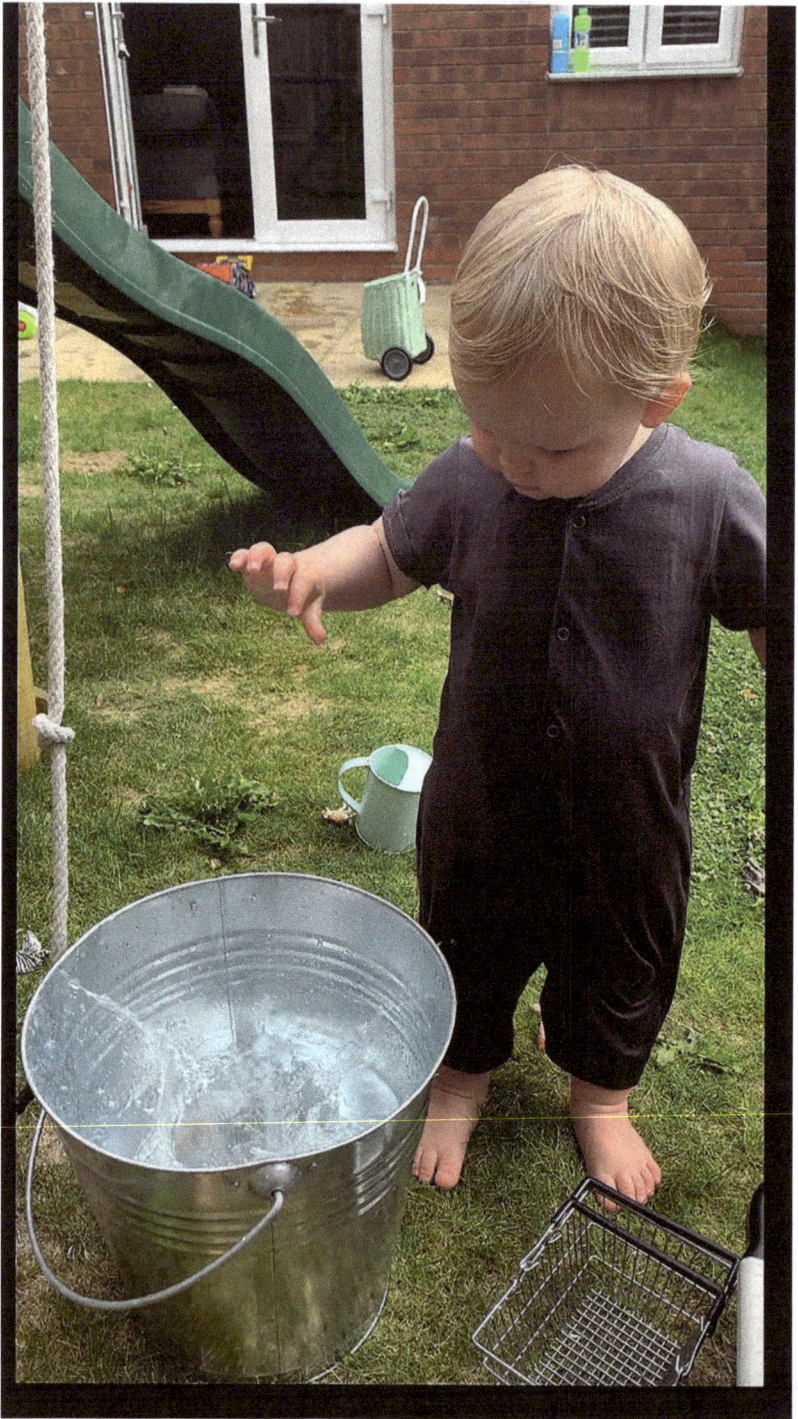

Figure 2.4

He then takes the lion and runs quickly to his 'luggy' (a trolley on wheels that he keeps his balls in) and selects a small tennis ball. He returns to the bucket and drops the ball into the water, followed by the lion (this time with his left hand). I say to him, '*Oh, the ball floats on top doesn't it . . . and the lion sinks*'. He takes the lion out of the water and drops it onto the floor. He immediately goes to the luggy and selects another ball – it is a tennis ball, but a pink and blue one – so appears to be different, but its properties are the same (perceptually different, but conceptually the same). He drops it into the water, and I say, '*Does that float as well?*' He picks up both balls in one hand and drops them back into the water together. He takes them out separately and drops them in separately. He does this several times – sometimes with one hand and sometimes with both hands.

Figure 2.5

Figure 2.6

Figure 2.7

Figure 2.8

Figure 2.9

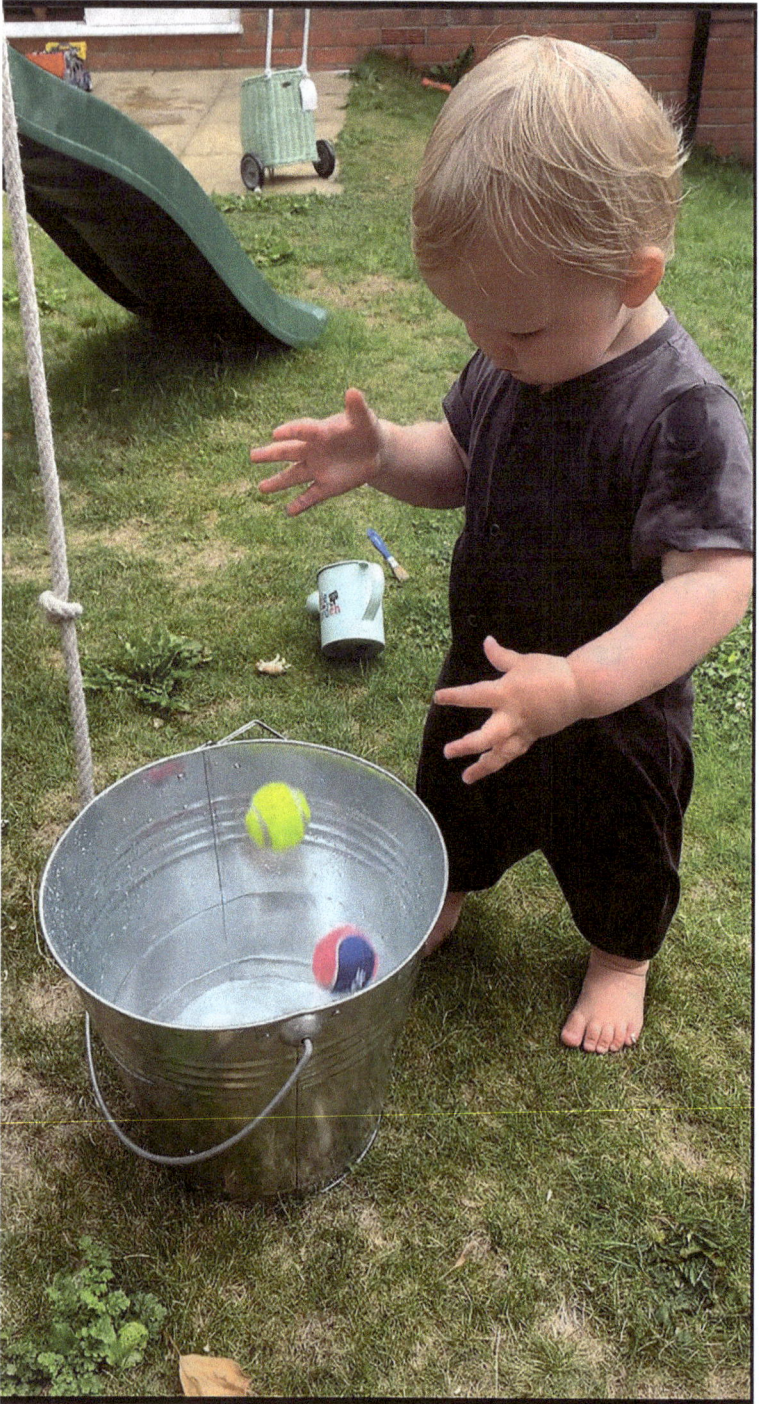

Figure 2.10

Ezra then drops both balls into the empty washing up bowl nearby. He does this several times and picks the lion up and drops it back into the water too.

Ezra then looks around the garden and runs and picks a small flower which he brings back to the bucket. He drops the flower into the bucket and agitates the water with his right hand.

Figure 2.11

Figure 2.12

As he stands up, I say, '*that floats on top too*'. He agitates the water more vigorously and then stands up and holds his hands out to say, '*where is it?*' I look and say, '*oh, it's at the bottom now . . . it's coming back up . . . there it is*'. He repeats this several times – usually with his right hand, but once with his left hand.

Some thoughts . . .

Here Ezra has very systematically used his *trajectory, containing and transporting* schemas (Athey, 1990) to experiment with objects that float and sink. To begin with, he identifies that the lion always sinks and then selects a ball which floats. In order to test out his hypothesis (which may be, at this stage, that all lions sink and all balls float), he selects another ball. He has the choice of balls identical to that which he has dropped into the water already, or balls that are different. He seems to purposely select one which appears to be different, as it is a different colour. This also floats. He experiments with dropping both balls from one hand and each ball from each hand. It is as though he is considering whether the ball floating is *functionally dependent* (Athey, 1990) on what *he* does or on the properties of the object. He then tries dropping the balls together and separately into the empty washing up bowl. I did not immediately see the significance of this. But now I assume that he is testing whether the balls behave in the same way as each other if he does something different to dropping them into water. They do. Ezra is *assimilating* (Athey, 1990) these experiences into his current working theory, which may be that '*balls behave in the same way as each other, despite what I do*'. When Ezra selects the flower, it seems that he has intentionally selected an item with very different properties to both the lion and the ball. Initially, the flower floats, but very quickly he agitates the water and the flower sinks and then rises to float again. He is again systematic in that he tries the same action with both hands and gets the same results. Density is the amount of mass something has in relation to its volume or size. Water has density. When the object dropped into the water has more density than the water, then it sinks (the Lion), and when it has less density, it floats (the balls and the flower). By agitating the water, Ezra may have created an 'eddy' (National Ocean Service, 2020) which is a circular current of water which both drew the flower downwards and, as the water calmed, allowed it to float back up.

Concepts that Ezra may be gaining partial knowledge towards, in addition to gaining understanding of the properties of different objects/materials:

• Floating
• Sinking
• Buoyancy
• Density
• Weight
• Gravity

Observation two

19 months and 5 days

Ezra has water in his bucket and has dropped all his animals into the water, and they have sunk to the bottom. The bucket is too big and heavy for him to lift. By pointing from the bucket to the washing up bowl nearby, he indicates that he wants me to pour the water and animals from the bucket to the bowl. He points to the bucket saying '*der*' *(there)* and the bowl saying, '*in der*' *(in there)*. I say, '*you'd like it in there?*', indicating the bowl as I lift the bucket up to pour its contents out. As the water and animals land in the bowl, Ezra does a little jump of 'chuffed-ness' (Tait, 2004), as Georgia says '*all your animals too*', meaning in addition to the water. He then directs me to pour the contents back into the bucket. As I'm doing so, he looks to Georgia and points to what I'm doing, and as the animals hit the bottom of the bucket, he makes a loud '*oooooooohhh*' sound. He is pleased with what is happening. He directs me to repeat this several times, each time paying close attention to the trajectory from one container to another (Athey, 2007).

Figure 2.13

Figure 2.14

Figure 2.15

Figure 2.16

Figure 2.17

Figure 2.18

Some thoughts . . .

Ezra experimented with dropping his lion into the water yesterday and see-ing that it always sank. Here he seems interested in what would happen if the water and animals were 'poured' or *transported* at the same time from one large container to another. Although Ezra is not actually the one doing the pouring, he is fully involved (Laevers, 1997) in what is happening and directs the play entirely. Is Ezra wondering if the animals will always be below the surface of the water – as the lion was yesterday? The force of the water was *functionally dependent* (Athey, 1990) on the angle I tilted the container at. Sometimes the angle was steeper, and the animals appeared to fall out within the water – as part of one 'continuous' trajectory. Sometimes the angle was shallow, and the water came out slightly before the animals, so they appeared as two different bodies, the water as a continuous flow and the animals as discrete objects, each creating their own trajectory. The animals hitting the bottom of the bucket seemed important to Ezra, as he vocalised loudly when they 'landed'. Was this confirmation that what he expected to happen did happen? Was he testing out whether, even when poured, the animals would end up sinking to the bottom? Ezra may have also been noticing what the water and animals looked like in the bucket and in the bowl. This might contribute in time to his understand-ing of conservation of amount and volume. The same amount of water was present when in the narrower bucket, which appeared deeper as in the wider bowl, appearing shallower. Therefore *'the quantity of water* [was] *equivalent in spite of apparent figurative differences'* (Athey, 1990: 35). The number of animals remained the same whether in each receptacle or in the trajectory from one to the other. As no animals were added or taken away, they *'represent conceptual equivalence'* (Athey, 1990: 35).

Concepts that Ezra may be gaining partial knowledge towards, in addition to gaining understanding of the properties of different objects/materials:

- Volume
- Capacity
- Conservation of amount
- Conservation of number
- Gravity

Observation three

21 months and 2 days

Going to the drains was a daily occurrence for at least two months. Each day when I arrived at his house, he would take my hand and say 'Dee?', mean-ing – I'd like to go and play at the drains, Coco. Ezra chose which drains to visit on which days, and on this particular day, he chose three different types of drain.

Figure 2.19

Figure 2.20

Figure 2.21

Figure 2.22

Figure 2.23

He became increasingly adept at knowing which objects fit in which drains. On this particular day, he went initially to the drain with the smallest hole first, ending with the storm drains with the largest gaps (seriation – this is the ability to sort objects according to characteristics, one particular characteristic might be size). Once at the storm drains, he was systematic in what he chose to put into the drain, often varying what it was to see the effects of his actions. I know that he had a plan in his mind as, at points, he would go to the border of stones and indicate that he couldn't find what he wanted by holding his hands out in a way that indicated 'all gone'.

Figure 2.24

I would support him to find whatever he hadn't just dropped down the drain – I knew that this was what he wanted from my previous experience of getting it wrong. The large stone sitting on the yellow drain, and subsequently on the storm drain, was a stone he took to all three drains but did not try to put down any of the drains. I believe this is because he already knew it was too large; he has '*accom-modated*' this learning from his previous experiments and so does not need to try it again (Athey, 1990). At points during his play, he would pick the large stone up and cuddle it, saying, 'ahhh'. I would respond with, 'do you love that stone, Ezra?' He took it home with him and added it to his collection of large stones that he played with at his mud kitchen. He continued with his agenda of dropping objects down the drains. As he dropped a large stone into the drain, he was splashed – this happened on more than one occasion and always made him laugh. He carefully watched what happened to the objects he dropped down the drain.

His Papa reported taking him to the drains one day and said that when he articulated to Ezra that he liked the sound of the 'plop' into the water, Ezra responded immediately and emphatically with 'Dat!', which at this time was his way to say 'Yes!'. Here it would seem that his Papa had tuned into Ezra's intent and was able to offer articulation that held meaning for Ezra (Brierley and Nutbrown, 2017).

Some thoughts . . .

We have seen from Ezra's behaviour that he has a plan in his mind. We know he is systematic and interested in what happens as a result of his actions. He has now demonstrated his capacity to estimate size and fit, with much success. The 'end point' of the trajectory seems important to Ezra. It has been at this point Ezra has demonstrated 'chuffedness' (Tait, 2004) by doing a little dance, or say-ing 'oooooohhh' emphatically, or in the observations at the drain laughing when the perceived endpoint causes a splash (it is only perceived as, of course, the stone will carry on travelling through the water). The splash is *functionally dependent* on the size of stone Ezra selects to drop into the water. In order to cre-ate a splash from the drain water, Ezra has to select an object that is both heavy enough to create a splash and small enough to fit through the gap in the drain. In a similar way to children in Athey's study (1990: 199), Ezra is '*speculating on the equivalence*' between the size of the stone and the space it has to fit through. Newton's third law of motion states, '*when two bodies interact, they apply forces to one another that are equal in magnitude and opposite in direction*' (Britannica Ency-clopaedia, 2020). This is what Ezra is experiencing through his play when he creates a splash as the result of dropping a 'heavy enough' stone into the drain.

Concepts that Ezra may be gaining partial knowledge towards, in addition to gaining understanding of the properties of different objects/materials:

- Size
- Fit
- Gravity
- Weight
- Sinking
- Floating
- Displacement
- Equivalence

As you can see, Ezra's cluster of schemas are giving him a wide repertoire of experience, which is contributing to his partial understanding of many different concepts.

A conceptually focused pedagogy

Before I take us back to thinking about trajectories, endpoints and Ezra being able to tolerate waiting for chocolate at 13 months, it seems important to consider the role of the adults around Ezra. What has been provided for Ezra is what Atherton and Nutbrown (2016: 8) refer to as a schematic pedagogy. We have tried to encourage 'conceptual thinking' as opposed to 'associative thinking' through the comments made on Ezra's investigations and our engagement with him (Athey, 1990: 42). Ezra's play is intrinsically motivated (Laevers, 1997), and as adults around Ezra, we have striven to support what he wants to do, often sharing in the 'awe and wonder' of his investigations and discoveries (Atherton and Nutbrown, 2016: 8). I have often also been in awe of the complexity of his thinking, demonstrated through his actions. Ezra has been, and is, viewed as capable and competent and has already developed a high sense of 'agency' (Bandura, 2006). He knows he can have an impact on the world around him, and his investigations support this – he is interested in what happens as a result of what he does – he is experimenting with *functional dependency* relationships (Athey, 1990). In the second observation, we could see how Ezra demonstrated 'agency by proxy' (Bandura, 2006) and instructed me to do something he was not yet physically able to do – i.e., lift and tip a heavy bucket and bowl.

Reflection within pedagogy

A notion I would like to see taken into account when considering pedagogy with the youngest children is 'reflection' and the encouragement of reflection. This comes from my observations of Georgia with Ezra. Georgia has always told Ezra what they would be doing each day, and when I arrived at the end of the day, she would say to Ezra, '*shall we tell Coco what we've been doing today?*', and the story of the day would ensue, in which she would emphasise those things that had seemed important to Ezra, or times where he had been upset or excited about something. Similarly, when John arrived home from work, Georgia and Ezra would also tell him about their day. Essentially Ezra was being told what the day might hold long before he could actually understand what was being said. Then he was experiencing the day and finally being part of telling others about the day. In effect, Ezra was experiencing reflecting on the day through Georgia's eyes and words, until he was able to articulate some of it himself. As a result of this, if I was looking after Ezra, I would mirror Georgia's actions and explain to Ezra what we were going to do and then encourage him to 'tell' his mum and dad what we'd done whilst away from them. For instance, today, I took Ezra out for a walk, and he wanted to watch the traffic. When we were telling Georgia about it, he articulated that we'd seen a 'blue bus' and 'motorbike'. Whilst we were out, he'd been very excited to see two blue buses and two motorbikes and had said, 'more motorbike', as he wanted to see more. Georgia told us at the beginning of this chapter how Ezra 'always wanted to revisit things'. Perhaps this is why: he has been given the opportunity to revisit events and share them with others, creating both a sense of belonging (Trevarthen, 2002) and a ritual. This is something I think we should consider more in early years, as it is through reflection that we develop self-awareness, which is a contributing factor to emotional intelligence (Goleman, 2004).

A line in Ezra's mind

Now I'd like you to think about the spoken narratives I have just described as trajectories with beginning points and endpoints, not too dissimilar to Ezra's trajectory play – as opposed to a sequence of events. If Ezra has an 'inner pattern' (Athey, 1990) that matches with this spoken narrative, or trajectory, then it will have significance for him – in the way the early images of a fence and a lion's cage did. The outer world may be mirroring his inner world, amplifying the idea of a 'line in his mind'. Although these observations demonstrate a cluster of schemas within each observation and in other examples I have shared, there has always been a trajectory or line aspect. He has looked at, listened to and created lines. He first looked at and listened to stories with lines, he has been part of a daily narrative about events (a spoken line), and he has created lines in his play. Firstly Ezra dropped items into a bucket; then he directed me to pour the water and animals from one container to another, focusing his attention on the trajectory flow; thirdly, he dropped objects down drains, creating a line with each object he dropped. If you can now think back to the example I gave early in this chapter about how Ezra, at thirteen months and two days old, was able to tolerate waiting for the chocolate he wanted. What I am proposing is that Ezra at this stage already had a 'line in his mind' and it was this line that allowed him to tolerate the wait, rather than 'flipping his lid' (Siegel, 2017), as might have been expected of a child at this age, not receiving immediate gratification. He wanted verbal reassurance during the walk to the shop, and he instigated this by pointing at himself and saying 'En?', to which we were able to respond and tell him what would happen, i.e. that he would get the chocolate soon – at the *'end of the line'*, so to speak. Shaw (2019) helps our thinking by pointing out that being engaged in container/contained relationships helps children to manage frustration. Ezra is in a container/contained relationship with the people he is closest to in his life. These relationships seem to allow him to work through and process frustration he experiences through symbolism (Shaw, 2019). On this occasion, I wonder if the symbol that allowed him to tolerate waiting for the chocolate was the 'line in his mind'.

Finally, I would like to end this celebration of Ezra with a nursery observation. Shortly after the third observation shared in this chapter, Ezra started settling into nursery. He was nearly 22 months old. Fortunately, Ezra is in a nursery where the practitioners understand schemas and their emotional significance, and support them well (Arnold and the Pen Green Team, 2010). This observation was shared with us via Tapestry, their online learning journal.

It evidences Ezra's processing of the feelings that arise when he is separated from his parents whilst at nursery; as you will see – there is a line that has a temporary, time-dependent disconnect.

Figure 2.25

> Good morning, Ezra settled very quickly this morning. Once he had said goodbye to you, he walked into the Nest and settled at the rainbow arches. He explored these in the same way he did with the pumpkins yesterday morning. He used the two large green arches and ensured these again were physically connected and then used the small blue arch to connect and disconnect it from the green ones. I really believe he is working out his separations and reunions.

The line in Ezra's mind is becoming more complex, and now, as well as having a beginning and endpoint, it also has units that can be separated and reconnected. In this instance, the units are symbolising him, Georgia, his mum and John, his dad. His play is both helping him to process the emotions he is feeling when separated from his parents as well as illustrating his understanding of their three-way relationship as one where they can be together, apart and together again.

Reflections and questions

I have loved the process of recording this small aspect of Ezra's schematic play. I think knowing that I was going to be committing words to paper helped me to think more deeply, notice more keenly and wonder more creatively. I tried to put myself in Ezra's shoes in order to notice the 'form' of things that appealed to him and was excited when I was able to notice the same things he had. I am humbled by the depth of his thinking and am left questioning whether we underestimate young children's capacity for complex conceptual thinking and learning just because we cannot always see what they see.

Recommended reading

Arnold, C. (1999) *Child Development and Learning 2–5 Years: Georgia's Story.* Oxford: Hodder and Stoughton.

Arnold, C. (2003) *Observing Harry: Child Development and Learning 0–5 Years.* Maidenhead: Open University Press.

Arnold, C. (2015) *Doing Your Child Observation Case Study: A Step by Step Guide.* Maidenhead: Open University Press.

Arnold, C. and The Pen Green Team. (2010) *Understanding Schemas and Emotions in Early Childhood.* London: SAGE.

3 Round and round

Learning about schemas in the Welsh Foundation Phase (FP) curriculum

Amanda Thomas

Discovering schemas

My own interest in schemas came about by chance. I had taught for 10 years as an early years teacher but I had never heard of schemas, and they certainly did not feature in my pedagogy. On moving from the early years classroom to teaching early years students in a Further Education college, I was asked to supervise a student's dissertation focusing on schemas. This was my first encounter with schemas and the work of Chris Athey. On reading Athey's book and her definition of schemas as, 'a pattern of repeatable behaviour into which experiences are assimilated and that are gradually co-ordinated' (1990: 37), I found myself remembering children I had taught and repeated behaviour that seemed random and haphazard, suddenly seemed to make complete sense, when viewed through a schematic lens. This led me to ponder if the Foundation Phase (FP) curriculum, with its emphasis on learning through play, active exploration and a learning environment driven by the child's interests, could nurture and nourish children's schemas. Therefore, when it came time for me to study for my PhD, there was only 1 topic I wanted to investigate which was exploring children's schemas in the FP (Thomas, 2018).

Findings from my PhD supported the realisation that, for some children, schemas are the ways they make sense of their world. Therefore, this chapter tells Lewis' story and how he used his rotational schema within the FP learning environment to construct his knowledge and understanding. It also tells my story as the researcher and that of the educators I worked with and how our growing knowledge and understanding of schemas shaped FP classroom pedagogy.

Introduction

In 2008 Wales broke away from 125 years of traditional education in the early years and introduced the Foundation Phase (FP). The FP is a learning

DOI: 10.4324/9781003224341-4

continuum for children aged 3–7 years with play at the heart of curriculum pedagogy (Thomas and Lewis, 2016). This curriculum is child-centred, holistic, experiential and starts with a child's interests and builds upon them (Welsh Government (WG), 2015). Here the educator is considered a play partner, supporting the child along the learning continuum.

The curriculum is delivered through a mixture of continuous, enhanced and focused provision across seven areas of learning (WG, 2015). The continuous provision is a constant of the learning environment on offer and allows consolidation of skills such as problem-solving, decision-making, teamwork and independence through playful activities. In the enhanced provision, the educator adds resources to the continuous provision based on the observed interests of the children, with links to the current classroom theme (Thomas, 2020).

The last part of the FP model of delivery is the adult-led provision or the focused tasks, which is where new skills are taught (Maynard et al., 2012). In the FP, there is an emphasis on observing children in the continuous and enhanced provision to note their interests, preferred ways of learning and how they constructed their knowledge and understanding. Building upon what has been observed in the continuous and enhanced provision, FP educators plan activities in the focused provision. Thus, providing children with:

> A well-planned curriculum (that) gives children opportunities to be creatively involved in their own learning which must build on what they already know and can do, their interests and what they understand.
>
> (WG, 2015: 4).

However, despite this emphasis on closely observing children to see their interests and planning a curriculum around those interests, schemas are not included in any depth within FP policy guidance and documentation. For FP educators, there is a mention of schemas as a window into a child's thinking in the 'Teaching and Learning Pedagogy' policy document. Here, schemas are mentioned on page nine under the heading, 'The Child as a Learner' where it states, 'By repeating a learning experience they develop schema or patterns of thoughts that are strengthened until they are able to make connections' (Welsh Assembly Government (WAG), 2008: 9). Further, there is a brief link between observation and schemas on page 22 of the same document, stating, 'Observation may draw attention to particular schema or patterns of thinking that predominate a child's play' (WAG, 2008).

However, there was no specific training or guidance offered to FP educators to develop their knowledge and understanding of schemas. This can be regarded as a missed opportunity within the FP for both educators and children. By nurturing and nourishing schemas, educators can gain an insight into the processes children go through in their 'coming to know' (Athey, 2007; Atherton and Nutbrown, 2013; Arnold, 2013). This enables the educator to have a window into a child's way of thinking and to shape the curriculum they provide. It facilitates the adult in being child-centred, holistic and supportive of the child's interests, all key concepts that underpin the ethos of adults working in the FP (WG, 2015).

Therefore, myself and three FP educators embarked upon researching children's schemas in one FP setting in South East Wales. We worked with children aged 3–5 years, and this chapter presents Lewis' schematic pursuits over two school terms.

This research can be deemed as the study of the social world as Bryman (2012: 28) states, 'The study of the social world requires a different logic of research procedure, one that reflects the distinctiveness of humans as against the natural order'. Proponents of such a study argue for an understanding of the lived experiences of those taking part in the research (Schwandt, 1998). Therefore, this research is conducted within naturalistic settings of an FP classroom environment, where it was possible to explore, in detail, the learning experiences of Lewis and the understandings gained by the educators.

Lewis' story

Lewis was 4 years old and in the reception class when the observations started. The educators described him as a very sociable and capable child who was always on the go. Lewis did not seem to have any one particular friend in the class, but he did like to be quite boisterous and loved to be outdoors. What had become apparent from the observations during the autumn term was that Lewis had demonstrated a dynamic circular (rotational) schema both indoors and outdoors.

A dynamic circular schema can be defined as 'an interest in all things that turn' (Mairs and the Pen Green Team, 2013: 9). Prior to observing Lewis in the spring and summer term, I spent the autumn term getting to know Lewis and for him to get to know me. Atherton and Nutbrown talk of 'gradualness' where children get used to the researcher's presence and a 'familiarity' develops (2013: 27). In addition, this first term was also an opportunity for me, and the three educators involved in the research, to develop our own knowledge and understanding of schemas.

As indicated previously, there was very limited policy guidance and training given to FP educators on recognising and supporting children's schemas. This lack of guidance and training was reflected in FP educators' knowledge and understanding of schemas within the research setting.

Through the analysis of responses from questionnaires given to all fourteen FP educators, at the start of the research, the following results were found:

Table 3.1 FP Educators' knowledge of schemas within the setting

Number of responses: (N = 14)	Responses given:
1	Based on individual needs
1	Behaviours shown by children
1	Exploring the world using sensory experiences
1	Schemas are learning styles
10	No Knowledge

Source: Thomas, A. (2018) Exploring the role of schemas within the Welsh Foundation Phase curriculum. Unpublished PhD thesis. University of South Wales.

Table 3.2 FP Educators' response to any training on schemas

Number of responses: (N = 14)	Responses given:
1	*Attended a training course at college that mentioned schemas, but I don't think I quite got it*
1	*Researched them when I was doing an assignment on Piaget whilst at university*
12	*Never had any training on them as a practitioner*

Source: Thomas, A. (2018) Exploring the role of schemas within the Welsh Foundation Phase curriculum. Unpublished PhD thesis. University of South Wales.

Although these responses are from one setting, within the larger PhD study, eighty-five FP stakeholders across South Wales were asked about their knowledge of schemas and if they had received any training on schemas; the findings were very similar to those evidenced above (Thomas, 2018). Therefore, the first term was spent developing a recognition and knowledge of schemas and how, once recognised, they could be supported within the FP learning environment.

Athey determined in her research the sequential levels at which schemas are explored, with the starting point as motor behaviours through to symbolic representations, then functional dependencies and then to thought (Athey, 2007). However, Arnold advises that we need a 'new way' to view schemas rather than operating at sequential levels as this confers a hierarchical view of development and 'the development of understanding and knowledge is more complex than this' (2013: 172).

Certainly, in the following photographs and observations of Lewis' lived experiences in the setting, he uses his rotational schema at all the levels depicted by Athey (2007). The photographs are used to supplement the narrative observations of Lewis in action. Cottle (2016) postulates that photographs allow for a rich insight into the child's world in the setting; they can provide a representation of a person's lived experiences within a given time and environment.

Today I am observing Lewis in the afternoon and he has chosen to play outdoors. He rushes over to the outdoor sand tray and picks up the sieve. The educator and I observe Lewis together. As we watch, he chooses a red sieve and twists it down into the sand (Figure 3.1). As he does this, it starts to fill with sand. Lewis looks up and seems surprised at the fact the sand is now inside the sieve. Lewis looks back down at the half-buried sieve, lifts it out of the sand and twists it back down, so it starts to fill up again. He does this repeatedly, as if he is checking that the sand does enter the sieve when he twists it downwards. The educator with me whispers, '*He is fascinated with that sieve and the sand*'. I nod and reply, '*Yes, if you watch he isn't using the sieve in a conventional way, but he is twisting it into the sand to fill it up, rather than pouring the sand into it. He seems surprised too, almost as if he did not expect that to happen. He is using his rotational schema as a way to get sand into the sieve*'. The educator nods her agreement, and we carry on watching him.

When Lewis was using the sieve, he was twisting the sieve downwards into the sand, which forced the sand upwards into the sieve. As Lewis seemed

Figure 3.1 Twisting the sieve into the sand to make the sand come 'up' through the round holes

Source: Thomas, A. (2018) Exploring the role of schemas within the Welsh Foundation Phase curriculum. Unpublished PhD thesis. University of South Wales.

surprised by this, it could be argued that he did not expect this to happen and that he was assimilating new information (the sand being forced up into the sieve) and needed to accommodate his understanding to take account of this new development (Piaget, 1936/1953). He then repeated this action to reinforce and consolidate this understanding. This could be an example of what Piaget meant by disequilibrium, where thinking needed to be adjusted to take account of a new (or surprising) development (Piaget, 1954).

This episode with Lewis emphasises the need for close observation along with a knowledge of schemas, as otherwise, this could have easily been missed. Meade and Cubey (2008: 152) proposed the idea of the 'novice adult' being an apprentice to schema theory. In this observation, the educator and I were able to view Lewis' actions through a schematic lens and note how his rotational schema supported a different way of getting sand into the sieve –developing his knowledge and understanding. Without a knowledge of schemas, this could have been missed or dismissed as Lewis just playing with a sieve in the sand tray. As Atherton and Nutbrown (2013: 109) write, 'A knowledge of schema theory can be enlightening. It allows for previously unfathomable behaviours to be understood for the conceptual exploits they actually are'.

Additionally, it could be argued that Lewis is also exploring functional dependency with the need to twist the sieve in order to get the sand inside (cause and effect). Athey (1990: 70) states, 'functional dependency relationships are manifest when children observe the effect of action on objects or materials'. Atherton and Nutbrown (2013), Nutbrown (2011) and Athey (2007) all agree

Figure 3.2 Giving a child a 'Razor cut'

Source: Thomas, A. (2018) Exploring the role of schemas within the Welsh Foundation Phase curriculum. Unpublished PhD thesis. University of South Wales.

that sensory and perceptual information alongside motor level actions leads to higher-level understanding. Here, Lewis has felt the force of twisting the sieve downwards into the sand and has observed the sand rising upwards into the sieve. He has repeated these actions to consolidate that this knowledge of downwards force leads to upwards movement of sand.

Today most of the children are sitting on the carpet watching a video on the interactive whiteboard. However, Lewis is not sitting but is standing over another boy (Figure 3.2). He is making a buzzing sound and he has four or five pencils in his hand. He begins to move the pencils over the boy's head in a circular motion. I carry on watching this go on for about a minute until Lewis says, '*You're all done, one razor cut that will be five pounds please*'. The boy pretends to give Lewis money who says, '*Thank you*' before moving on to the next child. He carries on 'cutting hair' until he moves to a little girl who is not happy and tells the teacher. Lewis is made to hand over the pencils and told to sit and watch the programme on the whiteboard. He does so but shouts out, '*It's not fair I want to cut hair. My dad cuts hair and I will too when I am big!*'

Lewis' dad is a barber and Lewis regularly spends time with him in his shop on the weekends. He used the pencils to symbolise the clippers and imitated the sound they made. Vygotsky discussed children repeating something they have seen others do. He declared that 'Play is more nearly recollection of something that has actually happened than imagination. It is more memory in action than novel imaginary situation' (1978: 103). In this instance, Lewis has recalled a memory of his dad cutting hair and has re-enacted this. Lewis was using his rotational schema to imitate the action of the clippers but was thwarted in his actions by being made to stop. Athey (1990) states that it is not necessary to love a schema; however, an attuned educator can find new ways to support children's schemas that are more acceptable.

Later that same day, when the educators and I were reflecting upon the observations and photographs, I suggested setting the role-play area up as a Barbers for a time with appropriate tools. This could support Lewis without annoying other children. Bruce (2011) argues for 'finding acceptable ways' for a child to use a schema and that schemas can help adults to support children in 'socially worthwhile directions' (Bruce, 2011: 104). The educators felt that perhaps they could adapt one of the wooden houses outdoors as a Barbers rather than change the whole role-play area inside. They wanted to keep the role-play area as an 'under the sea' theme in keeping with the topic that term. This was added to the planning for the next FP meeting and was agreed as a suitable way to support Lewis.

Once the outdoor Barbers was set up, Lewis chose to play in it each time he went outdoors; he used a number of 'tools' such as old (non-working) clippers one of the adults brought in to 'shave' children's hair. Each time he made the buzzing sound as he rotated the clipper over the children's heads.

Today, Lewis is sitting next to one of the educators at the writing table. The week before, I had brought twistable pens into the setting, and Lewis is showing her how to twist the pen to get the nib out (Figure 3.3). She listens to him attentively and shows Lewis how she writes with the pen. She asks him to copy her and he takes his pen and draws some lines on the paper. The educator turns to me and says, '*Lewis has been doing some lovely writing with these pens Mrs Thomas, haven't you, Lewis?*' Lewis looks at me and nods. I say, '*I can see Lewis, can you show me how to make these pens work?*' Lewis picks up another of the pens and begins to explain, '*You have to twist the top bit like this see, round and round, then the nib bit comes out, and then you can write with it*'. I take a pen, copy Lewis, and make a mark on the page. Lewis claps his hands and says, '*Yes that's right, like that, it is all twisty it is*'.

Another boy comes over and asks Lewis to come and play, so Lewis wanders off. I sit with the educator and she tells me that the pens have been a real hit with Lewis and that he loves to show others how to use them. They have also been a way to encourage Lewis to sit and do some mark-making as prior to this he would never choose to sit at the writing table.

In this observation, I have become the 'attuned' adult (Atherton and Nutbrown, 2013: x). Prior to this, Lewis had shown little interest in mark-making, but the introduction of the twistable pens had focused his attention and he was

Figure 3.3 Explaining that twisting the pen makes it work

Source: Thomas, A. (2018) Exploring the role of schemas within the Welsh Foundation Phase curriculum. Unpublished PhD thesis. University of South Wales.

keen to explain to anyone who asked how they worked. I had noted this eagerness and asked Lewis to show me how to use the pens and this, in turn, encouraged Lewis to mark-make. Here Lewis' schema has provided an opportunity or opening for the educators and myself to find a way to persuade Lewis to mark-make. Bruce (2011) makes the point that integrating the curriculum with an understanding of schemas allows educators to enhance and add to the learning environment. Athey (2007: 90) confirmed that 'graphic representations are based on schematic form'. The twisting actions that were required to make the pen work allowed Lewis to use his rotational schema and to proceed to mark-make.

In a follow up the educators put some of the pens in the outdoor Barber's shop and encouraged Lewis to 'write' down the names of his customers and to design an open and closed sign for the shop.

Lewis is mark-making on the shed today when I walk over to observe him (Figure 3.4). He is painting with water and he spent a long time repeatedly painting all over the shed. Lewis painted both large and small water circles all over the shed and he gave a running commentary to the girl with him, '*Look I have done an O, I can do big ones and small ones.*' Lewis further added that, '*Its ok to do it wrong as it goes away and I can do it again better.*'

Deguara and Nutbrown argue in their research, 'children's semiotic drawings could reflect their schematic understanding and meaning-making' (2018: 6). Here, Lewis has used water to make a letter 'O' as a symbol. He has chosen an 'O' as it is supportive of his rotational schema. As stated previously the educators

Figure 3.4 Painting circles with water

Source: Thomas, A. (2018) Exploring the role of schemas within the Welsh Foundation Phase curriculum. Unpublished PhD thesis. University of South Wales.

had found it hard to engage Lewis to sit and do any sort of mark-making. During this observation they noted his enjoyment in mark-making with water as it afforded him the opportunity and confidence to make mistakes that disappeared. They decided to use other malleable material with Lewis to encourage letter formation such as coloured sand and clay as these materials could be easily transformed, and like the water, any errors could easily be rectified.

There was a growing awareness amongst the educators of understanding how to engage Lewis through resources such as twistable pens and malleable materials that supported his rotational schema. This was the window into Lewis' thinking and the key to getting him enthusiastic about mark-making. The educators were again becoming the attuned adults (Atherton and Nutbrown, 2013).

When I begin to observe Lewis today, he is sitting at the writing table (Figure 3.5). He is using the twistable pens and he selects a green one. He concentrates on drawing his picture for several minutes, and then he says, '*Finished*'. He holds the picture up for me to see and I take this as a cue that he is happy to engage with me. I say, '*I love that picture, can I take a photo for my schoolwork?*' Lewis nods, so I take the photo. I ask, '*Would you like to tell me about your picture so I can write something about it for my schoolwork?*' Lewis points to his drawing and says, '*It is a man going to the moon. He had this round helmet so he can see and breathe*'. As he tells me, he rotates his hands round and round. He continues, '*Then when he gets there, he will have a round space machine that will let him land and then he will get out and run over the moon. There will be aliens there and he will make friends with them*'. I nod and say, '*That is a really good explanation of your picture;*

Figure 3.5 Going to the Moon

Source: Thomas, A. (2018) Exploring the role of schemas within the Welsh Foundation Phase curriculum. Unpublished PhD thesis. University of South Wales.

I can see exactly what you have drawn – there are lots and lots of round things'. Lewis nods and then he picks up the picture and takes it to the 'Going Home' box.

Later, when I shared this observation and photograph with the educators involved in the research, they told me that they had been reading a book about aliens and the moon, and Lewis has been really engrossed in the story and all things to do with space. They also tell me again that the introduction of the twistable pens has really encouraged Lewis to sit at the mark-making table much more often than before.

In Figure 3.5, there is a co-ordination in the development of Lewis' drawing of the 'spaceman'. Here Lewis has added vertical lines and spirals to his picture with evidence of an enclosure representing the space helmet. Lewis has attempted to draw features inside the helmet, of eyes and a nose. This is an example of 'vertical order between elements' within a figure (Athey, 2007: 63). He has talked of the man going to the moon – the man has transported himself from earth to the moon. Here Lewis has indicated a thought process of a journey to the moon and has represented this on paper.

Piaget (1969) identified two types of cognitive patterning: figurative, linked with perception and operative, linked with action. Lewis' figurative aspects of his rotational schema could be evidenced through his mark-making. This is an acknowledgement of what Athey meant when she argued, 'mark and model making are abstractions from the child's own movements' (2007: 75). Lewis had used his actions previously to represent rotational and transporting movements, and this – in Athey's terms – has translated into the marks he chose to make.

Further, this resonates with Piaget and Inhelder (1956: 77), who stated that mark-making was derived from physical action and was 'based originally upon a sensori-motor . . . action'.

Lewis was able to tell me a whole story about his picture and conveyed his interest in a rotational schema through his words and drawing. He was able to represent the round space helmet and the journey to the round moon in a round machine.

This drawing also supports Lewis' new fascination with Space, and this picture can be viewed as a drawing becoming a 'constructive process of thinking in action' (Cox, 2005: 123).

Atherton and Nutbrown (2013) urge adults to connect to children's forms of thought both dynamically and figuratively. Educators have done this through providing Lewis the opportunities to mark-make using water and the twistable pens. This has provided an insight into Lewis' thinking and allowed educators to nurture his schemas both indoors and outdoors. As Atherton and Nutbrown (2013) attest, to extend Lewis' thinking, there needs to be 'an environment enriched with content' with 'understanding adults' attuned to children's ways of thinking (:90).

Final thoughts

The above observations and photographs portray Lewis' lived experiences and his ways of 'coming to know' in the setting over two school terms. They have shown Lewis using his dynamic circular (rotational) schema in the setting to make sense of the world. Lewis has purposively explored the continuous and enhanced provision in the setting both indoors and outdoors to nurture and nourish his schemas. This is an example of what Bruner (1966) termed an 'enactive' child, exploring and using the resources in the environment to assimilate and accommodate understanding. Lewis was physically and mentally active as he remembered previous events from observing his dad at work and re-enacted them using his schemas.

The adults in the setting had recognised and supported Lewis' actions, although, at times, they needed to consider alternative ways for Lewis to pursue his schemas. An example being when Lewis was 'cutting' a child's hair and they became upset. Here the educators were able to plan other activities that would allow Lewis to use his rotational schema in ways that were considered more suitable.

Athey (2007) argues that when actions are viewed schematically, they can be interpreted in a positive light. Bruce (2011: 101), however, states that adults should not feel they must support unacceptable behaviour because it is part of a child's 'schema cluster'. Instead, Bruce argues that educators need to find ways that are more suitable for a child to use their schema (2011). Therefore, spending time with educators reflecting upon the observations and photographs was such an important part of this research. This facilitated a discussion resulting in setting up a role-play area outside as a barbershop to allow Lewis to 'cut hair' as he had seen his dad doing. In addition, in analysing the observations and photographs of Lewis, the educators and I were able to add resources such as the twistable pens, which encouraged Lewis to mark-make, something he had not been eager to do before.

Links with home

Whilst writing this chapter, I went back to Lewis' mum to ask her permission to include his story in this book. Lewis is now 11 years old, and I asked her if Lewis still had a fascination with roundness. She told me that he loves '*Formula One*' and he has a habit of 'fiddling *with things like wires, scarfs etc . . . I suppose I can describe it as rotating it in his hands, he tends to do this in private and when I've questioned him about it he says it helps him think or imagine things*'. This resonates with the work of Bruce (2011: 107), where she stated that 'schemas continue to be important throughout life. . . .' Lewis still uses his rotational schema to help him think and imagine, the roundness of the rotational movement seeming to support his 'threads of thinking' (Nutbrown, 2011: xv).

Mum also recalled that at the time of my research, '*he would watch the washing machine for ages, he would also love to pretend to drive cars and loved being in the car. He's grown out of all that now though*'. Perhaps Lewis' rotational schema can provide a link here between his past interests and his present ones. The rotations of the washing machine and the car's steering wheel in the past to his current love of 'Formula One' and the need to twist wires and scarves whilst thinking.

This also illuminates how schemas are influenced by both biological and sociocultural aspects. Babies are born with a repertoire of schemas that are biologically determined, but additionally, experience (sociocultural aspects) influences the development of schemas from childhood into adult life (Bruce, 2011; Arnold and the Pen Green Team, 2010). Lewis may have developed his rotational schema through having numerous opportunities to watch the washing machine spinning and being taken out on regular car journeys. As he has grown, his rotational schema – still present – has manifested itself in different ways through watching motor racing and in quiet moments, using rotational movement to help him think.

Timely

This research is timely as Wales is embarking upon a new 21st-century curriculum, which aims for greater educator autonomy (Donaldson, 2015). There is an opportunity for educators to rethink their pedagogy and to include schemas. However, to date, there is not any mention of schemas in the new curriculum documentation. Yet, as this study of one child's schematic pursuits in an FP setting has shown, early years educators need an understanding of how to recognise schemas and how children use them to construct their knowledge and understanding. This requires a reshaping of how children's actions are understood and viewed, with an acknowledgement of the complexity of schemas and examples provided for educators of how schemas can be embedded into curriculum planning and provision (Thomas, 2020).

Finally, this research has supported findings from Nutbrown, who has argued that it is crucial for adults working with our youngest learners to be 'tuned in to young children's thinking, open to their ideas and responsive to their ever-active minds' (2011: 149). This research has demonstrated that when educators **do** nurture and nourish a child's schema, they can become that tuned-in adult with an insight into a child's thinking. They can use a schematic lens to develop their pedagogy, to shape current and future curriculum provision, thus providing a truly child-centred, child-focused and child-led 21st-century curriculum, not only on paper but in practice too.

Reflections and questions

Throughout this chapter, I have explored Lewis' rotational schema in one FP setting over one academic year. However, even now, after having researched schemas, I still have questions, and perhaps this chapter has also led you to reflect and have your own questions. The following questions are what I still ponder upon:

1   Why do some children show clear evidence of dominant schemas and other children do not?
2   Are all schemas still evident in adulthood in some way?
3   Why do some early years curricula provide more recognition of schemas and others do not?
4   If educators use themes to inform their planning and resource provision, can this constrain some children's schemas?

To support educators in Wales, one output from my PhD was a schema toolkit (2020). This was developed in the setting to support educators in recognising and supporting schemas in the current FP curriculum but also in the new proposed curriculum for Wales. It has been published on the Welsh Government website (HWB) and can be accessed using the following link:

Schema Toolkit Available via the HWB

https://hwb.gov.wales/search?query=schemas&strict=true&popupUri=%2FResource%2Fe0ef76fe-334f-45ae-a6c8-7aa630e64310

4 Schemas and language

Emma Hewitt

Discovering schemas

I was initially introduced to schemas at the beginning of my early years journey – Early Years Professional Status – and was first drawn to Athey's (2007) ideas about content and form – parents and practitioners thinking not only about *what* a child is playing with (content), but what *interests* them about it, what they are *doing* with it (form) and how we adults can support learning by tuning in to both.

Later, I discovered Arnold's work on 'schemas and emotions' in Pen Green, which I felt explained a lot of my own experiences engaging with two-year-olds. When I was then employed by Pen Green, I had the opportunity to explore this interest further, and I continue to enjoy conversations about how schema theory can help parents and practitioners to understand and better support young children through their formative years.

Alongside this interest in schema theory, I developed an equally early fascination with the ways in which young children learn language – a complex learning process that often seems to happen as if 'by magic' (Gross, 2013). This particular interest was driven by the notion that 'the ability to communicate – to say what you want to say and to understand what other people are saying – is fundamental to life chances' (Gross, 2013: 1).

Speech, language, communication . . . and schemas

In this chapter, I aim to explore the relationship between two professional interests of mine: young children's schematic play and their early language development, to consider additional ways of thinking about and supporting young children's early learning and, therefore, future opportunities. I began

DOI: 10.4324/9781003224341-5

this exploration by engaging in case study research (Thomas, 2016) with four children and their families in the Pen Green Centre. What follows is a discussion of my initial research, which I hope contributes towards overall early years practice, and specifically, support for children's speech, language and communication development across the sector.

I focused my investigation into this relationship around the following research questions, which have intrigued me for some time:

- Are young children 'communicating' through schemas?
- Are children's schemas and early language linked, or not? How so?
- How might language strategies such as 'commenting', 'expanding' and 'recasting' be used in a meaningful way?
- How do young children learn and come to use new words and phrases?
- How might parents and practitioners further support children's language development?

I hope that a better understanding of these issues might help address some of the current concerns about young children's speech, language and, crucially, communication (ICAN and Royal College of Speech and Language Therapists (RCSLT), 2018). Ultimately, I believe, like Bayley and Broadbent, that 'each and every one of us talks with most interest and enthusiasm when speaking about the things that are important to us!' (2013: 41). Therefore, I hope that through closer examination of young children's schemas and really tuning in to their early language use, we might be able to offer support and appropriate opportunities for important language development in a way that is meaningful to each individual child.

In practice, I am mindful that some children have the additional complexity of learning more than one spoken language. Athey (2007: 78–80) demonstrates the benefits of nourishing a child's schemas in terms of learning English as an Additional Language (EAL) when telling Kamal's story, who started at the nursery with little spoken English. If any of these case study children had had more than one spoken language, this would have been a significant point of reference for me; however, on this occasion, this was not the case.

Schemas and language development – what is already known?

As previously discussed, Piaget (1936/1953) first referred to schemas as 'units' of information young children gathered about the world, which were updated (assimilation) and refined (accommodation) in line with new experiences (disequilibrium) or developing understanding (equilibrium). Later he referred to 'schemas of action' or 'co-ordinated systems of movement and perceptions . . . capable of being repeated and applied to new situations' (Piaget, 1962: 274).

Building on these ideas, Athey defined schemas as: 'patterns of repeatable actions that lead to early categories and then to logical classifications' (2007: 49), which I concur with.

Mercer (2004) linked this to children's development of language in that when children experience disequilibrium, or 'cognitive conflict', it is likely to be mediated by accompanying language. He states: 'language provides a means for resolving [cognitive conflict], by engaging in some joint thinking with an adult' (Mercer, 2004: 124). I am particularly interested in this relationship between schema and language – the cognitive aspect and the role of the accompanying adult. Atherton and Nutbrown refer to the adult's role too, stating that 'careful observation by practitioners can be used to understand and support future learning encounters through . . . practitioners developing a schematic pedagogy which focuses on structures of children's thinking' (2016: 63). The concept of 'schematic pedagogy' links closely with Athey's (2007) thoughts about constructivist teachers and Arnold's belief that we can support children by comprehending 'current understanding, particularly when it comes to very young children, who may not yet be able to guide us with their questions' (2015b: 728). This, too, is how I was beginning to consider the relationship between children's schema and their language development.

I began to wonder if the link in my interest in the two concepts, schema and language, was that they are both symbolic. Whitehead suggests we should have a 'keen awareness of the role of play in infant communication skills and early language, and in a most significant form of human thinking – the symbolic' (2001: 18), adding that 'symbolic thinking . . . is essential when we need to think about difficult and abstract ideas which cannot be touched, tasted or pointed to' (2001: 19). Although this is a reference to language and literacy – shared symbols (words, letters) needed to exchange ideas – I was beginning to think about children's schemas in this way too. Cath and Sue explore this idea further in their chapter.

Piaget and Inhelder state: 'the function of schema is to enable generalizations to be made about objects and events in the environment to which a schema is applied' (1973: 382), but what if it said: the function of *language* is to enable generalisations to be made about objects and events in the environment to which a *symbol/word* is applied? Schema theory is often referred to as another 'lens' through which to view children's learning (Bruce, 2015) – but what if we re-thought about it as another language? Is it a way for children to communicate their thoughts, feelings and understanding about the world around them? Bayley and Broadbent suggest that to support early language development, 'children need access to adults who really value what they have to say about their child-initiated learning and who make time to listen to them' (2013: 44), and schema theory offers practitioners an alternative way of 'listening' to young children. Indeed, Arnold refers to utilising schema theory to 'try to interpret' and to 'come to a closer understanding of' (2015b: 727) her pre-verbal granddaughter's intentions, something I hope to emulate in my own practice.

In carrying out these four case studies, I have focused on the development of children's spoken, or expressive, *language* in the form of their *speech*. I have considered whether we might consider children's schematic interests as an alternative form of *communication* regarding their cognitive and emotional concerns, providing further understanding that we might use to support traditional language development. I recognise there are additional considerations for those engaging with children with Special Educational Needs and Disabilities (SEND) or learning English as an Additional Language (EAL), but hope this chapter offers some initial 'food for thought'.

Although there are a number of theories (Chomsky, 1986; Vygotsky, 1986; Piaget, 1962), unfortunately, we 'do not know exactly how children learn language' (Macleod-Brudenell and Kay, 2008: 165). As with schematic pedagogy, however, we do know that adults have an important role to play. Routines, shared with familiar people, provide an important first step in learning language and, as Piaget (1962) suggests, through these recurring experiences, children develop schema (a mental image or collection of ideas) used to organise existing knowledge and make sense of new experiences.

> Learning to play with a ball provides a good example of the way that children's 'schemas' for objects and events are developed. Children need to touch, smell, roll, drop and throw a ball to develop the concept of 'ball'. Part of this concept includes the sound of words that are used by familiar adults when playing with balls. . . . Most of this learning occurs when children play regularly with a consistent partner.
>
> (Bochner and Jones, 2003: 12)

The above explanation, which refers to physical, social and cognitive aspects of learning language, fits very well with my own thoughts. Although Hart and Risley's (1995) much-referenced work on the 'word gap' claims that children's 'exposure' to language at home is most important, I align my views with those who challenge this notion (Johnson, 2015) and suggest that for children to learn and use new language it needs to be relevant to them and their current experiences. This is where knowledge about schema theory can support parents and practitioners in offering appropriate language for children.

The research process

To compile these case studies, I completed naturalistic observations (Mukherji and Albon, 2015) of the children in their nursery environment, incorporating a five-minute video observation once they each appeared 'deeply involved' (Laevers, 2000) in their learning. I then used these observations as prompts for discussion about the children's learning during semi-structured interviews

(Mukherji and Albon, 2015) with each of the children's parents and their key person (Elfer et al., 2012) within the nursery. I have applied existing literature regarding schema and language to help make sense of our (parents', professionals' and my own) initial understandings and identified key themes across the learning.

I subscribe to the notion that ethics are the moral compass which help guide researchers through a project, and I adhered to McNiff and Whitehead's (2011) three aspects of ethical consideration: negotiating and securing access, protecting your participants and assuring good faith. The Pen Green Centre developed through a process of democracy, and across the organisation, there continues to be a strong focus on the importance of involving others (Fletcher, 2014); it was important to me that I continued this. It was essential that parents and practitioners felt included throughout this research process, particularly when identifying the findings, recognising that through collaborative research, we could collectively find out about any relationship between schema and language.

Introducing: Robert, Ethan, Annie and James

Robert (2 years and 2 months):

> Robert attends nursery three days a week, in one of the birth to three spaces. Sue, his key person (Elfer et al., 2012), provides for his strong interest in water play. Robert became a big brother to Jullian at the age of eighteen months, and Jane, his mother, is pleased that their relationship has positively developed more recently.

During my observations, Robert demonstrated his keen interest in water play. He spent time filling different sized containers either from the tap or by submerging them in water. I was interested in the fact that he never seemed to fill the containers to the very top and, often, after filling them, he would pour the contents out immediately and start refilling them, saying 'more water'. I wondered if this was a comment he had heard previously and accommodated (Piaget, 1962) into his own vocabulary; on occasion, I noticed practitioners playfully asking, 'not *more* water Robert?' as he returned to the tap. Schematically, Robert seemed to be interested in containing and, also, scattering the water (Athey, 2007) – on one occasion, he sprayed water from his mouth quite spectacularly! In an earlier observation, Robert spent time selecting all the smaller sea creatures from a small world box, discarding larger or non-sea creatures. He contained (Athey, 2007) these creatures in a plastic jar and then used the tap to add water to the same container. Realising there was still space left in the jar, he then returned to add more small sea creatures. Robert used very little language during this sequence of events – he seemed truly engaged, in a personal state of 'flow' (Csikszentmihalyi, 1990: 4).

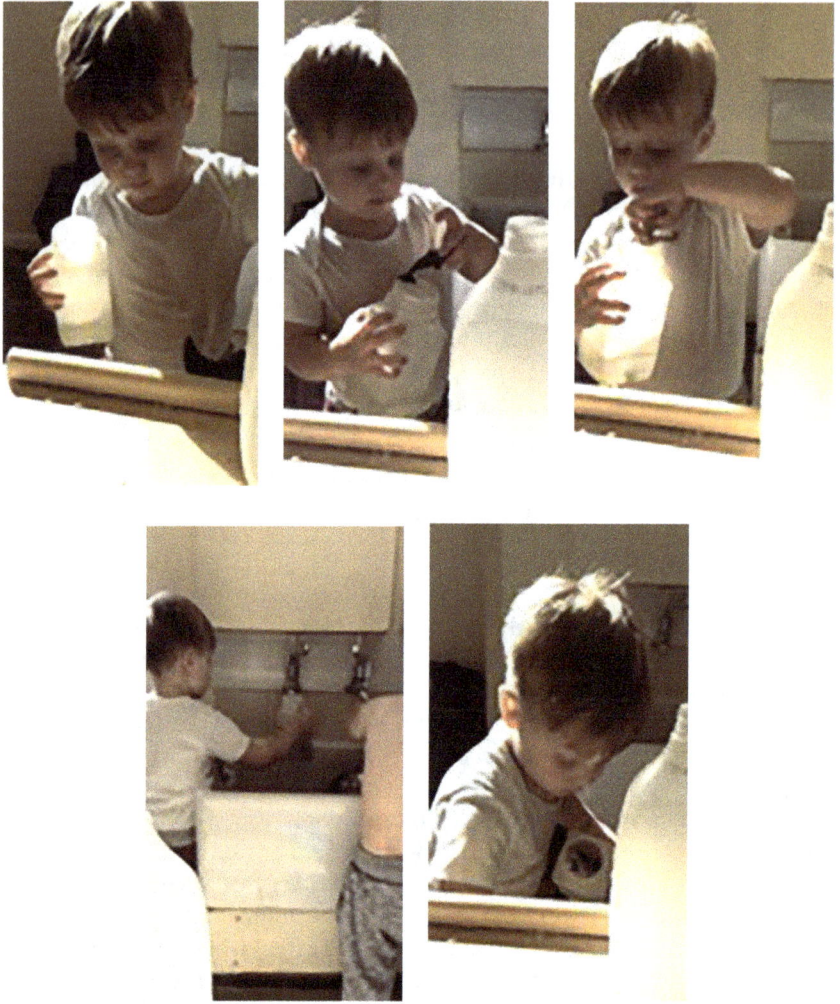

Figures 4.1–4.5 Robert discarded larger sea creatures, checked space for the smaller ones, added water to the bottle and then returned for more smaller sea creatures.

When I met with Jane and Sue, I shared my thoughts about the container of sea creatures, which reminded me of the proverb about a jar which once filled with rocks looks 'full', until you add pebbles, which 'fit in' around the rocks and make it 'full' again, until you add sand which also 'fits in' around the stones and makes it 'full' again, until you add water which 'fits in' still.

I likened this to Robert's understanding of the emotional 'space' that is available for him, now that there is a little brother to 'fit' alongside. Jane and Sue both agreed this was an interesting idea. Jane supported this by saying that Robert is very interested in relationships at present and refers to a family friend as 'my Hayey' [*sic*], instructing her: 'Jullian down' when she holds his younger brother. I wondered if this was about Robert re-creating a space for himself to 'fit' into, thinking about things that are the same and different – both to each other and from before.

Robert further demonstrated his interest in sorting and classifying objects (Arnold, 2003) as he built a tower using only the same sized blocks and paired them according to their colour. During this observation, he ignored my suggestion to include smaller, flatter blocks in the same tower – perhaps, because they were different, like the non-sea creatures, and therefore they did not 'fit' his original thoughts? This led me to think again about the notions of assimilation and accommodation (Piaget, 1962); children either exercise existing schemas or amend them to make sense of the world around them. Similarly, during a later observation, Robert had sorted 2D shapes into groups of squares, triangles and pentagons – the latter of which he referred to as 'a circle'. During this activity, Sue introduced the word 'pentagon', counting the five sides of the shape for Robert. On this occasion, however, Robert appeared not to have the necessary conceptual understanding and therefore did not accommodate and begin using the new vocabulary introduced to him, despite the fact that it was relevant to the situation. Jane confirmed that, at home, Robert correctly recognises and names squares, triangles and circles; his existing conceptual understanding, or schemes of thought (Piaget, 1962). By contrast, and building on his schematic play around containing, during later observations, Robert had also started containing or enveloping (Athey, 2007) in his mark-making. In one observation, he spent time drawing around my hand, his hand and his foot. As he engaged in this activity, I repeatedly asked who and what he wanted to 'draw round', and as he did so, he said to himself, 'round and round and round and round. . .'

Ethan (1 year and 11 months):

> Ethan has attended a birth to three space in nursery for six months, accessing two afternoon sessions a week. Kate, his key person (Elfer et al., 2012), recognises his keen interest in the messy play area and, his mother, Rachael, often encourages him to settle in the sand pit or water tray during his horizontal transition (O'Connor, 2012) into the setting. Ethan is an only child with five cousins, four of whom are older than him and spend alternate weekends with him.

During my observations, Ethan focused on resources in the messy play area, often engaging in sand or water play initially. It was clear this area offered him comfort, alongside a strong relationship with his key person (Elfer et al., 2012), and I was interested in the fact that he seemed to seek out opportunities to contain (Athey, 2007) during the initial separation from his mother. During later observations, Ethan became comfortable enough to talk about his absent mother, asking 'mummy, where mummy?' and replying 'no, home' when I asked if she had gone shopping. I was interested in this connection, considering the link between schemas and emotions (Arnold and the Pen Green Team, 2010) and Mercer's (2004) thoughts about language helping with children's cognitive conflicts. Ethan seemed able to regulate his emotions through the schematic action of containing (Arnold and the Pen Green Team, 2010) and was then able to use his emerging language to verbalise his internal, emotional concerns and seek comfort in addressing these. Whitehead agrees that 'language creates and extends our ability to think about abstract and complicated ideas' (2001: 10), such as, in this instance, absent parents.

In the sand and water, Ethan spent long periods of time over-filling and emptying various containers. He began to develop his understanding of capacity as he transferred sand or water from different sized containers, often lifting the empty container to look inside, seemingly silently questioning, 'are you empty now?' Reflecting on this, in relation to Robert's observations, it might have been an appropriate time to have introduced the words 'empty' and 'full'; however, I did not offer this vocabulary at the time. Stewart suggests that 'it is challenging to be effective as a conversational partner and co-thinker with young children, and we all have occasions where our approach misses the mark. We wonder whether we might have contributed in a more helpful way . . .' (2011: 89). For example, I was interested in Ethan's understanding of the different concepts associated with this type of play – full and empty, heavy and light, here and gone – and how these may have reflected some of the emotions he was experiencing as his mother left him to play at nursery. I wonder if offering some of this vocabulary might have supported Ethan's thinking? Atherton and Nutbrown refer to this as being conceptually attuned to children, and, throughout their many observations of young children, they 'focused on [the] aspects of thinking, learning and development that young children reveal in their schematic behaviour' (Atherton and Nutbrown, 2013: 3). Although I do not personally agree with the use of the word 'reveal', as I think it implies the unintentional discovery of something hidden, I agree that observing Ethan's schematic play certainly helped deepen my understanding of his possible thinking. More agreeably, Brock and Rankin suggest that 'even before they can talk in words children are keen to share their ideas through sounds, gesture and body language . . . [and that] talk helps children understand what they experience' (2008: 9). Although I consider myself to have 'missed the mark' this time, Atherton and Nutbrown suggests that 'a determination to take time to attune to children's own significances is at the route of accomplished pedagogy' (2015: 76).

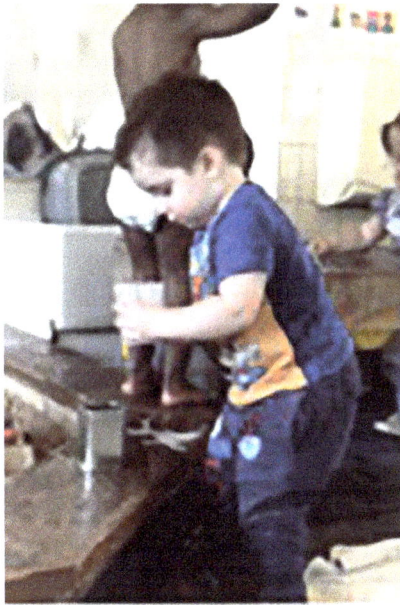

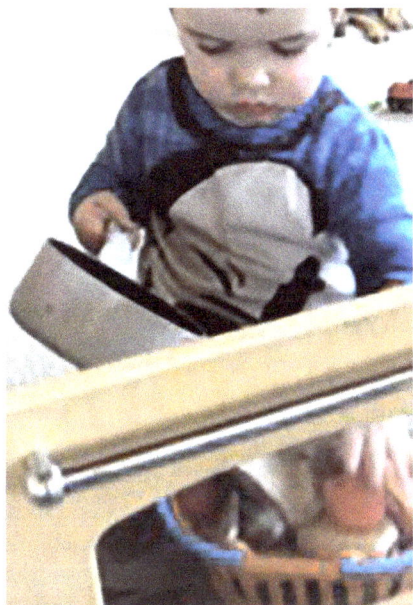

Figures 4.6–4.9 Ethan repeatedly explored capacity, checking if different containers were full or empty

Ethan seemed particularly interested in containing and transporting (Athey, 2007) objects, which might demonstrate the beginnings of a cluster of schemas that Athey (2007) states develop into later concepts. During one observation, Ethan emptied a container of toys before submerging the container in the water tray and trying to lift it out to carry around. Kate commented, 'that's heavy!' as he struggled and continued to explore. A little while later, another child tried to pick up the same container and Ethan exclaimed, 'my heaby!' [*sic*] as he looked at Kate to get it back. It seemed he had accommodated (Piaget, 1962) the significant language, even if he did not use it entirely accurately.

Mercer (2004) suggests that we 'appropriate' ways of using language through interaction with others and that, for children, like Ethan, 'recycling' language heard may be an important way of assimilating collective ways of thinking about the world around them. This idea links to Matthews' (2003) thoughts about the language offered to children by adults acting as a 'pivot' to group together repeated experiences in the brain and help children to form early concepts about the world around them. It would seem Ethan was beginning to develop his understanding of the concept of 'heavy' at the same time as Kate providing the word. Tomassello also refers to words that children use 'with a wide variety of object labels (e.g. "*more* milk", "*more* grapes", "*more* juice") [as] yielding a schema such as " *more* . . ."' (2009: 76). He refers to these as 'pivot schemas' or 'constructions' (Tomassello, 2009) that children adopt, reflecting how I then observed Ethan begin to apply the word 'my . . .' to different objects in his play, often when appealing to an adult to help him get an object back. Arnold, too, in her research into how action schemas are reflected in young children's emerging language, concluded that it is contextual learning that is important: 'when topics make "human sense" to children and their explorations are child-initiated and supported by adults, the learning occurs naturally and most effectively' (2018: 12). This experience demonstrated a link between two important, but abstract, concepts about the world that Ethan seemed to be grappling with making sense of – the weight of items and his connection to objects and other people. In conversation with Rachael, I learnt that, at home, she is trying to introduce the concept of 'sharing' to Ethan, as his cousins spend time playing with his toys.

Annie (3 years and 9 months):

> Annie attends one of the three-plus nursery spaces, five mornings a week, term time only with Jen, who was also the key person (Elfer et al., 2012) for Annie's older siblings. Annie also has a younger sibling, and her friend and neighbour Courtney attends nursery in one of the other spaces. Jen previously supported Annie's mother, Faye, to make a referral to a Health Visitor regarding Annie's communication and language development. However, this has improved significantly since Annie started attending nursery last year, and there is no ongoing support from additional services.

To begin with, I noticed that Annie was fairly non-verbal during my observations, although she always appeared to get her thoughts and ideas across to important adults and other children. Annie seemed to be an enigmatic character, and practitioners often asked her a series of questions to initially engage with her. Early in the research process, I observed Annie instruct a familiar practitioner to draw an entire A3-sized picture without seeming to utter a single word! Instead, Annie communicated only through eye contact, pointing, nodding and smiling. This illustrates the power of non-verbal communication, particularly for pre-verbal, less confident children, like Annie, or those with SEND and learning EAL. Like many, Gross argues that 'language (the speech that comes out of a child's mouth) is actually only a small part of a bigger picture. More important are the building blocks that underpin speech' (2013: 14), such as early interactions, attention and listening, playing, comprehending and, finally, expressing (National Health Service (NHS), 2018). It appeared that, although she sometimes chose not to use spoken language, Annie was still able to communicate with important people with whom she had existing relationships. Faye and Jen both reported that these relationships or connections are very important to Annie – for example, she will often seek out particular practitioners on arrival at nursery. I, too, noticed that when observing Annie playing with her long-term friend, Courtney, in one of the other nursery spaces, she seemed much more confident and was instead using lots of language to communicate rather than relying on non-verbal cues.

During these later, more animated observations, Annie was very interested in both containing and transporting (Athey, 2007), a cluster of schemas (Athey, 2007) evident throughout the many role-play scenarios she enacted, which included going shopping, going on holiday, a picnic and taking the baby for a walk in her pram. During these observations, I noticed Annie narrate her play, saying 'I close the curtains' and 'I make cereal' as she engaged in these pretend tasks. This links to Vygotsky's (1986) thoughts about 'private speech', which he suggests children engage in from around 3 years old, as a link between social communication and internal thought – essentially a child's thoughts spoken out loud. Vygotsky (1986) believed children resorted to private speech to facilitate problem-solving at times of difficulty in tasks; however, private speech has also been linked to accompanying children's activities and enhancing imagination, as I believe Annie was using it here. Berk suggests that 'private speech serves as an external instrument of thought, functioning as a plan that has been conceived but not yet realized in behaviour and assisting the child in guiding and controlling the self's actions' (1986: 671). This relates to Piaget's (1962) discussion regarding 'schemes of thought' or ideas about the world which children explore through different 'schemas of action'. I began to wonder if close observation, really 'tuning in' to children's private speech, alongside the application of schema theory, might further support our understanding of verbal children's emerging thoughts about the world, as well as their cognitive and emotional concerns. This idea challenges my practice when I consider children whose 'private speech' may be in a language different to my own.

Building on learning observed in Robert and Ethan's case studies, it was evident that Annie had started to use some of the language introduced to her relating to space and capacity. During one important observation, Annie seemed to use this to her advantage; she had packed a small rucksack with items 'for school' and brought it over to show me. She removed the items one by one, identifying what they symbolised (for example, a wooden block was 'milk') and then returned all items to the rucksack. As she was re-packing it, her friend Courtney added an item and Annie looked unimpressed. With the additional item inside, Annie struggled to do the zip up and contain (Athey, 2007) the items sufficiently. I asked her if it all fit, and she replied, '*this* doesn't fit', identifying the item added by her friend. She removed the unwanted, additional item and placed it on the table. Looking satisfied, she was then able to successfully do up the zip, contain (Athey, 2007) all her items and take her bag 'to school'.

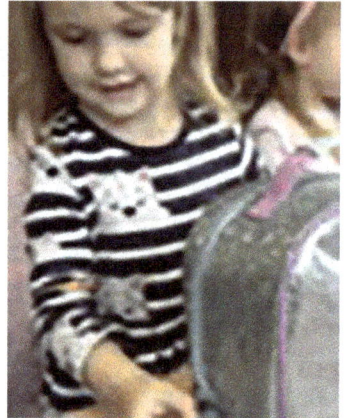

Figures 4.10–4.13 Annie empties and re-packs the backpack, minus the unwanted item

James (3 years and 8 months):

James attends one of the three-plus nursery spaces, five mornings a week, term time only. He has one older, primary, school-aged brother and his very close family friend, Charles, attends nursery alongside him. James' key person (Elfer et al., 2012), Carol, has known him and his mother, Anne, for several years, and both recognise his strong interest in making and sustaining relationships.

During my observations, James demonstrated a strong interest in following a trajectory schema (Athey, 2007), which is something Anne and Carol reiterated when I spoke to them. James seemed to enjoy running and chasing, climbing up and sliding down the slide, building towers and connecting train tracks, and climbing up towers of larger blocks to sit at the top.

During one observation, James and Charles spent over five minutes going up and down the slide, at first together and then, later, racing each other to the bottom. Anne and Carol confirmed that James is very competitive and, during this same observation, after he came last down the slide, I noticed James shout, 'first one to the gate is the winner!' as he ran towards the open gate. This demonstrated an important connection between James' schematic interest in a trajectory action and the possible language associated with it. As he develops his understanding of 'line', both stationary and in motion, James is beginning to recognise and use some important language relating to mathematical concepts, such as number and order. Arnold recognised similar connections as she observed her grandson, Harry, thinking about schema and mathematics: 'Harry initiates many actions that help him to understand his world and his particular culture; he uses the mathematical signs (like numbers), practices (like using the phone) and words (like "on top", "behind" and "before") with which he is familiar to understand emergent mathematical ideas' (2003: 93). Arnold (2003) also refers to Piaget's (2001) idea that thought is children's 'internalised actions', which made me begin to wonder whether James' actions, and those of the other children in these case studies, were, therefore, their *externalised* thoughts, providing us with an opportunity to offer relevant and meaningful language to support children's development.

Figures 4.14–4.18 James demonstrating his interest in a trajectory schema (Athey, 2007)

In a later observation, and as an example of schematic pedagogy (Atherton and Nutbrown, 2015), James had been provided with some pens and paper to draw smaller lines and create an invitation. As I arrived to observe him that day, he dived straight into an animated description of the dinosaur party in London that he had invitations to, showing me the lines on the paper proudly. As Bayley and Broadbent suggest:

> Child initiated learning offers such a wonderful context for supporting, developing and extending talk . . . . When children take on the responsibility for organising their own learning they will engage with things that interest them . . . . If we can find out about the things that are interesting to them and then provide access to those things in a culture of encouragement and support, talk will flourish!
>
> (2013: 45)

This example demonstrated how schematic pedagogy (Atherton and Nutbrown, 2015) – practitioners who are tuned into children's interests – can support both cognitive and language development. When I spoke to Anne about this afterwards, she confirmed that James was very excited about the party invitation he had received and had brought it in to share. Anne then shared another anecdote from this period, which further supports our understanding of James' interest in a trajectory schema and his close relationships, regarding his fascination with one practitioner's pregnancy. Anne described how, in all seriousness, James had offered to 'catch the baby when it comes out', with an understanding that he would then 'give it to [practitioner] with a blanket and nummy' [*sic*]. This demonstrates that James seems to believe the baby will arrive via a trajectory motion – which requires someone to 'catch' him or her – and also that he recognises the significance of the relationship between himself and the practitioner, but also between mothers and their babies.

What I have learnt about the relationship between schema and language

There is a strong theme relating to children's 'thinking' or 'thought' running through each of these four case studies. In terms of the relationship between schemas and language, this appears to be the connecting factor. Children's action schemas (Athey, 2007) reflect their emerging and developing thoughts about the world around them, including complex concepts such as 'here and gone'. Children develop their thinking by repeatedly engaging in these actions, which 'lead to early categories and then to logical classifications' (Athey, 2007: 49). Language then offers children a socially-constructed method of labelling these thoughts about the world around them, but 'these symbols have no meaning in themselves', they must be 'socially learned' (Hayes, 2016: 9). For children acquiring more than one spoken language, this process is potentially more complex; however, it does support the social-constructivist view that children learn language through conversation and experience. A criticism of this theory is that children only learn what we, as adults, want them to know; instead, Gross suggests that 'adults who take their lead from the child have a more positive effect on language development than those trying to direct the child' (2013: 17). This is evident when Sue tries to introduce the word 'pentagon' to Robert; although it is relevant to the situation, it appears that he is not interested in the concept and therefore does not accommodate (Piaget, 1962) the new vocabulary.

It is true that throughout these observations, children appeared to accommodate (Piaget, 1962) new language when it is related to their current thinking or troubling thoughts – often reflected in their schematic play – and it might be suggested, therefore, that language supports equilibrium (Piaget, 1962) and, subsequently, learning. Atherton and Nutbrown suggest that viewing children's actions through the schema lens 'enables adults to accompany children as they explore and investigate in a way which attunes to their *forms of thinking* and so provides a match for their conceptual concerns' (2013: 4) – we saw this accompaniment when Kate offered Ethan the word 'heavy' for example, at a time that it matched his physical and conceptual understanding. Hollich et al. (2003) refer to this as 'word-to-world mapping' when describing the different ways in which children learn words. Atherton and Nutbrown also suggest that 'an informed understanding of schemas gives practitioners insights into the richness of children's thinking and helps adults to be thought-provoking in a relevant way as they unite with children on their learning journey' (2013: 23). Although, as evidenced by my 'missing the mark' with Ethan, this is not always the case – by not offering the language relevant to his interest in containing at times of transition, I demonstrated that I was not truly united with him.

If thoughts are children's internalised actions (Piaget, 1962), then perhaps action schemas (Athey, 2007) are their earliest thoughts externalised. It is no surprise that previous researchers have referred to schemas in this way – Athey referring to them as 'systems of *thought*' (2007: 153) and Nutbrown (2011) as 'threads of *thinking*'. Atherton and Nutbrown made the same connection between the thoughts and actions of very young children when they stated, 'babies and toddlers learn with their whole bodies and all their senses, they are *physical thinkers*' (2015: 65). In terms of the 'Means, Reasons and Opportunities Model' (Money and Thurman, 1994), schema offers an alternative 'means' of communication for children, and for practitioners who are willing to 'listen' to them, an opportunity to support their traditional, language use through the offering of relevant words. As Atherton and Nutbrown summarise:

> Seen through the lens of schematic theory, those working with children can reflect upon and shape their practice in an effort to provide a cognitive match in learning encounters. It allows accompaniment in learning to be a relevant and pertinent occasion which affords children the respect that they deserve.
>
> (2013: 91)

Reflections and questions

Athey suggests 'the more a person knows the more he or she wants to know' (1990: 44), and I certainly intend for my learning in this area to continue, so for now, I offer merely a summary of my developing learning thus far.

Throughout my research, I observed children benefit from several 'attuned, matched learning encounters' (Atherton and Nutbrown, 2013: x) because the adults around them were aware of both schema theory and each child's schematic interests. I was reminded of the 'the importance of a conceptual response to children's *patterns of thinking*' (Atherton and Nutbrown, 2013: x) and, as a result of this conceptual tuning in (Atherton and Nutbrown, 2013), I noticed opportunities for practitioners to suggest appropriate language relevant to the individual child and therefore support overall development.

In practice, this means that, when planning, time and space should be allowed to consider children's current and ongoing conceptual concerns, so that all practitioners might be aware and therefore able to offer appropriate language which will support children's thinking and, possibly even, offer equilibrium (Piaget, 1962). Alongside a rich understanding of the individual children and their contexts, practitioners should then be able to support language development by appropriately 'commenting' on what children are doing in relation to their action schema (Athey, 2007), responding to their initial utterances with 'expansions' relating to their conceptual concerns or 'recasting' back what they say in the right form, without correcting them (Gross, 2013: 18).

Although some of my introductory research questions have been addressed, I feel my knowledge is still partial (Athey, 2007), and therefore, I would like to continue to explore certain aspects of the relationship between schema and language and encourage others to do the same in practice:

Do you too consider schemas an alternative form of communication about the world, especially for non-verbal children (i.e. young children, those with SEND or learning EAL)?

Do you utilise language strategies to comment, expand and recast words and phrases that are relevant to children's schematic interests?

Do you discuss what children may be communicating through their schematic play with parents/carers?

A brief word about parents and the home learning environment

Hopefully these case studies highlight a link between schema theory – as a method of identifying children's conceptual concerns – and the role of practitioners, *and* parents, in offering appropriate and meaningful 'word-to-world mapping' (Hollich et al., 2003), which is matched to each child's interests, and therefore more likely to be accommodated (Piaget, 1962) into young children's ever-growing vocabulary bank. Schema theory provides practitioners with an additional, practical approach with which to engage with parents regarding their children's learning and to encourage their involvement (Whalley and the Pen Green Team, 2017).

Gross recognises that 'how parents interact with their children is a powerful predictor of the child's language development and learning' (2013: 136). The Conservative Government, together with the National Literacy Trust and Public Health England, agree, recognising that: 'language skills are shaped and nurtured by the child's home learning environment (HLE)' (DfE, 2018: 6). In line with the Bercow reports (DCSF, 2008; ICAN and RCSLT, 2018), current policy states that 'the quality of the HLE is a key predictor of a child's early language ability and future success; positive experiences can have lasting and life changing impacts' (DfE, 2018: 21). For this reason, I encourage early years practitioners to support parents in utilising schema theory (Athey, 2007), to help tune into children's worlds (Arnold, 2015b), and therefore offer relevant 'word-to-world mapping' (Hollich et al., 2003).

Recommended reading

Atherton, F. and Nutbrown, C. (2015) 'Schematic pedagogy: Supporting one child's learning at home and in a group', *International Journal of Early Years Education* 24(1), pp. 63–79.

Hollich, G., Hirsh-Pasek, K. and Golinkoff, R. M. (2003) 'What does it take to learn a word?', *Monographs of the Society for Research in Child Development* 65(3), pp. 1–16.

Acknowledgement: This chapter is derived from an article published in *Early Child Development and Care* 20.07.2021 Copyright: Taylor and Francis, available online: www.tandfonline.com DOI: 10.1080/03004430.2021.1954628

5 Schemas and metaphor

Cath Arnold and Sue Gascoyne

Discovering 'schemas'

Cath: I first came across schemas, as we think of them today, when I joined Pen Green Nursery, as a family worker (Early Years Educator), in October 1988. Although I was a mother to three children and had worked in nurseries for 12 years by then, I had not heard the term used to describe young children's repeated actions. It was as though 'the curtains opened' for me at that point, and I have been studying and trying to learn more ever since, mostly from children but also from parents and colleagues and the literature. Schemas and the link with metaphor was something Chris Athey and I discussed briefly before she 'passed on the baton' to speak metaphorically. I write from the perspective of an early years teacher/researcher.

Sue: Reflecting upon my journey as a parent and educator and now a play therapist, I can pinpoint three discoveries which have fundamentally influenced me:

• Discovering schemas as a parent was quite literally like a lightbulb being switched on in a dark room, illuminating what had previously appeared as my children's intriguing, and at times frustrating, behaviours! I had always intuitively known that their actions were not random or lacking purpose, but knowledge of schemas gave me the confidence to trust and respect them, providing a possible decoder for understanding why it was simply not possible to walk to school without collecting pocketfuls of stones or swinging round the lamppost and walking carefully along a low wall, no matter how late we were!

• Many years later, when researching messy play for a book, I stumbled across Deci and Ryan's three psychological needs

DOI: 10.4324/9781003224341-6

(2000) (Gascoyne, 2019). (Sue's book entitled *Messy Play in the Early Years* is a great read.) This focus on the need to belong, to feel competent and have some sense of agency, helped open my eyes to understanding my own and other's feelings and behaviours, both personally and professionally. This was particularly relevant for me during the Covid-19 lockdowns when it was difficult maintaining feelings of connection, self-control and mastery (feelings which may also resonate in Amber's observation below).

- My final key inspiration came in a book provided by my mother-in-law. It was the compelling childhood memories of adults in Brenda Crowe's book *Play is a Feeling* that helped guide me to trust my instincts about the wondrous capabilities of babies and children, at a time when nurseries were openly saying 'babies don't do anything, we only care for them!' Reading the adult's vivid memories helped me challenge this and underpinned my fascination with all things sensory and how children learn.

Discussing this chapter with Cath has brought all three of these influences to the fore in being curious about what a child might be doing and showing me, giving me the confidence to not make assumptions about children's actions and motivations, and recognizing the importance of schematic actions in supporting children's fundamental psychological needs.

Time and again in our discussions, we found ourselves drawn to questions about the potential links between schemas, emotions and metaphors. At times our thinking was like feeling in the dark; at other times, sharp and lucid. Sometimes we thought we'd reached an understanding only for it to vanish, leaving us with a sense of something important still eluding us! To use a metaphor, this chapter feels like it has arisen from the ashes of our deliberations like a baby phoenix. The resulting fledgling ideas are offered not as facts, but wonderings to spark further reflection. We begin with a focus on metaphor.

What is metaphor?

Definitions of metaphor are far from clear-cut. According to google scholar, 'metaphor' is about language and thinking and the metaphors we use influence our thinking (Thibodeau et al., in press). The dictionary describes metaphor as 'a figure of speech', privileging language over other ways of expression. In fact, most definitions seem to view cognition and the brain as taking precedence over the body, inferring an artificial body/brain split. Loris Malaguzzi's emphasis upon the hundred languages of children, not just speech, helps to redress the balance, with examples of young children using metaphor in actions as well as language in Reggio Emilia settings (Reggio Exhibition, 2018). Modell (2009) states that 'Metaphor is the organizing template that establishes the categories of emotional memory' (:8). He suggests that we look for similarities in situations and environments to make sense of our emotional experiences, suggesting a curiosity which feels relevant to the observations shared in this book.

In Cath's PhD, she considered children's schemas and, alongside parents and workers, tried to work out the links between their actions and their emotions, using attachment theory in her analysis (Bowlby, 1997; Arnold, 2007). Cath found that 'The schema [seemed to] serve as a transition between an experience or feeling and understanding that experience or feeling' (Arnold, 2007: 368). One of the children studied, whose parents were preparing to separate, seemed to repeatedly use 'enveloping' to possibly 'imagine' or 'begin to work out' how life might change in the future in relation to her father moving out of the family home (Arnold and the Pen Green Team, 2010: 89) or possibly to recreate a sense of containment to fill this gap? 'Sam seemed to envelop objects with different materials to symbolize concepts like "sleep", "death" and "jail" and seemed to explore "here and gone" [object permanence] in a variety of ways over a long period of time' (2010: 103). This was prior to her father moving out of the family home. Cath coined the term 'reflective expansion' to describe how the children she studied 'reached back' and appeared to use repeated actions to make sense of an experience or event beyond their current comprehension (Arnold, 2007: 356).

As well as supporting the child, noticing and valuing children's repeated actions and behaviours also affords adults with an important insight into what the child might be experiencing. As a therapist, Sue likes to describe this as a bit like being a behavioural, schematic and emotional detective, trying to unpick clues. However, we need to be tentative about attributing meaning to children's actions, as without (and even with) the 'sub-titles' provided by language, context and the input of families and key workers, we may never really know their meaning. This positions adults as key in noticing and being curious about children's actions and behaviours to help gain a better insight into their emotional states and needs as well as their cognitive development. This involves a process of understanding, which will no doubt develop and change as we are privy to more pieces of the 'emotional jigsaw'. Crowe cautions us that 'There need to be times when we stand back and watch our children, just as an ornithologist watches a bird focused sharply in his binoculars and strives to take in every detail before it flies off again. Only then do we begin to understand the significance of what we see, and act more easily in accordance with what we understand' (1983: 74).

In Cath's work as a teacher and researcher, studying the child along-side their parents and keyworkers helps ensure that she 'does no harm' and also shapes and furthers her understanding. In contrast, when working therapeutically with a child, confidentiality is paramount, and Sue needs to draw from the child's context, environment and communication through symbolic and creative play, using a combination of theoretical knowledge and intuition as guides. Viewing the same observations from different ends of the lens, so to speak, has been fascinating for us, providing challenge, enrichment and fresh perspectives which have prompted new wonderings. This has also served as a useful reminder that we cannot definitively inter-pret children's actions, but the process of wondering may trigger different ways of us responding to, providing for and supporting young children's complex emotional, cognitive and physical needs. Building upon these points of difference, we have chosen to present both lenses within this chapter, to hopefully illuminate children's potential seeds of inquiry. Since we are all shaped by our own unique experiences and contexts as well as those which we share, we invite you to listen to any additional and alterna-tive interpretations that resonate for you, rather than being limited to those offered here.

Freud (1915) and Jung (1946) emphasise the importance of the unconscious and serve as important reminders that the meaning of a child's actions may be out of *their* own awareness. Piaget referred to 'secondary or unconscious sym-bolism' giving an example of a child 'who has been made jealous by the birth of a younger brother and happens to be playing with two dolls of unequal size, will make the smaller one go away on a journey, while the bigger one stays with his mother' (Piaget, 1951: 171). He inferred that the child was expressing an unconscious wish to be rid of his brother and could not safely express the underlying emotion of jealousy but could feel it and express it symbolically (or metaphorically?).

This resonates with Lakoff and Johnson's understanding that 'The essence of metaphor is understanding and experiencing one kind of thing in terms of another' (1981: 5). We know how important sensorial and physical expe-riences are for children, underpinning their understanding of themselves, others and the world around them, so it is fitting that metaphors have an 'experiential basis' derived from firsthand physical experiences and are rooted in 'embodied experience' (Lakoff and Johnson, 1981; Gibbs, 2008). Turner distinguished between 'action schemas' and 'image schemas' as the source of metaphorical thinking (1996), explaining that we 'project structure from a "source" we understand to a "target" we want to understand' (1996: 17). So, returning to the example of Sam, who 'enveloped' various objects perhaps to work through and understand what life would be like when her parents separated and her father moved out of the family home, Sam may have used the image created when she 'enveloped' objects to explore 'here and gone' in relation to her father and the changing family situation. In this chapter, we hypothesize that the chosen schema or repeated action may be the structure that enables young children to try to make sense of experiences that are either beyond their comprehension or too emotionally difficult or painful to process. Schematic play may help children work on gaining this understanding unconsciously as well as physically, intellectually, sensorially and spatially. Turner argues that bodily actions such as 'grasping' are 'some of the earliest spatial stories learned by a child' (1996: 34). Every small repeated action can be conceptualized as a story. The links with language are apparent as later we 'grasp' opportunities that are less tangible. According to Cattanach, cognitive psychologists suggest that 'we take in fragments of information and organise them in a narrative form' (1997: 5) to make sense of them, and this feels relevant to some of the children's schematic actions described in this chapter.

Crowe (1983) signposts the value of metaphors for children when 'dealing with very powerful feelings within themselves'. She goes on to consider that children sometimes can't take the value from the metaphor 'unless it comes to them at one (step) removed' (1983: 90). This seems relevant to several of the examples provided in this chapter, as if the schematic actions afford the child an 'otherly' experience, at one step removed.

Turner's explanation made us think about how children sometimes project relationships and feelings onto objects, environments and ourselves spatially, through 'lining up', 'seriating', 'positioning' and using 'proximity' or 'distancing' of objects which may represent important people. Susan Isaacs described a little boy distressed when his mother left him, being comforted by placing two blocks close together. Isaacs explained, 'here . . . we see a child comforting himself and overcoming feelings of loss and terror by a symbolic act with two material objects' (1952: 116). Parallels are also evident in Example 1 below.

What distinguishes symbolic play as metaphoric?

Another issue that has become part of our discussions is whether symbolic play is always metaphoric? Athey (2013: 9) describes the different ways schemas are explored, including 'symbolic representation', i.e. 'When something is used to stand for something else' in which children use 'actions, mark-making and other graphic forms and speech' to re-present their experiences. In many instances, children may be aware of what they are replaying and representing; however, sometimes children may repeat actions and reveal feelings of which they are unaware as well as unable to express and understand. The repeated action may give them some control over what they are feeling and may go some way towards visualising and aiding their understanding.

In this chapter, we offer five examples of young children's schematic play that can be seen as metaphorical, in the sense that the play may be helping a child or children understand, process and accept something beyond their current comprehension. Examples from Cath are of individual children and include discussions with parents. Sue's examples are drawn from observations of several children in a therapeutic setting and do not include discussions with parents.

- The first two examples focus on 'lines', 'connecting' and 'disconnecting'.
- Examples 3 and 4 focus on 'enclosing' and 'enveloping'.
- The final example shows 'stacking', 'lining up' and 'crossing a boundary'.

Example 1 – pumpkins

Ezra was 1 year and 11 months when he started nursery. Despite the Covid restrictions, his parents were able to settle him into nursery over nearly four weeks. This observation was made just after he was settled in and left without his parents/carers for the first time. The online journal shared by practitioners and parents to record children's play is an important link between educators and parents. Ezra's family worker at nursery shared the following observation with his parents:

> Ezra, saying goodbye to mummy was hard this morning and after working through this together, you then went to explore this separation further. Ezra, what you did next amazed me.
>
> You became very excited to see the pumpkins and immediately became interested in the small ones. You chose three and lined them up next to one another. You became very precise about the way in which each one sat and it became very apparent to me that you were ensuring each one was touching in the same way.
>
> After looking intently at the three connected pumpkins, you chose to move one to the other side of the (wet) messy area. However, whilst doing this, you never took your eyes off the two connected pumpkins you had left behind. You would then repeatedly walk back and reconnect the third pumpkin to the two others. Ezra, you spent a long period of time taking this one away and reconnecting it again.
>
> Ezra, I wondered if the pumpkins represented your family and you were using them to explore the separations and transitions that take place in your life?

Figures 5.1, 5.2 and 5.3 Ezra positioning the pumpkins

Reflections from Ezra's parents

'The observation with the pumpkins occurred the day after we tried putting Ezra in his own bed to sleep, so this may have been on his mind and connected to separating from us to sleep as well as to attend nursery'.

Reflections

Using and moving the toy pumpkins in this way, it appears that Ezra was able to physically and spatially recreate connecting, separating and rejoining to re-enact the separation that he was experiencing both in attending nursery and being encouraged to sleep in his own room. The physical act of separating and reconnecting provides both a visual representation of the situation and an opportunity to perhaps view this from an external perspective, as if a 'fly on the wall', separating him from the painful emotions. This sense of visual and spatial separation seems key both to Ezra's intentions and potentially his resulting understanding. It is interesting that he chooses to maintain a visual connection through eye contact with the pumpkins, reflecting perhaps his mother and him keeping each other 'in mind' (Winnicott, 1965/2006: 26). The separation of these pumpkins by a messy play area, distinguished by lino flooring, is also potentially intriguing on a metaphorical and emotional level, as well as the schematic opportunity that this gives for transition and going across a physical (and metaphorical) boundary. Playing out the changing relationship dynamics of connecting and disconnecting seems to offer Ezra an important opportunity to experience a sense of agency and control – an essential component of wellbeing and our psychological needs (Deci and Ryan, 2000).

The back-and-forth movement and repetition seem to provide a reassuring rhythm to the process and a sense of consistency and stability. The importance of an attuned educator in this situation should not be underestimated. The family worker provides Ezra with permission and space in which to attend to these concerns, noticing his feelings and providing an anchor and safe 'container' within which he could explore his understanding of, and feelings about, separation (Bion, 1962). Her summary also provides an opportunity to talk with Ezra about his play. (We saw in Chapter 2 that 'reflecting' with Ezra on his day is a strong feature of his parents' practice. This observation also links with his play on the following day with 'arches' featured at the end of Chapter 2.)

Example 2 – sticky tape

Connecting, disconnecting and going through a boundary are also key themes in children's schematic behaviours in Sue's therapeutic work. Often capitalizing upon the affordances of sticky tape, particularly its strength, length and sticking qualities, children have used this in a variety of ways within a therapeutic context. In several sessions prior to a holiday break from school, children used tape to attach Sue, or the play therapy resources, to themselves, as if reluctant to end the sessions and their connection with her and the safe space. Frequently having connected Sue to a table, door, chair or even a sensory tent or sink, they finished the session by cutting this tie, as if taking control of the 'ending' by physically and visually detaching from Sue, whilst leaving her still attached to the space!

Sometimes sticky tape has been used to keep something safe or to lock up (contain) something 'dangerous' or negative to prevent it from escaping. In these instances, separating out the sensory and physical experience from the metaphorical dimension is impossible as they appear to be inextricably interlinked. For example, wrapping a box or other container with sticky tape can involve rhythmic movements as the child encircles it, either with hands or their whole body. Sometimes considerable force and a strong trajectory motion are needed to counteract the resistance and unravel and extend the tape, making this a very physical and empowering act. Being curious about encounters like these led Sue to consider not just the sensory and physical experience and its calming and regulating affect, but also the affirming qualities of its visual representation and potential symbolic meaning.

In still other examples, tape appears to have been used by the child to provide a sense of separation and restrict access. In this way, Sue wondered if the child was able to experience much-needed agency and mastery and, in doing so, to visualise and try out different roles, positions and viewpoints? Sometimes a simple line traversing the room was sufficient, with the child choosing where Sue should be and whether on the same or a different side to them. In other situations, a more complex system of connections was created, effectively separating the space into three distinct zones. Sometimes these lines were imbued with special powers, whether as laser lines or poisonous wire, to be avoided at all cost. This provided the child with further agentic control as they chose when to turn off or trigger the switch! It also introduced moments of discombobulation for the adult, as they were not in control.

Example 3 – trapped

Amber, aged 3 years and 3 months, had recently started attending nursery. Amber's parents describe her as being 'very vocal' and 'into everything'. When Cath first spoke to her parents, Amber was predominantly into making lines and towers. However, around the time of her starting nursery, her mother (a childminder) noticed a fresh repeated pattern of enclosing and enveloping:

> In the first video, Amber was on the settee with a cushion and blanket completely covering her. Her dad lifted the blanket to peek in and Amber said 'Close the door' and 'In my house' and 'I'm going to stay here, Daddy' followed by lots of giggling and finally 'I'm trapped'.

In the second video, Amber is standing in the shower (fully clothed) with the shower curtain pulled around her so that she cannot be seen. She emerges to explain to her grandmother that she is Trike (the triceratops from her favourite TV show 'Harry and a bucketful of dinosaurs') and that she is hiding from her granddad, who is T Rex. At one point, she mentions that Trike is 'trapped' and when her granddad tries to get to her, she is tightly wrapped in the shower curtain. When he finally finds her, there is loud giggling.

In the third observation, she was sitting on the carpet and used her finger to draw a circle into the fluffy carpet around her, saying, 'look, I'm trapped'.

In the fourth observation, Amber squashed herself inside the oven of the play kitchen. She kept asking for the door to be closed, saying, 'It's very dark' and 'I'm stuck'.

Figure 5.4 Stuck in the kitchen

Figure 5.5 Using circles

Reflections from Amber's parents

'She's only just begun going to nursery so we think it could be related to the [Covid] restrictions and her being stuck at home for so long! At nursery, they cornered off areas, so they were enclosed. Even their outdoor space had barriers all around to separate the bubbles. I'm not sure if she's trying to process this lack of freedom.

She also questions why we haven't been to the farm, why she can't go shopping with us, why we can't go into nana's house too? She seems to have a fear that things she enjoys don't last long. She panicked when we explained nursery's closed for the holidays and became upset as her experiences of things closing last a long time'.

Reflections

Amber's choice of the word 'trapped' is interesting as it is such a strong emotive word. This may have come from the TV programme, but certainly resonates with how many of us felt during lockdown. Amber may have been making sense of and communicating her feelings of a lack of control, change and limits through these repeated actions. This could also have provided her with positive opportunities to experience being in control of her enclosure and feeling of trappedness.

In this way, she has managed to show the adults around her that she wants to be on her own through her describing words ('Close the door' and 'I'm trapped'), her request for adult input and her choice of a tiny space (the kitchen sink – see image) that no one else could fit in. It is interesting how the line on the carpet (a temporary line 'drawn' by squashing the fluff) is so much less physical and boundaried than the other forms of enclosure described. Although obvious initially, the carpet line is also very temporary and transient. Possibly having worked through this preoccupation, she no longer needed to experience enclosing in such a physical or sensory way, but more metaphorically?

Reflecting upon her squeezing herself into the play oven, Sue wondered whether this gave her calming and reassuring proprioceptive feedback and spatial awareness to increase her awareness of her own body (where her body begins and ends and the space around her body). She may also have been exploring her anxieties over bubbles and safety, hence the importance of people not being in her bubble?

Footnote: As time has passed and activities have re-opened due to an easing of Covid restrictions, Amber has ceased to engage in this type of play, inferring perhaps the importance of environmental factors on children's inquiries?

Example 4 – enveloping

For several children, the presence of a tent within the therapy room appeared to offer the child safety and containment. On entering the room, some children's ritual was to dart instantly into the tent (as if they were not there). Sue's response was to initiate a game of hide and seek wherein they were given control over their own safety and readiness to be found. Only after then did they venture into the room 'properly', ever ready to return to its safe containment if needed (Bion, 1962). In those moments, Sue felt that both the containment and separation that this afforded were significant, reminiscent of an air lock or birthing canal perhaps. Once safe enough to be enclosed within the space, they could take on the role of a baby, scared animal, aggressor or dangerous monster, without the need for making eye contact, which, in violent situations, they may have found to be unsafe.

For some children, the tent seemed to represent a safe space for them to simply be on their own. At other times it became a space from which they could ask to be rescued, with Sue always checking with them first to make sure they felt in control. For other children, it was important for Sue to join them within the tent, where the child then locked them in, creating a comfortable space for self-nurture and being vulnerable to others. In all these instances, it seems that the act of containing enabled them to feel safe, in control and ultimately process at a much deeper level.

Example 5 – crossing a boundary

Lillie was 2 years when Cath first spoke with her parents. She was just starting to attend nursery. Lillie's parents describe her as 'very sociable'. 'She loves playing with other children and her language is well developed'. Lillie and her family have a very supportive extended family and Lillie frequently spends time with grandparents at their home. Lillie's parents shared several video clips and photos with Cath.

> In one video clip, Lillie is stacking square wooden blocks on the floor. She does so quickly, not appearing to be bothered about carefully lining them up or positioning them in a specific order. Her tower fell once it reached seven blocks and she immediately started to rebuild the tower, deftly positioning all the blocks from a nearby upturned wheeled container. Once the container was empty, she moved to some toys nearby and, one at a time, got a block to add to the tower. When stacking the 12th brick, the tower, now about two-thirds of her own height, fell, and Lillie looks disappointed, asking her mother for help.
>
> In another video clip, Lillie is playing with seven small play figures on a boldly patterned rug. She places them in a line and her mother comments, 'You've lined them all up!' As the line of toys is in the middle of a large pale grey diamond on the rug, it looks like they are enclosed by the pattern of the carpet, as if in their own 'bubble'. Lillie runs around the figures several times (as though further containing them), appearing to follow the lines of the diamond pattern as she does so. She says something, which her mother thinks is 'Lined up', possibly echoing what her mother said. Whilst still running, her mother asks, 'What are you going to do now?' Lillie replies, 'Going to count them'. Lillie counts '1, 2, 3, 4, 5, 6'. Lillie then holds one up, saying, 'What's that?' Her mother replies, 'That's doggy – that's Paw Patrol', and Lillie places it within the thick black frame (of the carpet pattern), repositioning it within this a few times. She holds up another figure, asking, 'What's that?' Her mum replies, 'Baba JJ' and Lillie positions it within the grey diamond next to, but not touching, the doggy. She picks up the doggy again and repositions it on

the edge of the black and grey pattern. She then repeats this with the remaining figures placing them close to each other within, and next to the black frame and extending into the adjoining red diamond. Lillie says 'Girl' when she places three of the Paw Patrol figures on the black 'boundary'. She uses up all the figures again, but this time her finished line goes across the boundary, connecting two coloured 'bubbles' on the carpet. Lillie counts saying '3, 4, 5, 6, 8'. She then runs around her line several times, broadly following the shape of the two diamonds, saying, 'I'm running faster' followed by (what her mother thinks sounds like) 'Olay!' or 'All of it!' several times.

Figure 5.6 An enclosed line of play figures

Figure 5.7 Play figures crossing a boundary

Reflections from Lillie's parents

Parental insight can be invaluable when trying to better understand children's actions and behaviours. We both found it more difficult to recognize the potential patterns in Lillie's play but felt that the longer clip of Lillie positioning figures on the carpet was particularly intriguing. We wondered, given the focus of play (and context of the Covid pandemic), whether Lillie might be exploring connections. Lillie's mother agreed that 'much of her play is underpinned by her relationships'. Her mother explained, 'she's very close to her grandparents. I do agree that could be one of the reasons she was moving to different colours on the carpet' (i.e., going between the families' homes). On further reflection, her mother further explained that Lillie has moved to a different space in the nursery as she was not finding the youngest children's area stimulating enough.

A conversation with Lillie's family worker added that at nursery 'Lillie likes to dress up, especially as Spider-Man, which may help her feel more secure in the new space' and give her 'agentic powers'. Tracy also added that 'Lillie noticed that some of the staff had moved and needed a little trip to see where Kerry had moved to'. This confirmed Lillie's strong interest in people, where they are located and the potential importance of this for feeling safe and having a sense of agency.

Reflections

Lining up and enclosing seem to feature in Lillie's play. It may have been significant that as she placed the figures, she said 'Girl' on three occasions. Could 'girl' be herself or her peers, we wondered. We can only speculate on whether the pattern on the carpet was important for Lillie in providing a 'boundary' to cross. Watching the video clip, the containment, and conversely, the separation afforded by the carpet pattern instinctively felt relevant, as did her whole-bodied encircling of the lined-up play figures. This could represent her going to stay with grandparents, feeling restricted by 'Covid bubbles' or, alternatively, in response to her move to a different space at nursery. Under normal circumstances, the move in nursery would have been more gradual and controlled by the child, with Lillie making several visits to the adjoining space to become familiar with the environment and the people, but due to Covid restrictions, the move may have been less gradual and more controlled by adults. Moving the play figures in this way, she may have been processing her feelings about the nursery move and its associated connections and disconnections, using the visual containers of the carpet as a tool. Of course, we will probably never know whether its position was accidental or intentional, but this does highlight the potential insight that small and seemingly incidental details may bring to our understanding.

A 'line' can also represent time, past, present and future, a concept difficult to grasp. When building a tower, she seemed intent on using up all the blocks she could find, not just those nearby. Perhaps her sad expression when the blocks fell reflected her lack of satisfaction at not completing her self-set task? When

Lillie 'enclosed' the 'line' by running around it several times, that felt celebratory, a kind of celebration of 'togetherness' or completion. Lillie performed this running 'around' when the figures were initially together, and again once she had repositioned them across the boundary between the two coloured 'carpet diamonds'. Could this reflect a finishing of the 'task' in a metaphorical full stop or her bringing together the before and now?

If we take the time to carefully watch everyday moments of play, such as those described in this chapter, this raises a host of questions about the child's intentions and seeds of inquiry, as well as how best for adults to support these. Just as adults 'follow a train of thought through loops and whorls as we try to get to the point of resolve' (Crowe: 79), so too a child's investigations may (if not interrupted by adults) continue until they come to 'what the child recognizes as the end' (Crowe: 75). Being able to see something through to its natural end is a key component of competence and autonomy (Deci and Ryan's three psychological needs), and this is potentially even more important for children, for whom much of their world feels beyond their control and at times like the pandemic, where individual's sense of agency and connection were limited.

Crowe (1983) reminds us of the importance of not interrupting children but watching first. We have all experienced the frustration of being interrupted or not being able to finish something and the niggling sense of frustration and lack of satisfaction that results. Sometimes we look at children's 'busy hands first, but if we could also look at the concentration on their faces we might perhaps leave them . . . more often than we do, to await the moment when a "proper" ending affords them the satisfaction that each of us knows so well in our own lives as we bring something to a conclusion' (1983: 79). It is in this respect that the adults around children have a vital role to play in allowing them to be in flow and involved in following their own preoccupations and interests (Crowe, 1983).

Reflections and questions

Considering schemas from two different perspectives has been extremely stimulating. Our backgrounds provided different foci, resulting in considerable discussion and uncertainty. Throughout this metaphorical journey, our purpose was to keep our minds open and to tolerate the discomfort of this uncertainty. We see this as a small beginning to understanding schemas and emotional metaphors. Inevitably, there is a lot more to metaphor than what we have focused on. Much of the historical emphasis within the literature appears to focus on language. Whilst children's verbal language is undoubtedly invaluable in helping to decode children's actions and behaviours, we suggest that this is only a small part of the picture. As Landreth so eloquently reminds us, 'toys are used like words by children, and play is their language as well as a portal not just to the conscious but the unconscious too' (2002: 12).

Inevitably, with a spotlight on the metaphors found in everyday actions and play, we have had to restrict the focus of this chapter and, in doing so, omit what in many ways would be far more obvious examples of metaphorical/symbolic play. However, we are both alive to the practice of children 'taking on a character' (both in mainstream and therapeutic contexts) and its potential significance in feeling more powerful and experiencing agentic control. Both Amber and Lillie appeared to take on a character in these observations, so this is certainly another fruitful line of inquiry. There has also not been space within this chapter to focus on the rituals used by some children, potentially to feel safe and provide reassurance that things are predictable; however, this is an area explored in Chapter 7 (on schemas and autism).

In the examples provided and countless others that we have observed, it seems apparent to us that schemas are prevalent; however, each child seems to explore and use them in their own unique way. With a wide-eyed and open-minded lens on children's play, actions and behaviours, inevitably, we are left with as many questions as we started with! Not the least of which: are children communicating with themselves (and potentially bridging any body/brain gap) through the use of schemas as metaphors? And how can we best respond to children demonstrating their feelings through schemas as metaphors or emotional containers? The intention of this chapter has not been to definitively pin down the answers to these and other questions, but rather to remind us of the importance of carefully noticing, wondering and giving children the space, time and permission to play.

Recommended reading

Crowe, B. (1983) *Play Is a Feeling*. London: Unwin Paperbacks.
Turner, M. (1996) *The Literary Mind: The Origins of Thought and Language*. Oxford: Oxford University Press.

6 Why do they do that, and how should we respond?

Kate Barker

Discovering schemas

Ever since I first embarked on my career in early education, as a reception class teacher in a small primary school, young children's thinking has fascinated me. I have often found myself wondering why a child has taken a particular course of action, wishing I could get inside their head to find out more about the thinking behind the action. When working as an early years advisory teacher, I was introduced to Pen Green's theoretical frameworks for working with parents (Whalley, 2001). I discovered in-depth analysis of observations as a way of deepening my understanding of children's thinking and learning, and by this route became interested in the use of schemas to explore and understand more about young children's explorations, play and thinking.

Boys and schemas

My particular interest in the ways boys play stemmed from two main sources: my own son and a boy whose play I studied as part of my MA studies, with a strong interest in Spider-Man. Analysis of my observations using a schema framework, as used by Athey (2007) in the Froebel Nursery Project, and Arnold (2003) in her analysis of observations of her grandson Harry, led me to the conclusion that his interest in Spider-Man was motivated by dynamic horizontal, vertical and rotational trajectory schemas. That study, plus a general impression that many boys have an interest in exploring trajectory, like superheroes, and frequently participate in active, boisterous play and playfighting, gained both at work and at home, led me to wonder about the reasons for these interests. I further explored this through a more in-depth research study involving four boys who appeared to participate in war, weapon and superhero play, which was submitted as my MA dissertation. I have returned to this research recently and will present my findings at the time, along with reconsidering some of my thinking in light of further reading, and more recent perspectives in relation to gender roles, stereotypes and brain development.

DOI: 10.4324/9781003224341-7

Participation in the research, and consent to use the findings to inform the wider early years community, was on the basis that the individuals involved would not be identifiable. Names have, therefore, been changed, and I will refer to the boys as Aaron, Bruno, Charlie and Dexter throughout, and their mothers as Kassie, Leila, Mel and Nina. Consent to observe and video the boys was also discussed with them. Upon commencement of my observations, the boys ranged in age from 37 months to 45 months. No photographs are included as parents did not fully consent to the sharing of images.

When I undertook the study, I appreciated that not all boys were interested in war, weapon and superhero play, nor were all girls dis-interested. Indeed, I have vivid memories of my grandmother watching Saturday tea-time American cop shows on television and declaring on more than one occasion, 'I love a good punch-up!' However, it seemed beyond dispute that the children predominantly interested in this type of play were boys. Considering this now, in some ways, we have come far with regard to expectations for boys and girls. There are numerous programmes and projects to encourage girls into science, technology, engineering and maths (STEM) routes in education and employment, and men into careers such as childcare. There have also been great strides into workplaces and educational establishments being more inclusive of people who do not feel they fit or feel comfortable with traditional thinking around gender identity or who are transgender, but it, unfortunately, remains a contentious issue and we are clearly not there yet. In addition, the media and advertising stereotypes I found over 10 years ago continue to abound, and it is no less difficult today to avoid the situation I experienced around 16 years ago, whereby a boy who had chosen his own pink and lilac pyjamas for the summer season at the age of almost 3, was reluctant to wear them the following year at almost four, saying 'they're for girls'.

I could write this whole chapter, or perhaps even a whole book, on gender identity. Much of what we thought we knew about the brain, and about being male and female, is being challenged by further research. Fine (2010) provides an interesting and helpful summary of some of the changes in thinking over the last 200 years or so, and the changes in direction that this area of study has taken in recent years, presenting ideas which challenge many of our old assumptions based on very limited, narrow, and often biased findings about areas such as innate skills, male/female brains and what we are capable of. I will return somewhat to this theme later; however, this is predominantly a book focussing on schemas, so I will first share a summary of my observations and analyses of the play I spent several months studying, which took me further down the schema path.

Observing and analysing through a schema lens

Aaron

Through close examination of Aaron's actions in his play, I identified a small number of seemingly strong interests which underpinned much of his play.

Aaron participated in a wide variety of types of play, with different tools and resources, both alone and with others. He participated in some calmer activities, for example, mark-making, drawing, exploring books, completing jigsaws and creating collages, but in a large proportion of my observations, much of his time was taken up with very active play, with lots of running about, chasing and playfighting using objects as weapons, and lots of throwing, batting, rolling and crashing of objects. This suggested to me that Aaron was exploring the trajectory of objects, making them travel, seeing what happened when they travelled through the air and when they stopped. These explorations involved a variety of methods, and he employed different parts of his body and objects designed for that type of activity, along with the creative use of objects and resources originally designed for other purposes. This creative use of objects links into the second common pattern that emerged from Aaron's play: transforming. I observed him engaged in transforming objects, himself, and other living things. Much of Aaron's play also involved symbolic transformation: he frequently used one object to represent another, either through physical action or the use of language. In one play episode, he transformed a single cardboard tube into a variety of objects and tools, both demonstrating and labelling its new identities. Other examples included transforming a pencil and conker into a golf club and ball, using them to play golf; exploring a range of uses for a cork mat; and using a conker as a pirate's eye patch.

In addition to transforming objects, through dressing up as Spider-Man, using language to label himself as someone else, acting out dying and playing dead, Aaron was transforming himself. He also participated in many activities where he was covering and uncovering living things and objects. I observed him covering bugs with soil, finding and re-burying worms, and covering wooden blocks and paving stones with mud he had made by pouring water into a tyre outside. It could be suggested that this is linked to an enveloping or containing schema (Meade and Cubey, 2008; Nutbrown, 2008; Athey, 2007), but I would also suggest that this links with Aaron's interest in transforming, as he was transforming the position of things when he covered them in soil, to being '*under* the ground', and transforming the state of the wooden blocks and the paving stones when covering them in mud. He also explored this through transforming the state of materials by mixing paint or soil with water and combining resources from the workshop area to make them into something else; during one session, he spent time making treasure to go and bury outside, explaining this purpose to an educator.

When I shared some of my video observations with Aaron's mum, Kassie, and with educators working with him, my thinking about what was underlying his play was given further credence. Kassie commented that he was very boisterous in his play and noted similarities in play at nursery and at home. She reported that he loved playing with elastic bands and would set up targets to hit and open drawers to try and shoot the bands into them, describing him as being 'quite passionate about that'. This helped to confirm my identification of Aaron's strong trajectory schema. Kassie also confirmed that he played at

crashing things at home, as was observed in nursery. She linked this to his interest in transforming, wondering if it was about him 'seeing the shapes of things
when they crash', which extended my thinking as I was considering the context of trajectory (travelling and stopping) alone. Kassie described an occasion
when Aaron had sat and untied every single one of a number of knots in an
apron string, thus transforming the string from knotted to smooth and returning it to its original state. I then wondered if there was a connection between
this and Aaron's digging-up and re-burying worms. If he was transforming
their state or position by digging them up, then by burying them, he was
returning them to their original state or 'un-transforming' them. Discussion
with Aaron's Key Person in the nursery confirmed that he frequently collected
worms then returned them to their homes. She also said he made games 'out
of random toys' and invented his own play. Transforming himself also came into
our discussion, as she described an occasion when Aaron had put on a dress and
said, 'Look, I'm a girl, I'm a girl!'

Aaron's obvious enjoyment of war, weapon and superhero play could be clearly
linked to his presenting schematic interests. The playfighting he undertook, along
with his use of imaginary weapons and aiming and firing elastic bands at people
and targets, all involved the exploration of trajectory. A common feature of superheroes is their transformation from a regular person into their superhero role.
Perhaps Aaron's involvement in and enjoyment of this type of play was because it
gave him a context to explore his strong schematic interests further.

Bruno

It was more challenging to identify the probable interests behind Bruno's play than
Aaron's, the main reason being that he often allowed his play to be led by others, usually Aaron, and I gained the impression that sometimes he was following
Aaron's lead rather than his own interests. I particularly felt this when I observed
him commence playing in one way, only to change his play if Aaron did not follow or suggested something different. This, however, did change over time, and
towards the end of my observations, Bruno began to pursue his own interests
more frequently and lead play episodes involving other children, including Aaron.
As with Aaron, much of Bruno's play was very boisterous and physically active.

Despite Aaron's influence and some of Bruno's play behaviours appearing
imitative, I observed subtle differences in the underlying nature of his play.
Bruno spent extended periods of time playing with cardboard tubes, mainly
using them as swords or lightsabers. He also used other objects such as pencils
for this purpose. Observing Bruno undertaking this type of play, I noticed he
focused strongly on the movements that he could make with the tubes and
other objects, often accompanied by sound effects. On occasions where his
play was influenced or directed by others, he invariably returned to his exploration of movement after a short period of time. I, therefore, reached the conclusion that the underlying motivator for Bruno's play choices and behaviours was
linked to the dynamic trajectory of objects and the force and movement that

is required in order for something to travel from one space to another. This trajectory interest sometimes focused on dynamic horizontal, at other times dynamic vertical. There were also a number of occasions where Bruno combined the two and explored dynamic diagonal trajectories.

In addition to exploration with objects, Bruno also explored trajectory using his own body. I observed him punching through the air, again with sound effects, running back and forth from the end of the garden to the nursery door, and climbing on and jumping off the climbing tower in the garden. This trajectory schema was also explored through mark-making. On all the occasions I saw Bruno participating in mark-making activities, he made vertical movements, often going back and forth over the same place on the paper. He did this on both a large and small scale, and also used similar zig-zag movements as a representation of writing his name.

Another less frequently observed schema was containing or filling, sometimes accompanied by emptying, which could be linked to movement, as the focus seemed to be on the action of filling then emptying, rather than on the end product of having filled something up. Examples of this type of behaviour included throwing balls into a net and putting soil in a wheelbarrow then using a spade to empty it.

As it had with Aaron, sharing some of my video observations with Bruno's mum, Leila, supported my interpretations of the play. Leila reported that at home, Bruno liked to play with items such as tubes, sticks, lightsabers and broom handles, moving them in the same ways as he did in the video clips I shared. From one clip, she also highlighted how one of the children was going round and round with his drawing, whilst Bruno was repeatedly going up and down. Whilst watching a clip of Bruno throwing quoits, I asked if his play at home involved much throwing; she responded that it was more about 'waving things around and battling'. An educator I shared the clips with commented on the impact Aaron could sometimes have on Bruno's, and other children's, play, saying, 'The others seem to look to Aaron to see if it's okay to do a certain thing . . . pick something up and look at Aaron and if he says "no" they put it down and follow what he's doing', which supported my impression that Bruno sometimes prefers to follow Aaron's lead rather than following his own particular play interests. Leila also commented that 'you can see Aaron is his best mate'. The change that I noticed later in the term was also picked up by an educator, who wondered if it was because Aaron had been absent, and Bruno had enjoyed leading the play during those sessions when Aaron was not present. It is possible that this is the case, or it could simply be that the longer he spent in the three-and-four-year-old room, the more confident and assertive he became, and the more able he was to lead play and follow his own interests.

Charlie

Although Charlie frequently played alongside or with the other three boys, particularly with Aaron and Bruno, the incidences of him engaging in war, weapon and superhero play were fewer, and he had a wider circle of play partners than Aaron, Bruno or Dexter. I found it extremely interesting that the educators had suggested his involvement in the project as they thought he engaged in war, weapon and superhero play; on closer observation, he did not participate in such play as frequently as I expected, nor as they thought. Two educators were quite surprised by this when I shared the video clips and discussed Charlie's play with them.

During several observations, Charlie appeared to be experiencing somewhat of a dilemma in his play. There were occasions when he clearly had interests that he would like to follow but was equally eager to be involved in play with Aaron and Bruno. On one occasion, he tried to involve them in his interest by drawing their attention to what he wanted to play with and moved back and forth between his choice (skateboards) and where they were playing. The desire to play with his friends was stronger and he went to join them. Eventually, however, he successfully tried again to persuade them to join him, taking a skateboard over to them – they stopped what they were doing and followed him.

Charlie did, on occasion, participate in play chasing and fighting with fabricated weapons, and much of his play was still of a physical, movement-based nature. As with Aaron and Bruno, many of the play behaviours I observed suggest an interest in trajectory, but again with a slightly different focus. Charlie seemed to be exploring his own trajectory more, as I frequently observed him walking and running in different ways, trying out using stiff legs, striding, taking tiny steps and taking straight and curved pathways, often retracing his steps. A similar interest was observed in his use of a skateboard when he retraced his pathway several times. He also explored movement trajectory using his arms, swinging them back and forth by his sides and across his body, and focusing on their movement when throwing quoits in the air. Another example of this exploration of trajectory was observed during play with a wheelbarrow and soil. This was linked to containing, as he was containing soil in the wheelbarrow, then flinging it onto the grass, watching its trajectory as he did so.

This interest in containing was evident in several other play episodes when I observed him filling containers with sand and water, completing inset jigsaws and containing himself in dens and through hide-and-seek. I also identified a possible link between this and a third strong interest – that of going round a boundary. On numerous occasions, I observed Charlie symbolically enclosing a space by running or riding around it, driving toy vehicles around it and also by mark-making round it. Perhaps by doing this, he was containing the space.

On sharing video clips with Charlie's mum, Mel, she commented that, at home, he frequently drives his toy vehicles around the edge of a large rug. This type of play was also discussed with one of the nursery staff who told me that Charlie had made lots of circular drawings on a piece of paper, then said they were worms. Mel also commented that he is very precise and likes lining things up; this linked into an observation of him playing at going on a bus with a line of chairs. During this play episode, he was very particular that the chairs had to be one behind the other, and no one was permitted to sit side-by-side with someone else. Mel was also very interested in the fact that he did not participate in the same levels of war, weapon and superhero play as his friends who were involved in the study.

Two educators with whom I shared video clips of Charlie commented on differences in his play compared to the other three boys observed. One reported that he is 'not as vocal as the others', whilst the other commented on one of the video clips where he is playing in close proximity to Aaron and Bruno, that he is very engrossed in what he is doing and 'not really bothering what the other two are doing'. Although Charlie's friends are clearly very important to him, what is more important is following his own specific interests. One educator wondered if the differences in his play were due to him having a female twin, and so more contact with 'typically female' play behaviours than the other boys.

Dexter

I found observing and analysing Dexter's play particularly fascinating, as I felt there were two dimensions to the main schemas I identified. He showed a very strong interest in connecting, and much of his play with toys and objects was centred on this. I observed him using construction toys to create 'Spider-Man bridges'. He was often very precise, ensuring that objects were completely touching when putting them together, checking there were no gaps when he had finished, and showed great satisfaction when he had done this. He also connected objects and connected himself with objects during play by bringing two objects together, so they were touching, and by very deliberately touching things with his finger. On one occasion, I observed him connecting a piece of guttering to the downspout from the outdoor canopy. At another time, when Aaron and Bruno were playing 'golf' with pencils and conkers, Dexter could not find another conker, so used a die instead, but was very interested in touching the die and the pencil together, getting the point of the pencil to connect with the dots. This connecting schema could also be seen in Dexter's creations: joining together cardboard tubes and connecting paper in collage pictures.

The thing that I found most intriguing about Dexter's obviously strong connecting schema, which was evident in the majority of his play, was that it was not limited to physical connections. Social connections also seemed to be extremely important to him; I observed many instances of him approaching others and instigating play with them in order to make a social connection. He seemed to do this by initiating play he thought they would respond to, often approaching Aaron and Bruno with playfighting behaviours and awaiting a response. At times the response was actually more than he could cope with, and he would retreat from the play, even though it was he who had started it off. This view was supported by comments from his mum, Nina, who described how he would only pretend to shoot at male play companions and would never attempt to involve her or his nana or female friends in that type of play. I then realised that this was also the case in nursery, as although he would involve himself in play chase scenarios with girls, he never approached them with weapon, superhero or playfighting behaviours.

This idea about the importance of social connections to Dexter was furthered by observations on a day when there were relatively few children in nursery, and of those who were present, a number had been given the option of going to play on the trim-trail in a separate part of the outdoor area. Dexter remained in the nursery with a small number of other children and was observed wandering around, seemingly wondering what to do, as he could not find anyone to play with. When it was his turn to go to the trim-trail, he took great delight in playing chasing games, and one educator who went with them told me how all the children participated in Dexter's game, where he was pretending to be a crocodile and chasing them around.

During his play, Dexter also showed an interest in trajectory. This was manifested in his weapon play, when he used objects to represent guns, pointing them at other children and shouting 'Bang, bang!' He also talked on several occasions about things 'going right up to the sky' and batted and threw objects into the air and into containers.

Although much of their play was very physical and involved play chasing, playfighting and the use of imaginary or fabricated weapons, and all four boys made reference to superhero-type characters (for example, Superman, Spider-Man, Power Rangers and Ben 10, or 'baddies'), these characters were not a prolonged feature of their play. Dexter was by far the most likely to mention superhero characters or act out their roles during his play. It seems possible that he saw this as something that the other boys were interested in and used it as a way of connecting with them. Or perhaps as he was relatively new to the three-and-four-year-old room and sometimes seemed to be a little timid around the other children; maybe taking on the mantle of a superhero made him feel brave enough to approach others and engage them in play.

Sharing video clips with Nina confirmed his connecting schema. She described how he liked fitting things together at home, including construction toys and jigsaws, commenting that 'he gets quite upset if things break . . . he tries to get them back together'. She also talked about his interest in watching videos of and imitating superheroes and his participation in playfighting with his dad. One educator commented that Dexter had developed some good relationships even though he had only been in the three-and-four-year-old room for a relatively short period of time, and described how he had particular friends and seemed to follow 'the louder ones'. This also supported the suggestion that social, as well as physical connections, were very important to him.

So why do they do that?

Cross-disciplinary literature contains a range of perspectives on why boys enjoy particular types of play. Through my own experience of working with young children, it seemed that, in general, boys tend to participate in more active, boisterous play and playfighting, and to like superhero characters. A great deal has been written about these types of play, for example:

Table 6.1 Types of play

Play type	Reference
Active play	Grant, 2008; Lindsey and Mize, 2001; Martin and Fabes, 2001; Campbell et al., 2000; Cupit, 1996; Paley, 1986; Eaton and Keats, 1982; Goldberg and Lewis, 1969
Hero play	Grimmer, 2020; Grant, 2008; Martin, 2007; Wood, 2007; Levin and Carlsson-Paige, 2006; Pellegrini and Gustafson, 2005; Browne, 2004; Maccoby, 2002; Nakamura, 2001; Bauer and Dettore, 1997; Paley, 1991; Rubin et al., 1983
Playfighting	Pellis and Pellis, 2017; Kalliala, 2006; Smith, 2005; Pellegrini and Smith, 1998; Cupit, 1996; Goldstein, 1995; Sutton-Smith et al., 1988; Isaacs, 1933/1967
Rough and tumble	Holland, 2007; Fry, 2005; Smith and Pellegrini, 2005; Maccoby, 2002; Martin and Fabes, 2001; Pellegrini, 1995; Boulton and Smith, 1992; Watson and Peng; 1992

Despite differences in classifications of play type, my experience-based notion being shared by others is evident in the literature. It is widely accepted that boys participate in rough and tumble play far more than do girls. This is supported by a great deal of the documented research (see Rough and tumble, Table 6.1), but not all. Although Smith and Lewis (1985) also found more prevalence of rough and tumble play in boys than girls, their research did show that girls do engage in that type of play, and they consider the small difference in their research sample to be insignificant. Blurton Jones (1974), in his studies of children's interactions with peers, found that amongst four-year-olds, there was no overall difference between the sexes in the incidences of rough and tumble play, but this is not frequently evident in other studies. Sex differences in play behaviours have been found to be cross-cultural by other researchers. Goldstein (1995) and Fry (2005) both found differences in play behaviours between boys and girls in numerous countries.

In addition to cross-cultural sex differences in play behaviours, similar differences have been found outside the human species. Smith and Pellegrini (2005) and Boulton and Smith (1992) report that rough and tumble play has been found to be more prevalent in males in other mammalian species. Play fighting is extensively explored, with specific reference to rats, by Pellis and Pellis (2017), who explore differences in male and female behaviours and the impact of hormones on behaviour.

These differences are not solely limited to rough and tumble play, but have also been observed in tool use. Pellegrini and Gustafson (2005) reported that research into tool use in chimpanzees discovered that females used sticks as a means of obtaining insects for food, whereas males used them as weapons against each other. This was mirrored in their research into object play in boys and girls, where they found that boys often played with objects within superhero-themed fantasy play, something which was evident in my own observations, and that they tended to weaponise objects more than their female counterparts. That said, Fine (2010) presents the suggestion that some of the historical research around the considerations of differences between male and female behaviours, and the concept of male and female brains, is the result of an element of bias, suggesting researchers saw what they expected to see, alongside the influence of gendered parental response to infants from their first days of life, and even before.

Both during my original studies and more recently, I have considered if boys and girls are predisposed to an interest in particular schemas due to biological and/or evolutionary differences. Holland (2007) suggests that trajectory is a commonly occurring schema in boys' war, weapon and superhero play, whilst Meade and Cubey (2008) describe a cluster of schemas, including trajectory, evident in one particular boy's superhero play. Does our hunter/gatherer ancestry have any bearing on boys' common interests in trajectory schemas and girls in containing and transporting? It sounds reasonable to suppose it might, however with my more recent reading, I encountered something which throws somewhat of a spanner in the works: Haas et al. (2020) found evidence of women as hunters in archaeological excavations, so perhaps differing roles in prehistoric societies weren't as clear cut as originally thought. When considering my own findings alongside this, with the surprise experienced by some educators regarding what they thought they knew about the boys and what I identified as differences in their explorations of schemas, it is not possible to give a definitive answer. Dexter seemed to use war, weapon and superhero play more as a way to connect with his peers. Movement was clearly the main event with Aaron and Bruno, but there were subtle differences regarding this. To give any particular weight to the hunter/ gatherer influence on children's presenting schemas today, it would require evidence from a large-scale study of schemas explored by boys and girls, alongside a secure picture of our prehistoric ancestors, to enable any secure conclusions to be reached.

Another possibility can be suggested by considering Abramov et al. (2012). Their studies examined differences in the eyes, and in visual processing, between men and women, finding that women had an eye for finer detail whilst men were more attuned to movement. Is this why boys are interested in exploring trajectory? Or could it be that, as the study involved people between the ages of 16 and 38, this is more a question of 'practice makes perfect' – perhaps men are more tuned into movement as that is what they have grown up focusing on. Would the common differences in interactions with, and responses to, girls and boys from birth presented by Fine (2010) be sufficient to impact on this too? Abramov et al. suggest testosterone as a factor in this, and testosterone is oft credited with differences in male and female behaviours. This has been extensively explored by Pellis and Pellis (2017) who found that altering testosterone levels in male and female rats impacted their playfighting behaviours. They also found, however, that male rats without augmented levels of testosterone demonstrated the same brain changes as ones with artificially higher levels after a period of time of being paired with them. This suggests that the behaviour, and possibly the hormonal state, of others may have a significant influence on an individual.

My observations of the children studied and conversations with parents, educators and the children themselves suggest some key points:

• There were patterns or schemas in the boys' play.
• The focus of these was slightly different for each boy.
• These patterns impacted the boys' play behaviours.
• What we think we know isn't always the case when we look a little closer.

The original process of undertaking the research and subsequently reviewing it have further cemented the view that it is crucial not to jump to conclusions about children's play or make assumptions based on brief, superficial observations of play behaviours. My work has shown that although interests may appear the same at first glance, on closer inspection, there could be some important differences.

Identifying what children know and can do, what they need to learn next and the best way to help them to learn it are key features of the revisions to the EYFS in 2021, alongside a move towards increasing time spent in interactions with children and a reduction in the 'gathering of evidence' of children's learning. Whilst these are, of course, admirable intentions, we also need to remember that in order for this to be most effective, we need to know our children well. Young children can often show us their thinking and what they are interested in more easily than tell us about it, and we need to take care not to lose sight of the fact that sometimes the best way to find out what children know, can do and are interested in, is to sit back and watch what they do without adult influence or interference. In addition, if we accept that children explore schemas through their play, it is important to give children the space, time, resources, support and language necessary to make those explorations in whatever way makes the most sense to them, and not to attempt to overly lead their play through our interactions.

In order to gain a secure understanding of children's behaviours and to put that understanding to good use to support their learning, it is important to observe closely and analyse thoughtfully. Athey (2007) discusses how focus can be made on the wrong aspect or interpretation of a child's interest. It is also wise to obtain different perspectives where possible – I learnt a huge amount about the individual children I observed through discussing my observations with their mothers and the educators who worked with them on a daily basis. Having failed in my attempts to discuss the observations with any of the children's fathers, and the educators in the nursery being exclusively female, an unfortunate gap in my work was a male perspective on both their play and my analysis of it. When planning experiences for young children based on their interests, in order for the children to engage in and derive benefit from these experiences, it is imperative to ensure that the true nature of the interest is addressed. We can never be entirely sure what someone else is thinking, but exploring our thoughts with the people who know children best will help to ensure we are as close as we can be to certainty. It may be that I was able to ascertain that true nature through my work, but it would have felt more secure if I could have explored this with the boys' fathers as well as their mothers.

Unconscious expectations?

My discussions with parents highlighted that there were differences in the way they responded to their children's play. Nina talked about how Dexter's dad would respond negatively to him expressing the desire to play with something he considered as a girl's toy. Even with parents who make a conscious effort to avoid responding to their child in a gender-stereotyped manner, it can still happen subconsciously. It is also impossible to avoid other outside influences, as considered by Music (2011) in his explorations of the impact of social and family context on the developing child. This was also considered by one of the educators, who wondered if, although we don't think we express different expectations of boys and girls, perhaps we do it without realising: we might ask boys if they want to make a rocket because we assume that that is what they would want to do. This fits with research findings; for example, Nakamura (2001) reported that despite Japanese preschool educators stating they treated boys and girls equally, observations showed this was not the case.

The natural inclinations of humans to be social beings and to want to belong also means that cultural considerations and sex-role expectations have an important role in the development of behaviours. This is particularly important in relation to gender and equality issues if we are to combat the potentially limiting effect of media and cultural pressures on children's experiences. Wood (2007) suggests the performance of gender stereotypical activities and roles may have a limiting effect on both children's own play choices and the choices of those around them. We have a huge amount of influence on the children we work with, which requires reflection on how we ensure children feel able to be their true selves. Cole and Cole (2001) consider that young children learn a great deal about expectations of the roles individuals play. The outcome of a negative response to a child's play choices, including the schemas they explore, because they don't fit with a cultural view of what boys or girls *should* be doing, could lead to children suppressing natural behaviours or becoming conflicted about who or what they are. We, therefore, need to think carefully about how we respond to children to avoid reinforcing stereotypes and how we challenge these if expressed by others.

Reflections and questions

Reflecting on whether or not I arrived at an answer to the title question, I recognise that there is a complex combination of factors that could no more be separated, and the relative contribution of each measured, than could the ingredients of a cake once it has been mixed and baked. It has also become clear that the recipe for each child is different. A simple answer that applies to every boy who enjoys this type of play clearly does not exist. Revisiting my original thoughts, and considering those against where we are in early childhood and society today, has helped identify some key questions that I would encourage educators to consider in their own particular context:

- How well do we understand the children we are working with?
- Do we have enough opportunities to discuss children with all parents/carers involved in the life of their child to deepen our understanding?
- Do we have a consistent response to supporting children to explore their fascinations, whatever these are?
- Do we respond differently to different children, whether deliberately or not, based on their sex, and does this limit the possibilities for our children?
- Do we have a consistent approach to recognising and challenging stereotypes, whether these be expressed by parents, children, visitors or educators?
- How do we combat any influences on children's play and explorations which may present as barriers that narrow their opportunities and limit their learning?

Recommended reading

Holland, P. (2007) *We Don't Play with Guns Here: War, Weapon and Superhero Play in the Early Years*. Maidenhead: Oxford University Press.

Meade, A. and Cubey, P. (2008) *Thinking Children: Learning about Schemas*. Maidenhead: Oxford University Press.

Music, G. (2011) *Nurturing Natures: Attachment and Children's Emotional, Sociocultural and Brain Development*. Hove: Psychology Press.

7   An exploration of schematic play in autistic children

Tamsin Grimmer and Sue Gascoyne

Discovering schemas

Tamsin: I first heard about schemas after I had been teaching and working in early years for several years. I became a Foundation Stage
Adviser for the North Somerset council and worked with a wonderful lady called Fran Kirkwood. She had been teaching students about
schemas for years and was surprised that I had not come across them!
It felt like I was viewing children in a whole new way and provided
an explanation for some of their behaviour I had thought was weird
and wonderful! Once I began delivering training and professional
development for early years educators, I was amazed at how few had
heard of schemas, and this led me to write my book, *Observing and
Developing Schematic Behaviour in Young Children* (Grimmer, 2017).
I hoped this would be an accessible read and help educators to re-
interpret behaviour in the light of schemas. I was inspired by the
schematic play of my own children whilst writing; however, at the
time, I was unaware that they were on the autistic spectrum.

Sue: I first became curious about whether autistic children might play
differently from their neurotypical peers when watching a baby
under 8 months old not interacting with the objects in a treasure
basket. She was later diagnosed with severe developmental delay
(Gascoyne, 2012). Watching older autistic children engaging with
the natural and household treasures in a treasure basket, I was struck
by the more ritualistic and repetitive way in which they counted,
lined up, rotated and manipulated the objects rather than using the
items for exploratory or pretend play.

Working in primary schools as a play therapist, I noticed a plethora of
schematic behaviours with children containing, connecting, transporting,
transforming and enveloping themselves, objects and creations as part of

DOI: 10.4324/9781003224341-8

their therapeutic play. However, it was only when discussing this chapter with Tamsin that these threads of thinking merged, and I reflected upon the schematic clues apparent within the play, actions and behaviours of the autistic children that I was privileged to work with. For some children, the act of immersing themselves in shredded paper, hiding in a dark, cramped cupboard or enveloping themselves in a sensory tent or blanket seemed to bring about a striking transformation to their emotional, physical and cognitive state. Conversely, for others, a lack of containment and the resulting overabundance of resources and over-stimulation manifest as overwhelming anxiety, quite literally stifling their actions. Noticing these striking and full-bodied responses to containing has, once again, further piqued an interest in understanding schemas and their potential value.

Introduction

Repetitive and ritualistic play that has a focus on detail is widely accepted as being typical of children with Autistic Spectrum Condition (ASC), which is why a child fixated with turning the wheels of a toy car (rotating) or lining things up (connecting or positioning) may be 'labelled' as autistic. However, this may be unhelpful, as the presence of schematic behaviours alone does not mean they are autistic. Autism is the term given to an alternative wiring of the brain so that an individual experiences the environment and its sensory and social inputs differently to a neurotypical person. It is characterised by challenges relating to social interaction, language and communication, sensory processing and repetitive and restrictive behaviours.

Autism is a condition about which we have vast gaps in our knowledge and research. There is still much to learn. For the purposes of this chapter, we are intentionally using the term condition rather than disorder to maintain a strengths-based approach and avoid a deficit view. The focus of this chapter is not to ascertain whether schematic play is a reliable indicator of autism, but rather to share observations of children diagnosed with ASC and shine a light on what value or purpose there could be for these children to engage with particular schemas. We are also curious about potentially what message this might be communicating about their needs or fascinations. This chapter will draw upon Tamsin's rich experiences both as an educator, and as a parent of three children with ASC who has witnessed a wealth of schematic play. It also reflects Sue's observations and experience of children's schematic play in a therapeutic context as a play therapist, an educator and researcher. In this chapter, we hope to convey the voice of the child, parent and professionals and, in doing so, to bring into focus our noticing of children's repeated actions and behaviours as potential insights into the child's world and clues to our role in supporting them.

Autism and repetitive actions – the misconception

Described as 'a lifelong developmental disability which affects how people communicate and interact with the world' (National Autistic Society, 2021), ASC is widely accepted as a triad of difficulties, focusing on, 'social interaction, communication and imagination associated with a narrow, repetitive range of activities' (Wing and Potter, 2002: 152). Wall includes rigid, stereotypical and repetitive or obsessive play when unpicking the classic features and specifically mentions lining up toys (Wall, 2010). ASC can also be defined as having challenges in the four main areas of communication, social interaction, sensory processing and repetitive and restrictive behaviour. Schematic play most obviously fits within the arena of imagination or repetitive and restrictive behaviour; however, if schemas are a child's way of understanding themselves and the world around them through bodily actions, then schematic behaviours may also have a valuable role to play in supporting social interactions and communication.

Several questionnaires which form part of ASC diagnosis mention repetitive or compulsive play which could be deemed as schematic, such as:

22. Does the child develop elaborate routines or rituals that must be completed? For example, lining up toys before going to bed.

(Garnett & Attwood, undated: 4)

34. Does the child like to spin things like jar lids, coins and coasters?

(Autism Research Institute, undated: 2)

37. (age 3–5) Does the child sometimes line things up in precise, evenly-spaced rows and insist they not be disturbed?

(Autism Research Institute, undated: 2)

However, although repetitive play can form part of diagnostic criteria, it is only a small part of a much longer list. It is, therefore, an unhelpful misconception to assume that schematic play alone is an indicator of autism. We suggest this is like trying to piece together the jigsaw pieces of a puzzle for which there is no picture on the box to provide a clue to what is happening. In addition, recent research suggests we revisit and question these common indicators and perhaps include other aspects such as difficulty with visual processing and theory of mind (Cashin and Barker, 2009). So, noticing a child repetitively lining up toys may trigger an adult to be concerned about a child, but they would need to build up as wide a picture as possible of their learning, sensory, social and communication needs and seek expert advice before drawing any conclusions.

Many children on the spectrum do engage in repetitive actions or play that is compulsive in nature, and we can observe many schemas in their play. This could be defined as 'restrictive and repetitive behaviours and interests', although this term is not widely accepted within the autism field (Fletcher-Watson and Happé, 2019). Examples of these behaviours and interests can also include needing to stick rigidly to rules, having to walk the same route to school every day, always wanting to eat the same food for breakfast or repeating movements or actions. There are many reasons why ASC people may act in this way, for example, 'enhancing the ability to function; reducing external stimuli and avoiding communication; coping with stress, distress and excitement; and coping with social communication' (Manor-Binyamini and Schreiber-Divon, 2019: 29). In addition, people with ASC may find these routines and repetitive actions calming, reassuring and pleasurable.

Tamsin's perspective

It is well documented that girls on the spectrum are harder to diagnose and are often diagnosed at a later age than boys (Carpenter et al., 2019). My daughters, Pippa, Hannah and Becky, were all diagnosed with ASC between the ages of 7 and 9 years old. At home, Pippa, Hannah and Becky need additional support in understanding what people mean, their intentions and perspectives and their autism sometimes manifests itself in high anxiety, obsessive and compulsive behaviour, sensory issues and difficulty in coping with their emotions. Routine is important and change difficult.

My children have regularly played in schematic ways, bringing me to the conclusion that repetitive behaviours help them understand the world around them, cope with their feelings and offer them comfort and security within familiar actions and routines. The National Autistic Society suggests that these behaviours may help calm autistic people when they are stressed or feeling anxious, but they may also engage in these behaviours simply because they enjoy them (2021).

When I originally observed Pippa, Hannah and Becky, I did so as a parent with a background in early years education and child development with a little knowledge about schemas and less about autism, and I did not know that they were on the spectrum. I have now revisited my observations and am reflecting on these with a new lens: the knowledge that they have autism. As well as showing me the importance of retrospective insight and digging deeper as an educator, this has inevitably also highlighted ways in which I could be a better parent if I had my time again! Above all, I see the value of reflective practice and have enjoyed revisiting these observations and discussing them with my children whilst writing this chapter.

Sue's perspective

As a play therapist, reflection is also a key aspect of my work. Watching children curiously, I try to understand what they might be communicating through their actions, play and behaviours and how best I can support them to meet their needs on their emotional journey. When we take the time to notice, schemas potentially provide adults with an insight into children's needs and preoccupations, vital clues for better supporting them.

In the following observations, Tamsin and Sue share some examples of schematic play with a view to better understanding these young autistic children's needs and what they might be experiencing and communicating through their

actions. These everyday examples are likely to resonate with parents and educators and hopefully shine a light on the role of adults in noticing, decoding and
accepting children's 'schematic voices'.

Tearing up paper – exploring (dis)connection and trajectory

Context

When Pippa was younger, she loved to explore how things worked. She still
has an enquiring mind with a keen interest in science and technology, perhaps
beginning with investigations like this while Pippa was staying at her Grandparents' house.

What happened?

Pippa (11½ months) was very interested in tearing up the magazine. She used
both hands and pulled the paper in two directions to tear it. She loved watching the paper fall and then looked down onto the ground at the little pieces of
paper. She repetitively tore this paper for a long time, showing high levels of
engagement (Laevers, 2005).

Figure 7.1 Pippa tearing up the magazine

Figure 7.2 Pippa pulling the paper apart

Figure 7.3 Pippa looking at where the paper landed

Figure 7.4 The torn paper on the floor

Schematic behaviours

Connecting,
Disconnecting,
Trajectory

Reflections

Pippa appeared to be interested in the way the paper tore into smaller pieces and how it fell to the ground, which could link with connecting and trajectory schemas. Perhaps she was exploring what we understand as gravity through trajectory play. However, Pippa could also have been exploring separating when a smaller piece of paper separates from the larger sheet from which it is torn. This is part of a connecting and disconnecting schema, and Pippa often found separating from Tamsin difficult, so perhaps she was exploring this concept here?

She may also have been investigating object permanence and change, comparing her expectations of what the torn pieces might look like with what they did. By changing the form of the paper and visually comparing it, she may have been more easily able to explore and make sense of concepts and feelings about same and different, together and apart, big and small, stability and change.

Implications for the role of the adult

Although tearing up paper could be viewed as a destructive or an unnecessarily messy action, the adults around Pippa saw value in allowing her to do so. This offered her the opportunity to develop hand-eye coordination and tracking skills, practise fine motor skills and potentially explore the concepts of connecting and separating, as well as cause and effect from the falling pieces. Part of the adult's role was providing appropriate resources, giving the child permission to freely explore and investigate these, and valuing her inquiry through the provision of time and acceptance.

A family of elephants – exploring connecting, positioning and containing

Context

Pippa regularly used to line up her toys at home, and on one occasion, she carefully lined up six toy elephants.

What happened

Pippa (2 years and 10 months) searched through the box of animals and found all the elephants. She then placed them side-by-side, beginning with the largest

Figure 7.5 A family of elephants

at each end. Pippa spent a long time putting each elephant in place and seemed to have a clear idea of where she wanted each elephant to go. Once finished, she proudly told Tamsin, 'I've made a family'. Describing the outside two elephants first as the mummy and daddy, she pointed and explained, 'This is the mummy elephant, this is the daddy elephant, and the big sister elephant and the big brother elephant and the little sister elephant and the baby elephant'.

Schematic behaviours

Positioning,
Seriating,
Connecting

Reflections

Reflecting upon her ordering of the smaller elephants between the two parent figures raises questions about whether she was exploring connecting and belonging as well as her role in the family and feelings of responsibility, relationship and security. She carefully positioned the elephants putting the parent elephants on the outside of the line and the children inside, which could link with ideas around protection, safety and containment as the two end elephants feel like they act as a strong container for the central elephants. Despite the family of elephants appearing as a safe structural unit, there is very little personal space for individual freedom as the elephants appear to be squished together. This could reflect the physical and emotional impact of making space for a younger sibling, as by this age, Pippa already had one younger sister and Tamsin was pregnant with her third child. In addition, perhaps organising her toys in this way helped her organise her thoughts physically and externally, as well as developing executive functioning skills, which many children with autism find difficult.

Implications for the role of the adult

Tamsin was available for Pippa, observing her play and ready to listen respectfully when she wanted to talk about the family of elephants she had created. On reflection, if at the time Tamsin had thought about the potential significance of the play in communicating Pippa's feelings of safety, security and belonging, or her worries about time, space and attention, being 'squished' by the changes, she might have reassured Pippa and talked more about family and her place and role within it. This demonstrates the value of reflection and how it can help us to respond appropriately. Schön (1983) calls this 'reflection in action' when we reflect on a situation as it is unfolding, and this links with Ephgrave's work around the importance of responding 'in the moment' to children (2018). It also underlines the importance of noticing and valuing children's actions in the same way that we would if they were verbally communicating these to us.

Waiting for the train – exploring positioning and connecting

Context

Pippa regularly lined up toys, often in one long line across the room. She wouldn't allow anyone else to touch these toys and would usually have a narrative alongside this play, which told a story.

What happened?

Pippa (2 years and 11 months) arranged the figures in one long line and the toy train in another. As she did so, she explained to Tamsin that all the people in the line were waiting for the train.

Schematic behaviours

Positioning,
Seriating

Reflections

Watching this unfold, it appeared to Tamsin that Pippa was exploring place value, ordinal numbers and thinking mathematically, exploring concepts

Figure 7.6 A line of people waiting for the train

like, 'Who is first in the line?', 'Who is second?' and 'Who is last?' Although interesting and visually striking, it is the story accompanying this photograph that potentially helps illuminate her thinking. The train was already almost full and there would not be enough space on the train for all the passengers waiting. Perhaps this links with feelings of separation and belonging or questions about there being enough space, as in the previous observation. With vehicles sometimes being associated with symbols of help, energy, regulation and transformation (Kalff, 2003; Ronnberg and Martin, 2021) in children's play, this could reflect the fact that within a growing family, sometimes first-born children will have to wait a little longer for their needs to be met.

Implications for the role of the adult

For Tamsin, her role as parent was to provide accessible resources, be available and listen when Pippa wanted to talk about the arrangement that she'd created. Similarly, a key part of an educator's role in supporting schematic play is ensuring access to open-ended resources and a stimulating and challenging environment together with an ethos which allows children to play flexibly with these. Within a therapeutic environment, Sue might have reflected that there were a lot of people waiting for the train and not enough space, to see if this facilitated greater self-awareness or gave the child an opportunity to share their concerns and find ways of addressing this, for example, through using a social story (Gray, 2015), if needed. She may also have wondered curiously where the train was going, in case this resonated with the child's inquiry.

Running water – exploring trajectory, containing and transforming

Context

Although not as notable as her sibling's schematic play, Hannah's fascination for containing, trajectory and transforming play has been evident. From an early age, Hannah loved any sort of messy play, whether mixing sand and water or making potions and mud pies. Her trajectory play is particularly evident in her enjoyment in playing with running water in any guise, whether damming rivers, playing with taps, hoses, sprinklers or water fountains.

What happened?

On visiting a water park, Hannah (3 years and 1½ months) was particularly interested in the fountains that spurted water upwards. She tried to stop the flow of water using her hands, feet and whole body.

Figure 7.7 Stopping water with hands

Figure 7.8 Stopping water with feet

Schematic behaviours

Trajectory,
Containing,
Transforming

Reflections

Hannah appeared to be particularly interested in how she could stop the trajectory of the water with her body and often explored containing the water in her hands. The water appeared to have a life of its own as it spurted out of the fountains and the resistance of the water and sensations this provided are likely to have given her satisfying sensory feedback, bodily awareness and agency, a fundamental component of wellbeing and our three psychological needs (Deci and Ryan, 2000). Hannah's engagement with messy play resources like sand and water seems to feature elements of the complementary yet, in many ways, opposing containing and trajectory schemas. Both these schemas were also apparent in Sue's observations of a 7-year-old's exploration of shaving foam in a play therapy session:

> He squirted it in the bowl (trajectory) and felt it with his hands, engrossed. He asked to clean his hands and carefully did so in the bucket before returning to the bowl of foam, covering his hands (enveloping) then tentatively clapped his hands together (trajectory) and smiled. He squirted some more foam (trajectory), seeming absorbed in controlling the flow then squirted it into the lid making this a container (containing).

Sometimes when children have an interest in a particular schema, they are also interested in the opposite action, so if a child enjoys containing, they will fill containers, but chances are they will also empty them! This could also be seen in Hannah's transforming play. When playing with sand and water, Hannah would love to mix them together, but when eating, she would not want her foods to touch each other, whilst at other times she would choose to mix it all together to make one big mush.

Implications for the role of the adult

When a child shows interest in following a line of inquiry, the educator can support this by offering an ethos of permission. This allows them to explore the concept to its natural conclusion, which may not be the same end point as adults envisioned. Sue has been reminded of this time and time again when watching children play with natural, sensory and open-ended objects. Frequently, the child's emerging thread of thinking is far more sophisticated than the adult's ideas which are sometimes restricted to colour or number! Giving children this freedom can be difficult with a trajectory schema, especially one linked to water play. Children may plug sinks, fill them until they overflow, or leave taps running with little regard for saving water, which can be easily misinterpreted as poor behaviour (Grimmer, 2017). However, if an effective educator or parent can recognise the child's natural urge to play schematically, they can find a way of redirecting this play in a more acceptable manner (Nutbrown, 2011) or preparing for and containing the resulting mess (Gascoyne, 2019).

As a parent, Tamsin learned to respond with understanding and acceptance to Hannah's need for agency in mixing or not allowing food to touch by providing opportunities for sensory mixing and providing separate plates or dishes as needed. Within therapeutic sessions, Sue has used creative approaches for satisfying children's need to experience trajectory with messy materials through imaginative approaches to containment and enveloping of the child and the environment. For one primary-aged child that Sue worked with, a plastic box in a school room provided the child with a target for squirting water at!

Hiding – exploring enclosing and enveloping

Context

Becky's engagement in schematic play has followed lines of enquiry that link with rotating, enclosing, enveloping, containing and connecting amongst other schemas; however, it is her enclosing and enveloping which has really stood out as a key theme.

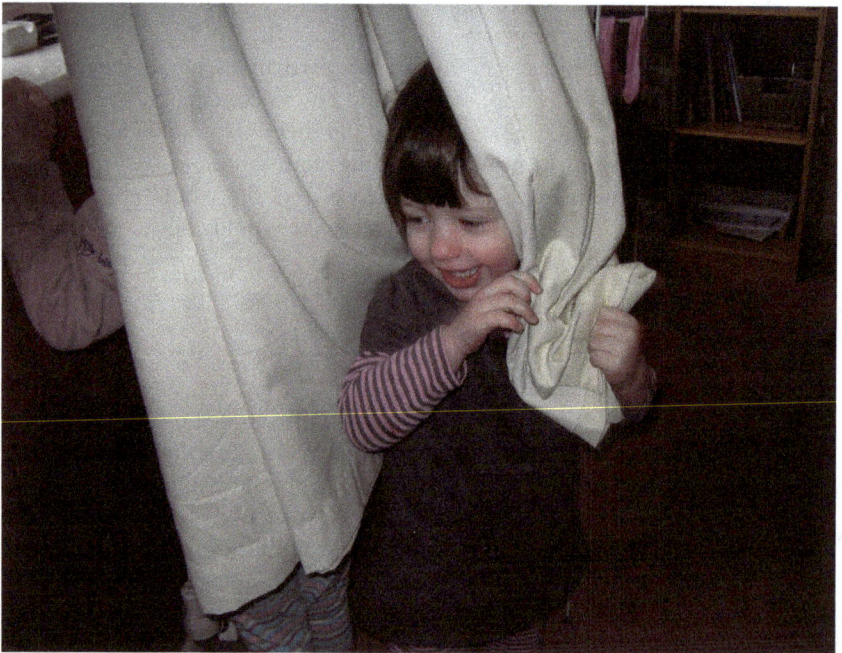

Figure 7.9 Becky hiding in the curtains

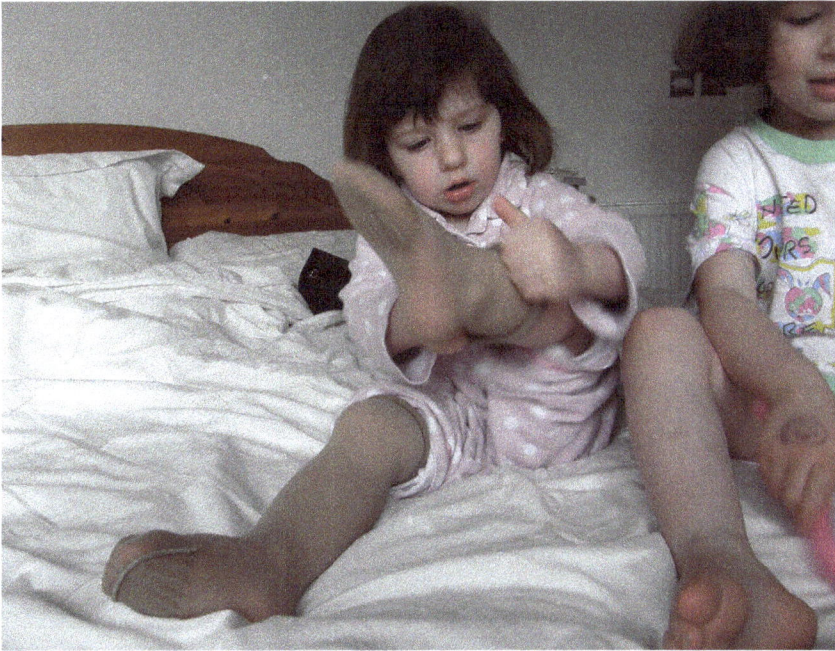

Figure 7.10 Trying on stockings!

What happened?

Becky's interest in enclosing began at an early age. As a tiny baby, she loved 'peepo' and having muslin draped over her face and then removed. Becky (2 years and 1 month) regularly hid in the curtains with her sister Hannah, giggling non-stop, so it was always obvious where they were hiding! Becky would often empty the toys from her large toy box so she could climb inside.

She also used to try on Tamsin's socks, tights and shoes, put Christmas stockings on her feet and loved to dress up in layers of dressing-up costumes or material.

There were also lots of links with enveloping play, which she loved so much that her parents gave her an empty cushion cover for her 3rd birthday! She used to put things in envelopes and loved wrapping presents, sometimes getting a cloth and putting it around a toy, taking it to Tamsin saying, 'Happy Birthday!' Becky's interest in enveloping continued in nursery as she regularly came home with paintings that were just a wall of paint. Her teacher would, sometimes apologetically, explain that there was a picture of a sun or a person under the paint, but Becky decided to paint over it, covering it totally with a wash of colour! Figure 7.11 (3 years and 8 months) clearly shows that Becky drew three people before completely colouring over them.

Figure 7.11 Three red people drawn in red pen and coloured over

Schematic behaviours

Enveloping,
Containing,
Through a boundary

Reflections

Becky's interest in enclosing and enveloping could be an expression of feeling safe and secure, a preoccupation with bodily sensations, or even exploring separation and object permanence. Enclosing ourselves in a small space can make us feel cosy and safe and provide calming, self-regulating sensory feedback as well as proprioceptive bodily awareness. When children play hide and seek, they sometimes experiment with feelings of being seen and unseen, lost and found, connecting and disconnecting, as well as self-worth, for example, will I be noticed and looked for? It is possible that Becky was exploring these concepts through her play.

Sue noticed the sensory benefits of enveloping in a therapeutic context for Charlie (7 years, pseudonym). Childhood trauma and a lack of attachment made it difficult for Charlie to focus in mainstream lessons, resulting in 'challenging' behaviours. Being assessed for ASC at the time, his body language and engagement differed markedly in play therapy, where he was alert, engaged and spoke enthusiastically. After a physical incident in class, Charlie came to his sixth play therapy session sad and subdued.

> He instantly got in the large tray of shredded paper and started pulling the paper up and over his head to cover himself with (enveloping/containing). He began smiling happily with twinkly eyes and asked me to take his picture as he played hide and seek in the shredded paper (enveloping/containing). He then asked if he could get into a large container of dried rice (containing). He sat in this as his hands scooped and sprinkled the grains of rice (trajectory).

Sue was struck by how quickly Charlie transformed from a seemingly sad and low energy state to an engaged, sparkly-eyed, happy child. Observing this, she felt sure that his immersion in the sensory resources – Jennings Embodiment stage (1990) – was a key factor in this change. Sue also wondered if his containment within the sensory resources mirrored and satisfied his need for emotional containment and nurture after being reprimanded in class.

For some children, the focus of their containing appears to be motivated by scientific investigations. For one child (approximately 6 years), a treasure basket, a basket of sensory-rich and open-ended natural and household objects (Gascoyne, 2012; Goldschmied, 1987), afforded very different play opportunities to his peer. Ben (pseudonym) had ASC, and his focus of interest was akin to watching a scientist at work, seemingly methodically testing his theory in a series of experiments. Selecting a small cylindrical metal tin and discovering he could remove its lid, he proceeded to try to fit different utensils inside the tin. Repeating this same action, each time with a different utensil, be it a honey dipper, small spoon, large-headed spoon, mini whisk and so on, he narrated out loud, 'Fits!', 'Doesn't fit!' In contrast, his peer initially explored the items individually and then together, moving through a continuum of single item exploration to multiple item exploration before using the resources for domestic role-play (Gascoyne, 2012).

For another primary-aged child, the same cylindrical tin suggested a different, but equally compelling mathematical seed of inquiry. Discovering some maize packing 'peanuts', Fred (pseudonym) began inserting these into the tin, counting them as he did so. Pressing firmly with his fingers, he persevered with squeezing as many of the packaging pieces as he could into the tin, focussing intently on this self-set challenge. In both these observations, the child's enveloping, containing and going through a boundary schema appear to be grounded in logical thinking. Their actions or counting created a rhythm and energy to the task and were characterised by high levels of engagement (Laevers, 2005). Their narration not only helpfully provides adults with a clue to their inquiry but potentially fulfilled the same function as Vygotsky's 'inner speech', in reinforcing what their body and senses were telling them as a 'physical thinker' (cited in Atherton and Nutbrown, 2016: 65).

Implications for the role of the adult

Aware of Becky's love of enclosing and enveloping, her parents fully embraced her play at home by providing lots of resources to enable her to do this to her heart's content. Fortunately, her nursery teacher also recognised the value of the process, not just the finished pictures! Perhaps in Becky's mind, her picture was not complete until covered with colour, so if she had been asked to stop and not paint or colour over what she had initially drawn, this may have caused unnecessary upset. Similarly, Charlie's need for whole-body engagement with sensory resources could easily have been denied, or worse, still have become a cause for shame if told he was too old for such behaviour. Time, permission and acceptance were also key to both Ben and Fred's investigations. Watching Fred's play, it felt important to show interest, curiosity and acceptance without intruding on his investigations. In this way, Sue was able to value his inquiry and witnessed a change in his body language and social connection as his confidence and mastery appeared to grow.

Moments like these underline the importance of adults reserving their own personal judgements and accepting the child's wishes and actions. Awareness of potential schematic underpinnings also help us value and appreciate behaviours so that we can accept what the child may be showing us. Although firm conclusions can rarely be drawn, reflections remind us of the potentially multiple benefits of schematic actions for a child, and also the value in repetitive behaviours which tend to be labelled as negative. Educators should remain curious about a child's seeds of inquiry and make more such opportunities available to meet this need.

Ropes, pulleys and more – exploring going through a boundary and connecting

Context

Becky's interest in connecting initially took the form of playing with toys that joined together, like construction materials and wooden train tracks. As she got older, she also became interested in knots and tying things together, such as tying together her dressing gown cord and skipping ropes to create zip wires for her toys. Her interest in enclosing and connecting continued for many years.

What happened?

Becky (5 years and 4 months) created a complex pulley system for a bucket on the climbing frame in the garden.

Figure 7.12 Creating a pulley system

Schematic behaviours

Connecting,
Going through a boundary

Reflections

Autistic children sometimes find it harder to express their feelings and interpret and understand emotions. This observation occurred a few months prior to moving house, so perhaps Becky felt the need to tie everything together and re-establish connections with an important anchor for her (the climbing frame) as her world changed around her. Being curious about her play, maybe her interest in connecting and joining things together was linked to her feelings of wanting to be connected emotionally. Unlike some children's connection to people and their environment by physically wrapping or joining themselves to these (see Chapter 5), Becky's investigations involve a sense of transition and venturing beyond, which may have been an important tool in processing difficult feelings about connection and disconnection.

Implications for the role of the adult

If Tamsin had recognised the significance of Becky's play in relation to their move, she may have created a social story (Gray, 2015) to help Becky understand more about moving house. In addition, providing resources and safe opportunities for Becky to tie things together was important for Becky, and, as a parent, Tamsin's ethos of permission ensured that she was able to safely play in this way. When children are choosing to play in ways that adults may deem to be risky, such as play with ropes or water, adults have a stronger role than ever in enabling children opportunities to safely navigate their seeds of inquiry. Key to this is considering how can we ensure that we listen to the voices of our children with ASC and value and respect their interests and fascinations.

Babies and teddy – enclosing and positioning

Context

Becky's interest in enclosing and connecting continued for years. When visiting her grandparents' home after moving house, Becky (6 years and 9 months) arranged her special toys to create the scene shown in Figure 7.13.

What happened?

Becky placed her favourite doll, *Mummy Baby*, in a nappy sack; she tied *Sister Baby*'s wrists together and enclosed her favourite teddy, *Splish Splash*, in between Grandma and Grandad's hats!

Figure 7.13 Enclosing her toys

Schematic behaviours

Enclosing,
Connecting,
Positioning

Reflection

Having moved 100 miles with her family to a new town and changing schools, Becky's world was more upside-down than usual when she created this impactful scene. With change extremely challenging for many children with ASC, she may have used the toys to express her feelings about the big life transitions that had occurred, playing out her feelings through these toys. Becky's interest in enclosing may be linked with her feelings of safety and security, with the toys representing her need for emotional security. This striking arrangement may also visually reflect her coming to terms with her disconnection from her grandparents and a medley of emotions, including anger, sadness and frustration at her parents for the move.

For some children being able to contain things and limit visual clutter seems to help make their world more manageable. Oscar (7 years, ASC) attended play therapy sessions to support his emotional wellbeing and help him cope with mainstream school during a difficult family time. On entering the therapy space for his second session (after a more structured introductory session), he was clearly overwhelmed by the large basket of toys and other resources available. With tense body language, shortness of breath and repeated sighs of, 'It's tricky', his discomfort was apparent, and he chose to leave the session early. Listening to his 'voice', Sue decided to remove some of the resources to help limit his feelings of being overwhelmed. In his next session, he instantly noticed that the basket of toys wasn't there and asked where it was, then went to the cupboard to get it out and placed it on the round mat. He paused, saying, 'It was tricky with so much' before adding more toys. As Oscar's sessions continued, he was increasingly able to tolerate a lack of containment and create mess.

It is very common for children with autism to find change difficult. This may be linked with control, consistency and familiarity adding to a child's feelings of safety. For Oscar, control over change was key to him experiencing a sense of agency, with containment key to this. Over several months Sue observed him transform from being overwhelmed by the lack of containment and structure, to being able to experience uncontained play, introduce connections and order and have an ability to tolerate uncontained play. Reflecting upon these sessions and the changes that were apparent throughout them with a schematic lens, the importance of containment versus a lack of containment in this child's journey is clear. Sue also wondered to what extent his physical being mirrored his sense of emotional containment.

Implications for the role of the adult

Noticing the potential message in children's behaviours and responding appropriately and respectfully is our aim. Reflecting upon Becky's enclosing and tying-up of her toys, it is clear that she needed the freedom to safely express herself without judgement and for an adult to interact and not interfere (Fisher, 2016). Many adults seek to control children's play or stop them if they see a child playing in ways they deem inappropriate. Since this play was not dangerous, her parents were later able to raise the important safety issue of not putting bags over our heads whilst appreciating how she had expressed herself.

Similarly, Sue was able to give Oscar agency by responding to his anxious body language without shaming. Once the child was able to communicate their overwhelming discomfort, Sue put resources away and used a mat to visually contain play on the floor. These simple changes to the environment appear to have made a big difference to the child's sense of structure and containment, enabling them to experience agency. In this way, the adult role was to notice and attend to the child's needs for containment, potentially mirroring or amplifying their schematic 'preferences' through the containing environment provided.

Conclusion

In this chapter, Tamsin's children, Pippa, Hannah and Becky, and the many children Sue has had the privilege to work with, have generously shared their play and behaviours so that we can gain potential insights into their play and lines of enquiry. As Dr Stephen Shore (2018) so wonderfully reminds us, 'If you have met one person with autism, then you have met one person with autism!' Autistic children are all different, and interpreting their schemas and schematic play can only ever be speculative because it is impossible to know why they have played in this way, and it is important, therefore, to remain tentative in any conclusions regarding these lines of enquiry.

For some of the most troubled children that Sue has supported, particularly in a sensory or messy play context, structure and containment have been vitally important themes. Sue has developed multiple ways of supporting children with this through her own body language, words, actions, and environments. Reflecting upon this and Tamsin's observations of her children in relation to connection and containment, we wonder if the security and potential amplification that this provided also supported their schematic investigations and helped them feel safe and secure.

As adults, we may not always notice how change affects our children; however, we are reminded that 'Something adults may consider to be a small or insignificant event can be quite traumatic for children' (Daly et al., 2004: 111). Observing children's schematic play and listening to what they say can give us an insight into their views, feelings and wishes, which links with the UNCRC article 12 which states, 'Every child has the right to express their views, feelings and wishes in all matters affecting them, and to have their views considered and taken seriously' (Unicef, 1989).

All children's behaviours are a form of communication (Mathieson, 2015), with our interpretations inevitably influenced by our own perspective. It is as if we are behaviour detectives (Gascoyne, 2020; Grimmer, 2022) attempting to work out what they are interested in and fascinated by and the implications of this for our role. Whether reflecting as a parent, educator or therapist, our key learning is the importance of valuing and respecting what children do, because the way they interact and play with resources is important to them. Educators must take time to notice and listen to children. In providing effective learning environments and resources and through the relationships we build, we can facilitate their play and, when appropriate, support and extend it.

Reflections and questions

Throughout this chapter we have shared observations of children with autism engaging in schematic play and reflected upon the possible reasons why they might play in this way. As well as demonstrating our acceptance, respect and curiosity for the children we love or work with, we see this as an opportunity for adults to really notice children's preoccupations and better understand the value, significance and benefits of their interests and fascinations. The following questions may help us reflect on the children we work with and care for:

How can we develop our noticing, not just of children playing in repetitive and restrictive ways, but also the impact of ourselves and the environment, and the child's sensory and emotional needs?

How might we be curious about the meaning, benefits and significance of children's interests, fascinations and patterns in play to enable them to feel valued?

How can we become better attuned to notice the many ways that children generally, and specifically those with autism may be communicating their needs so that we listen to the voice of children with autism?

How can we adopt a strengths-based approach to supporting children with autism?

Recommended reading

Gray, C. (2015). *The New Social Story Book, 15th anniversary edn.* Arlington, TX: Future Horizons Firm.

Grimmer, T. (2022) *Supporting Behaviour and Emotions.* London: Routledge.

Higashida, N. (2013) *The Reason I Jump – One Boy's Voice from the Silence of Autism.* St Ives: Sceptre.

Wall, K. (2010) *Autism and Early Years Practice.* London: SAGE.

8 Feeling at home in the world

Linking schemas with landscape and embodiment understandings

Jan White

Introduction

Outdoor environments have the most potential to become enabling and empowering 'third teachers' when we think about them through child development lenses, such as schema and embodiment theories, along with ideas from Landscape studies. I will mine this very rich and productive interface, bringing together some deepening ideas about:

- What schematic behaviour might be for.
- How young children mobilise their moving bodies to interact with the world they are learning to inhabit.
- Ways of thinking in evolutionary and environmental psychology.

This chapter is very exploratory. In it, I will be bringing together thinking from several fields where I have been seeing resonance and investigating the synergy that emerges as the ideas interact with each other. I will also be asking questions, opening up avenues for thinking more deeply about child development, but not necessarily being able to present answers. We certainly do not yet know enough about schemas, nor do we yet fully utilise the potential of the set of ideas that we call 'schemas' or 'schema theory' – I wish to model this uncertainty, questioning and pushing at the boundaries of these concepts.

I focus this investigation of schema on physical life in the material world whilst being very aware that schemas have great relevance to emotional, social and cultural life also – as explored in other chapters in this book. I hope to bring new perspectives to our collective thinking about the concept we call 'schemas' and will conclude with some thoughts about how this understanding can help us design and create more powerful environments for young children's wellbeing and development. In particular, I hope that the analysis presented here will influence how we look at schemas as a core part of life and development.

DOI: 10.4324/9781003224341-9

Discovering schemas

I was introduced to schemas as a useful tool that helps us notice what children are doing and might be thinking when my own children were at primary school and found the ideas resonated well with what I had encountered through their early years. I have been adding deepening layers of understanding over the many years since, a journey that has given me the strongest experiences of Piaget's notions of disequilibrium and accommodation I have ever had!

New perspectives have repeatedly brought me back to question my current understanding and to think more extensively about the idea. Each layer adds another fascinating dimension to how this very useful concept might illuminate the process of a child's self-construction. Very briefly, my developing layers of understanding about 'schemas' have been:

- Themes or threads in action and behaviour patterns (Nutbrown, 1994).
- Ways of exploring 'big ideas' (Isaacs, 1930) about how the world of things, forces, events, people and relationships works.
- A physical way of making sense and meaning, self-awareness and identity through embodied intelligence (Johnson, 2007; Claxton, 2015; Dent and the Spatial Reasoning Study Group, 2015): we think in all the ways we experience.
- A scientific method of exploration and experimentation through constructing 'working theories' (Carr et al., 2010): data gathering, theory building, predicting, testing, refining and applying to new situations.
- Creation of mental structures (neural networks) that support the development of both thinking and 'thinking tools' that can be used in other situations and for different uses. Building the architecture of one's own brain through bodily interaction with the external material world (note that this neural architecture is a complex, integrated, brain-body system) (Claxton, 2015; Eagleman, 2021).

What might specific schematic behaviours be for? – a pressing question

Over many years, there has been a lot of focus and work on identifying the patterns in young children's behaviour – the underlying ideas that link what a child is doing. Although there may well be a long list of 'threads of thinking' (Nutbrown, 2011) that we can identify, a few themes seem to stand out as especially common across time and cultures (e.g. Yuejuan, 2004). At the heart of my interest in schemas is the question: Why *is it* that some themes stand out so strongly? I have long been wondering, why *do* we see these specific patterns so often – what could explain why *these particular* lines of enquiry by young children are so common?

If these themes occur in multiple cultures and in very young children (where cultural influences might not have had such a strong influence yet), this suggests that these behavioural patterns have a biological basis. If so, how come these *particular* patterns? Are they important or even necessary types of behaviour for wellbeing or brain/body development? What is it about these specific themes that make them so significant in child development? How is it that a child is tuned to possibilities in their world for making these behaviours? What do they represent in the development of the brain and thinking/learning? And further, is it the *idea* that they are exploring, or is it the *behaviour* that they need to be carrying out? Or, are both of these going on – perhaps in an interrelated way?

Looking from ecological and landscape perspectives

I have an academic background in soil science and ecology, both strongly relational disciplines that explore interactions and complex relations: how things influence each other. This has framed my interest in how young children experience the world and see their environment – what they are attuned to, what they see as possible and how they react.

I witness the environment 'speaking' to the child and the child answering in an ongoing conversation that continually impacts and alters each participant – always in relationship and never fixed; always changing in light of the other, always developing: a constant becoming. What do young children notice in their environment and what draws them to respond? Why do they interact and behave in the schematic ways we so commonly see?

Several years ago, I was introduced to some intriguing ideas and understandings in landscape and evolutionary/environmental psychology research (in particular Jay Appleton's 1975 habitat theory) and realised how much some fundamental environmental characteristics matched up with very commonly observed schemas, such as transporting and trajectory. Starting from a fascination with why young children need to move so much (White, 2015), I have also been developing my awareness and understanding of movement, sensory development and embodiment theories, gaining the understanding that the brain is inextricably enmeshed with the body and the brain/body is embedded in the world (Johnson, 2007; Claxton, 2015; Dent and the Spatial Reasoning Study Group, 2015). We think, learn and know in all the ways we experience in, and with, the world.

These three strands of interest coalesce in this chapter to explore:

- How landscape and environmental psychology perspectives add to thinking about 'schemas'.
- How movement and embodiment perspectives add to understandings about 'schemas'.

- How these interacting perspectives can help us to provide the right kind of foundational developmental work for the child.
- How combining these perspectives can enable us to design a powerful environment for early childhood care and education.

How schemas link with landscape elements

I have long been fascinated in the way that young children are in 'dialogue' with their environment and have been observing children at play (that is, following their own interests and desires) to find out what messages environmental features and characteristics send to young children: 'The world of children is a world of action in which things are valued as a function of their handiness or efficaciousness in play' (Werner (1948: 383) quoted in Wood, 1993: 16).

The concept of 'affordance' (Gibson, 1986; Heft, 1988) captures this well as it describes the specific opportunities that arise from interaction between the properties of the environment at this time with the interests, ideas and intents of an individual child in that moment. It is a very relational and inclusive way of thinking about the 'opportunities' that an environment provides, as it focuses on what it *affords* individuals in the here and now – what individual children are actually able to do in and with it – rather than being general to all the children present. What each child 'sees' in the general opportunity will be different and unique.

It is not always clear 'who' starts off the conversation, but the child notices (or is seeking and looking for, so very ready to notice) a possibility for action that something in the environment proposes – a signal or invitation. What the environmental feature offers depends on what the child is internally driven to do and what they actually *can* do depending on their physical abilities at that time – and this is constantly changing, both as they mature and as they gain experience and expertise.

By responding to this invitation through an action (behaviour), the child feels themself against the world, gaining sensory feedback information simultaneously from inside their body and from everything surrounding them. Their action causes a reaction from the material environment, which they can then receive as another invitation or prompt. This action-response–further action, back-and-forth conversation creates an ongoing experience that generates a huge amount of data about the world, their own body and, crucially, how they operate in this complex world.

As I watched for these signals and invitations, I realised that there was a strong alignment of some of the major patterns in play with landscape characteristics that have been studied from evolutionary and environmental psychology perspectives (Appleton, 1975) and are well known in landscape and garden design (e.g. Hayward, 1993; Dannenmaier, 1998). This alignment seems significant in being able to design children's gardens that both feed schematic interests and meet bodily and psychological needs. It also feels likely to give us insight into the question of *why do we see these big patterns? Why are these particular strands of enquiry by young children so common?*

In the following sections, I will explore how the two areas align in six examples of schema and landscape overlap, illustrating the degree of connection. I will then explore how this might be significant for early childhood education. Figure 8.1 maps the alignment, drawing together the salient features between child development aspects and elements of landscape/environment and providing an overview of this interesting association.

Design feature or characteristic	Landscape theory	Schema theory	Other child development aspects
Pathways Straight paths Winding paths Wide and narrow paths Variety of surfaces Stepping stones Steps Tunnels Bridges	Tracks & trails Linkage & Connectivity Unity of space Readability Complexity	Trajectories (horizontal dynamic) Grids Connecting Transporting Going through	Mobility and movement Semiotics – messages Journeys Here and there Adventure/imagination/mystery Following where others go Personal routes (quick way/short cut) Mapping the space Winding and straight Motor control & vestibular stimulation Meandering and reverie Vision – 3D, space, movement
Prospect Topography Slopes Hills Mounds Steps Platforms Veranda Windows Doorways	Being high up Being able to survey the landscape Mapping Landmarks & pathways, Sources (food, water, safe places)	Up and down (vertical dynamic)	Perspective Big picture Understanding large environments Understanding space Power, control Vision Spatial awareness Height & distance Long & panoramic view
Boundaries & places to go through Fences & walls Vegetation Gates, Stiles Edges Arches Doorways Tunnels Bridges	Boundaries Terrain Territory Thresholds Escape routes Connectivity Permeability	Edges Boundaries Enclosure Going through a boundary In and Out	Landmarks and mapping out Territory, protection Perimeters Thresholds – entranceways Portals (imagination) Multiple access to dens – choice of entry/exit options Gaps & holes Squeezing-through places Traps Look-outs, peep-holes & spying

(*Continued*)

Figure 8.1 (Continued)

Design feature or characteristic	Landscape theory	Schema theory	Other child development aspects
Refuge Dens Enclosure Vegetation (especially along boundaries) Mosaic of spaces Corners, steps Behind the shed Nooks and crannies	Refuge Shelter Safe haven	Enclosure Boundaries Envelopment Containment In and out Going through a boundary	Nurture, intimacy Safety, protection Familiarity – home feel Comfort (physical & psychological) Withdrawal, sensory reduction, control and management Hiding, being secret, unseen Fears – being lost; danger (baddies) Personal space, privacy Me-sized, body/space awareness Self-created: autonomy, agency How do I fit in Inside and outside Shape and space Place identity
Source Water Vegetation Natural materials Digging	Food & water Seeking Searching Foraging Gathering	Collecting Gathering Placing Grouping Containing	Hoarding, stashing Emotional security Safety Comfort Treasure Discovery Hiding, caching Ownership Personal worth Gifts and giving (food especially) Categorising and attributes (same/different)

Figure 8.1 Linking landscape understanding to child psychology and development

Links between *dynamic horizontal trajectory* schema and pathways

Schematic behaviour identified as 'trajectory' is where movement in lines, arcs or curves (in the horizontal or flat plane) is explored, building the child's ability to think about, and operate within, three-dimensional space. The child will use their own body to explore the ideas of moving in a particular direction, giving them a personally felt meaning of the movement or direction. It is imperative to move the whole self, many times, as well as to convey objects or be the one that causes objects to move along these

Figure 8.2 Children are compelled to respond to pathways

lines in order to build up embodied feelings, which then create *felt meanings* (Laevers, 2003) and an *intuitive* (bodily held) intelligence that sits under and enables more abstract, conceptual thinking about space, distance and movement of objects.

Lines are fascinating and underpin an extraordinary amount of knowledge, thinking and application (Ingold, 2007, 2015). Making lines both horizontally and vertically gives us the ability to think about space and how movement can occur in it and also utilise these ideas well beyond their physical meaning. This dynamic exploratory pattern involves gaining an understanding of along, to and fro, here and there, there and back again, start and stop, beginning and ending, position, how things link, past and future, cause and effect, and so many other emerging ideas!

Landscape architects and garden designers are well aware that paths play a deep psychological role, exerting a powerful influence on people (Hayward, 1993), especially children (Dannenmaier, 1998; Keeler, 2008; Striniste, 2019). They also play a significant and multi-faceted role in how an outdoor (and indoor) environment operates for those inhabiting it. As Hayward (1993: 5) describes, 'The path, then, is far more than a means of getting from here to there on dry, solid ground. . . . It is a way to organise space and clarify meaning

Figure 8.3 Paths provide varied experience of horizontal trajectories

of your whole garden. The well-designed path is irresistible. It invites, even pulls people into the garden. Put a curve into a path that disappears around a corner and [people] will yearn to know what is around that corner. [Paths make the] garden become coherent while simultaneously offering intrigue, surprise, movement, variety and ever-changing perspectives'.

We have a natural inclination to follow where others have gone before – this beaten track signifies a safe route that may well lead to a source of interest and benefit. Because pathways enable us to move around safely, know where places and things are located and how to find them and map out the entire space – coming to know and understand it as a whole, tracks and trails have been extremely important to our survival as a species over the millennia. As a result, the effects of paths run deep in our psychology, affecting how we feel and how we behave (the concept of Trail: Appleton, 1975; Sobel, 1998, 2008). Pathways speak loudly to children, and they are compelled to respond to them (Wilenski and Wending, 2013)!

A labyrinth-like hierarchy of pathways and journeys offer a variety of perspectives and ways of travelling, enriching ways children and adults can perceive and interact with the environment and each other (Shaw, 1987).

Links between *transporting* schema and pathways

Pathways also strongly suggest, invite and enable transporting activity, being especially valuable as a stimulus to move, to journey, to convey and to relocate both oneself and others.

Children exploring the schematic behaviour identified as 'transporting' are strongly interested in moving themselves and things/others from one place to another. They might move objects, collections or materials such as water and sand by carrying them or using some form of transport – they are especially drawn to transporting other children in carts, on trikes and with any other mobile device available. They will do this repeatedly and in many different ways as they continually explore and investigate this very big area of under-standing about how everything works and fits together, building the capacity to think about how things and people can be located and relocated in space, and about motion itself.

Through this action, they will be physically experiencing *mobility*: that things *can* be moved in space, *how* things can be moved, how things behave as they are moved, their size and weight and how they handle in space and gravity. They will also be generating a growing sensory database of felt knowledge about *movement*: such as position, direction, length travelled, speed and how they

Figure 8.4 Transporting is invited and enabled by pathways

move in relation to other things in the same environment (which may remain static but appear to move as the child moves themself). This is big physics, and also critical bodily held intelligence that enables safe and effective control and management of the body in complex environments throughout life.

When children push, pull, carry and heave things that have size and weight in order to move them, they receive considerable 'pushback' from the world through gravity, friction and inertia. This feedback feels wonderful as it stimulates the internal body-awareness sense called *proprioception* (White, 2015), releasing the neurotransmitter dopamine that makes us feel good. Activation of this sensory system provides feedback about the child's own body and actions in the world – young children are constantly seeking opportunities for this stimulation so that its development keeps up as they grow each day. Moving along pathways also creates excellent stimulation of vision and the motion-detecting *vestibular* sensory system, which integrate to develop good balance and body control (White, 2015). Both sets of feedback give rich, embodied experiences of being in and operating in the world.

Because the nature of a path so much affects emotions and behaviours (Hayward, 1993), a variety of different pathways – from wide, open and straight tracks to narrow, enclosed and winding trails – will prompt and provide a wider range of movement and translocation experiences. If these paths cross and interact, the complexity of discovery and information gathering can greatly

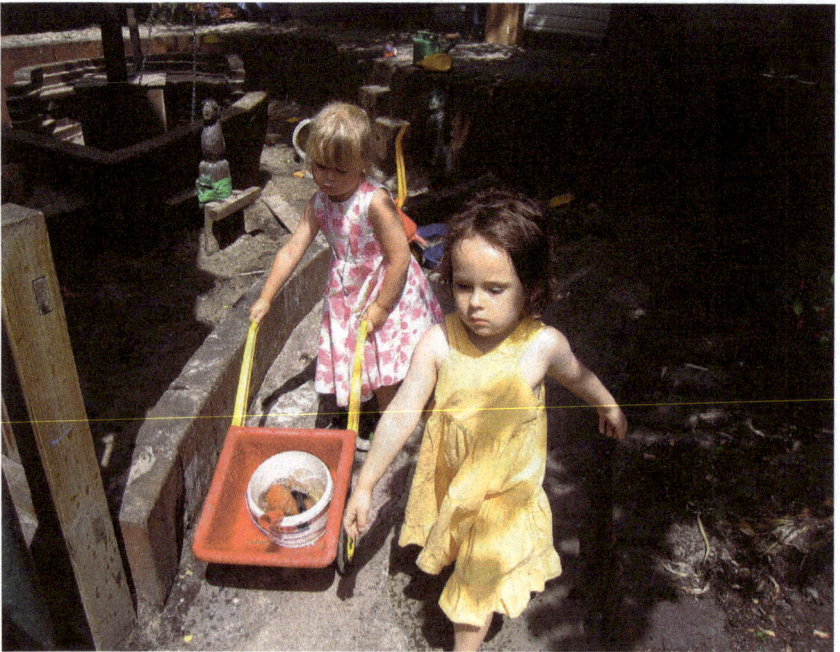

Figure 8.5 Transporting is a deeply felt, whole-bodied experience

increase (Harding, 2005; Herrington and Lesmeister, 2006), creating embodied experiences for the development of spatial awareness, mental mapping and spatial reasoning and feeding fascinations relating to the schemas of connection, junctions and grid. 'Pathway', 'way', 'route', 'course', 'track' and 'avenue' are also valuable metaphors for thinking about actual and potential progress through space and time. A future result of embodied sense-making *with* the world in physically making your own path is the capacity to consider 'making your own *way* in the world' or 'forging a *path* through life' (see also Chapter 5).

A wide range of transportable materials and containers with handles, wheels and runners will support deeper and fuller exploration of these big concepts, as will added challenges of gradients, bumps, dips, obstacles and different (soft, hard, loose) surfaces.

Linking *dynamic vertical trajectory* schema with topography and prospect

Humans love to be high up, seeking high places, vistas and scenic viewpoints, especially when visiting somewhere new or having a favourite place to sit and relax. The emotions and pleasure derived from 'prospect' is a long-recognised landscape concept, which has been harnessed in landscape and design from parklands to gardens: 'A lookout brings a sense of power and exhilaration' (Harland Hand quoted in Hayward, 1993: 3).

Children also show this desire strongly: they love to climb up on and walk along a flat-surfaced wall, to find raised surfaces such as mounds and platforms and to be off the ground in trees, even when (or perhaps because) this is quite a challenge. Babies at the crawling stage are driven to climb stairs even before they can walk. Being up high gives a new and very different perspective ('I can see the whole world from here') and does seem to generate powerfulness and a sense of control (the feeling of 'I'm the king of the castle!').

The interest in up and down relates to two elements of landscape in a nursery garden: *topography* with the opportunity to move oneself and other things or people in the vertical dimension by one's own endeavour, and *prospect* that enables the child to survey the landscape and be able to map out its parts in relation to each other, providing the big picture (linking parts into unified wholes is a feature of Froebelian pedagogy). Being able to navigate a large and complex environment to locate and find what is needed for survival is a clear evolutionary requirement, and both of these landscape elements would require plenty of time and experience to master, so it is perhaps not surprising to see these drives in children's play from an early age. Movement in lines or arcs in the vertical or upright plane should build capacities for thinking about a three-dimensional landscape and how movement can occur in it, slowly becoming able to perceive, process, predict and plan ahead so as to be safe and effective in it.

An 'up and down scape' with lots of level changes and ways to move between them is clearly much more valuable for toddler's and young children's physical and cognitive development than a uniform and flat expanse (Olds, 1987; Fjortoft, 2004; White, 2015).

Figure 8.6 From a very early age humans are drawn to height

Figure 8.7 An up-and-down landscape feeds vertical trajectory explorations

Connections of the *going through a boundary* schema with edges, boundaries and thresholds

Many young children show a strong interest in boundaries and this may be linked with perceptual/psychological development: the world is full of edges and boundaries – both physical and social – that need to be recognised and understood.

In a video of Bobby at 3 months, her attention seems to be drawn by edges – the roofline, the top of the hedge and fence, especially those outlined against the sky where there is strong contrast (Siren Films, 2010a: 3.53–6.06). In my interpretation of this observational material, I wondered whether Bobby's schematic interest in edges and boundaries was developing perceptive ability that would allow her to see things as separate objects against a background. This attention might, in addition, be constructing neural architecture, enabling her to begin to interpret the vast amount of visual information being received and for this to be organised in a systematic way (White, 2010). In another sequence, 18-month-old Yasmine appears to be mapping out the edges within the nursery garden, getting to know them through moving her body (Siren Films, 2010b: 44.14–47.41). Through noticing where the ground is worn in nursery gardens, I have also found that children particularly explore the external boundaries and that this is a popular place to play.

A common aspect of a fascination with boundaries is exploring ways to go across or through them. The 'going through a boundary' schema is described by Arnold as a physical experience of 'causing oneself or material or an object to go through a boundary and emerge at the other side' (1999: 22). In his 1986 study 'Childhood's Domain', Moore (2018) recorded children's interest in 'squeezing through' places where children pointed out small gaps and secret ways as landmarks important to them, and Harding (2005: 151) shared the popularity of their gate and kissing gate (see Figure 8.9). Entry-exit options were noted by Kirkby (1989): escape routes are an important part of the ability of dens to provide refuge, and their doorways can become much embellished with time. Thresholds in the environment can play significant roles in offering crossing points – or portals – into imaginative worlds (Duckett and Drummond, 2014).

Within an early years garden, boundaries help to separate and define areas/zones for different kinds of play. However, these provide the most value for children when they are 'permeable', providing multiple ways to signal and encourage 'crossing'; permeable boundaries are boundaries for *going through*. 'Physical elements that enclose zones and contribute to the fluidity among zones are objects such as low walls or stumps, which can be climbed over, or plant material, which can allow children to pass through its walls' (Herrington & Lesmeister, 2006: 72).

Opportunity for boundaries and places to go through abound in an outdoor environment through walls, fences, doorways, gates, gaps, stiles, arches, bridges, tunnels, tall or thick vegetation providing sides and even a ceiling, and

Figure 8.8 Young children explore boundaries with their whole body

Figure 8.9 Gates are fascinating ways to go through boundaries

looking through peep-holes. Paying attention to boundaries in the physical environment and how they can be crossed – experiencing and creating edges, separation and in and out – seems likely to provide some very foundational processes for understanding how the world works and how the child can operate in it, storing up intuitive intelligence for a great deal of symbolic and metaphorical application later on.

Linking *enclosure*, *envelopment* and *containment* schemas with 'refuge'

From a very early age, young children are drawn to and seek out small and enclosed spaces in the environment they are in, noticing all sorts of nooks and crannies and responding to the invitation to fit their bodies into the enclosed space (Striniste, 2019). A seemingly universal aspect of children's play across childhood is the finding and elaborating of small hideaway spaces or the making of dens (Sobel, 2002) – although these have interestingly different names around the world, such as cubbies, hideouts, forts and bush houses. Writing almost a century ago, Margaret McMillan noted, 'To put up some kind of house, to fix some kind of tent and to sit inside – that is the aim of and desire of all the children. And the making of this house is a more popular occupation than any other, except of course the making of mud hills and trenches and the

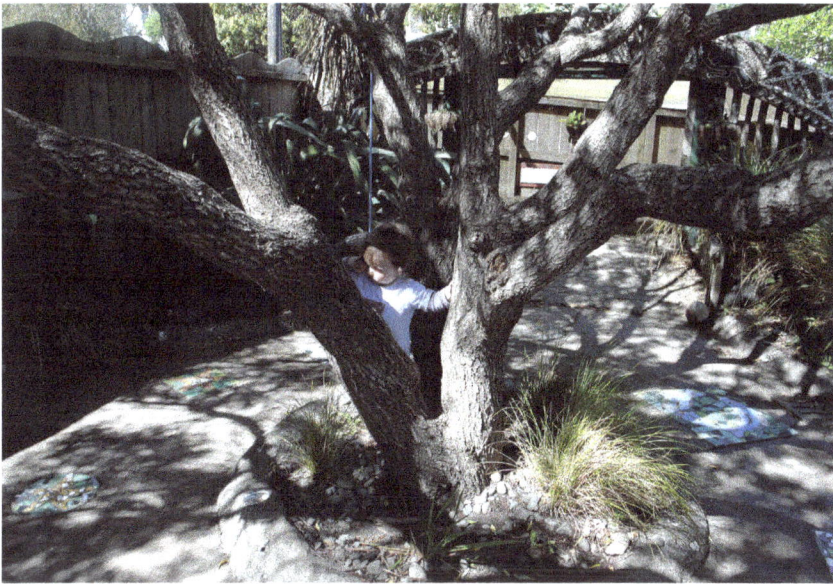

Figure 8.10 Children seek out the physical experience of being enclosed

filling of dams and rivers' (1919/1930: 26). Through interacting processes of building and imaginative play in them, these places become self-made, personal, homely, nest-like and under the child/children's control (Dixon and Day, 2004).

My personal fascination with why children were so commonly interested in small, enclosed spaces, making dens and playing in them stems from many memories of such play across my early and middle childhood. My understanding grew immensely once I came across 'habitat theory' and the idea of 'refuge' (Appleton, 1975; Hildebrand, 1999). Through this evolutionary biology lens, we can see the deep psychological significance of such behaviour, manifesting the survival need for a refuge that is hidden from or inaccessible to predators, providing a secret place to 'see out without being seen' (Kirkby, 1989: 7; Dixon and Day, 2004) which ensures safety, shelter and comfort. 'Children love enclosed, nest-like spaces, especially when they can see out but remain hidden. Researchers believe that this childhood tendency stems from an early survival instinct to seek unobtrusive places in which to hide from predators, with easy escape access and unblocked, long-range views' (Dannenmaier, 1998: 72). In meeting this biological survival need for safe haven – being both hidden and held – we experience a security that calms the limbic part of the brain where emotions are processed and generates pleasurable feelings. This is just the right state for encouraging intimacy, friendship and imaginative play, including dealing with troubling concerns and fears such as baddies and monsters.

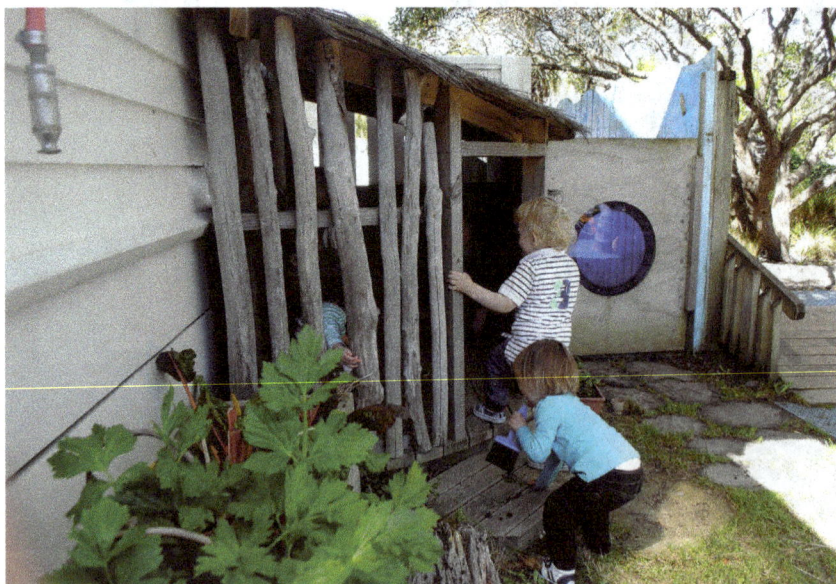

Figure 8.11 Enclosed spaces provide refuge and a safe haven

This evolutionary and psychological perspective on nooks and crannies has a very interesting resonance with the possible emotional aspects of enclosing, enveloping and containing schemas explored by Arnold and the Pen Green Team (2010). Making nests and dens and playing in them clearly also provides children with a great deal of experience for dynamically and bodily exploring how things, others and themselves can be inside or outside something, be covered and be wrapped or enclosed, uniting the embodied feeling of being contained with understanding space as a container. Since dens also have entrances, exits, windows and lookouts, this kind of play is also rich in investigations of boundaries and going through them. Lots of ideas for creating nooks and crannies in an outdoor space can be found in Dannenmaier (1998: 72–85) and Striniste (2019: 148–157).

Relating the collecting, grouping, heaping, placing schema cluster with 'source' and foraging

Cath Arnold has suggested that schemas of gathering and hoarding might have emotional security links to sibling rivalry (Arnold and the Pen Green Team, 2010). She comments that the physical gathering of materials, keeping them together and exerting and displaying power over them is a common motive in young children and that Isaacs (1933/1967: 221) pointed out 'the common wish of little children to have exclusive possession or at least the biggest share or main use of whatever properties are the centre of interest at the moment'. She also notes that this might also be linked emotionally to personal worth: '[h]aving lots might be a symbol of needing lots of love and also of being worth lots of love' (p59), with the child drawing satisfaction from this gathering and possession. She suggests that for some children, this might help to cope with the difficulties of sharing parental love with siblings, especially new ones, a common experience for young children. I think this could also relate to the survival requirement of having enough food as well as sufficient attention and care.

There are very many cognitive ideas that such gathering activity might support, such as building the ability to think about properties and attributes, sameness and difference, how things belong together and how they can be categorised. However, Arnold describes how a two-year-old 'derived satisfaction from this gathering' (Arnold and the Pen Green Team, 2010: 60) and this cluster of schemas seems strongly related to hunting and gathering behaviour. I found that my understanding of collecting, grouping, placing and heaping schematic behaviour could be taken to another level through the application of habitat theory from environmental psychology (Appleton, 1975), in which 'preferences for particular landscape features are seen to correspond with an evolutionarily ancient and deep-seated psychological drive to ensure that our survival needs are met' (White and Woolley, 2014: 31).

This theory proposes that conditions in the environment favourable to biological survival give us pleasurable sensations and we seek them out: the 'habitat' need for refuge (safe haven), 'prospect' (high points and look out places), 'trail'

Figure 8.12 Young children often show fascination with collecting from the environment

(routes between places) and 'source' (places with food, water, building materials etc.) have become coded psychically through the process of evolution. As adults, we are drawn to, prefer and enjoy these elements in our environment, whether that is inside a building or outdoors, but we see these elements particularly strongly in children's play: hiding (refuge), climbing (prospect), travelling (trail) and digging and collecting (source). 'The impulse to hunt and gather is still very alive in children's psyches' (Sobel, 2008: 53), visible in their play as an enthusiastic drive to forage, collect, hoard and arrange, and relating to gathering and placing schemas. Foraging for food is, of course, an ancient drive in humans, and a feeling of having plenty is likely to satisfy at a bodily, physiological level. As Appleton suggests in the concept of 'source', from a genetic perspective, we are still hunting and gathering organisms; searching for and gathering anything compels us with the lure of 'treasure', capturing the imaginations of countless seekers, young and old alike (Sobel, 2008).

Baskets are the original container for gathering, holding and carrying foraged sustenance. Arnold also comments on the emotional content of holding on to something through containment (Arnold and the Pen Green Team, 2010: 59): with an enduring motive of possession, '[c]ontaining materials or objects enabled Caitlin to carry them about, keep them together and exert or display her power over them'.

Figure 8.13 Processing the gathered materials generates feelings of pleasure and satisfaction

How does the understanding of schemas support our thinking about designing outdoor environments for young children?

The analysis given above has foregrounded the importance of recognising the value of schema for deep physical, emotional and cognitive development during play outdoors. The outdoor environment is a potentially powerful place for children to engage in schema-based experiences because of the space, stimulus and possibility for activating the whole body and movement senses (White, 2015). However, although schematic behaviours are often seen more when children are outside, adults may be less aware and work less with them than indoors (Yuejuan, 2004).

   Alongside actively developing awareness and attention, ensuring that this potential is harnessed comes through ensuring that the special nature of the outdoors is fully captured in both provision and practice, so that a rich menu of possibilities is constantly available in the whole environment (White, 2011). But we can take this further when we combine the child development lens of embodied schema exploration with ideas from environmental psychology and landscape studies. This combination offers valuable guidance for designing powerful outdoor environments that enable a child to explore the world, themself and themself in the world in a richly embodied way. 'The key is to understand what nourishes our children and use this awareness to inform every step of the design process' (Olds, 2000 quoted in Striniste, 2019: 7).

How can we design an environment so that children can pick from it what they need for the foundational development work their mind/body is focusing on? Harnessing 'schema theory' as a design tool for the creation of early childhood care and education environments should focus on how elements in the outdoor space can act as vibrant play partners, for example:

- Providing several different kinds of *pathways* to enable complex investigation of trajectories, transporting, connection, grids and boundary-crossing.
- Providing a good *variety of materials* with different properties and the means of containing and transporting them via bowls, baskets, buckets, guttering, carts and vehicles.
- Creating a *multi-layered, 'topographical' landscape* with many different ways of exploring this vertical dimension.
- Adding a variety of *boundaries* within the outdoor space and making them *permeable* to encourage interaction and discovery.
- Making a *mosaic of spaces* through built elements and vegetation that create plenty of *nooks and crannies*.
- Offering abundant supplies of *collectable natural materials* and the means to hold and carry them.

Taking this approach emphasises the notion of children's 'gardens' rather than playground-like 'playspaces', moving further towards meeting cognitive, psychological and bodily needs to create valuable places for wellbeing, relationship and development through play.

How does understanding from landscape and embodiment studies develop our thinking about schemas?

I am intrigued by the amount of correlation I have described here. Bringing the three areas of schemas, landscape and embodiment together demonstrates to me just how much *sense-making* relies on being in and actively working with the material world, how the 'embodied' mind develops entangled with, and enmeshed in, it. 'An embodied view of meaning looks for the origin and structures of meaning in the organic activities of embodied creatures in interaction with their changing environment. It sees meaning and all of our higher functioning as growing out of and shaped by our ability to perceive things, manipulate objects, move our bodies in space, and evaluate our situation' (Johnson, 2007: 11).

I feel that the degree of overlap of such commonly witnessed schematic behaviour with landscape elements that have significance in evolutionary biology and environmental psychology is compelling; this resonance must have something valuable to tell us. Schematic interests appear to orientate children towards interacting with the landscape for learning *with* the body and knowing *in* the body. Realising the powerful role of landscape elements in the psychology of children's drives to learn how to inhabit the environments in which they spend their lives adds a new dimension to understanding children's schematic behaviour, emphasising the role of embodied meaning-making in cognitive and emotional development. As Michael Follett puts it, '[a]ccess to a rich material environment is essential in order to be able to build understanding of what the world is made of and how one relates to it. . . . These schematic behaviours are not just about coming to a static understanding of the nature of the material world, they represent *the way children act in that world* to maintain an ongoing and ever-changing relationship with it, based on the actions and experiences they generate' (2017: 21–22, my italics). It seems to me that young children's action-oriented schematic play is *a way of communicating with and inhabiting the world* through a lively conversation of interacting, relating and continuous becoming.

With this way of being in the world, through bodily interaction with the external material world, the child actively constructs the architecture of their own integrated brain/body. By responding to invitations in the environment through an action (behaviour), the child feels themself against the world, gaining information simultaneously from inside their body and from everything surrounding them – the feeling of *being* a body *in* the world. This action generates a huge amount of data about the world and their own body and, crucially, is continuously updating how they operate in this complex world. As David Eagleman describes, '[o]ur DNA is not a fixed schematic for building an organism; rather, it sets up a dynamic system that continually rewrites its circuitry to reflect the world around it and to optimise its efficiency' (2021: 10).

This is an enormous task, and it needs ongoing experimentation all day, every day, for many years! But it also needs strategies for *attending to what matters most* so as to collect the most useful data as well as creating the means (constructing neurological architecture) for processing incoming information, integrated from internal body signals and external data gathered through the five externally orientated senses: sorting it all out, making sense of it and making it useful for the future. These networks then provide tools for thinking and learning. Eagleman asserts that our 'machinery' (the brain-body) shapes itself by interacting with the world (2021: 3) – 'our brains invite the world to shape them' and 'distributes its resources according to what's important' (2021: 10–11) – by paying attention to what matters.

So, what *does* matter? What are the important features of the world, and life in the world, that must be given lots of attention during the early years of life? And are the 'patterns of children's exploration of the relationship between themselves and the material world' (Follett, 2017: 21) that we call 'schemas' related to these? Returning to my big pressing question about *why we see these specific patterns so often*, I suggest that common schematic behaviours might be building the foundational brain/body architecture required for organising the sensory information that allows us to comfortably exist, think and operate in the world.

In summary, I want to put forward the idea that there might be *core features of the world* that children must learn to inhabit, exemplified by the landscape elements that young children are so ready to have a long conversation with. I propose that the schemas so commonly seen represent the way to pay deep and prolonged attention to what matters in terms of coming to successfully inhabit the 3D physical/material world. Could these themes be some of the foundational ways 'our brains invite the world to shape them'? Might they actually be big patterns of the natural world in which we evolved, which must be worked with in an ongoing way in order to shape us to 'optimise our efficiency' (Eagleman, 2021: 10)?

If so, schematic behaviour would be a significant route to feeling truly *at home* in the world.

Reflections and questions

Having contemplated my original 'pressing question' with the lenses of embodiment and landscape understandings, I am excited to continue this fascinating journey with plenty of further questions to pursue!

Do schemas invite the world to build the child?

I want to pursue the idea that 'schematic behaviours represent the way that children act in the world to maintain an ongoing and ever-changing relationship with it, based on the actions and experiences they generate' (Follett, 2017: 22), enabling them to actively 'invite the world to shape [their brain]' (Eagleman, 2021: 10) – although I would be careful to think about a unified body-brain system (Claxton, 2015), rather than separating them!

Are schemas about inhabiting the world?

Are schemas patterns of the natural world? Could the ideas of Alexander et al. (1977) about an architectural 'pattern language' help us to look more deeply into the relationship of schemas, as patterns of behaviour and meaning-making, to evolutionarily significant environmental features for humans inhabiting the physical world? Might this illuminate the roots of some foundational exploratory behaviours in early childhood? As Sarah Robinson (2011: cover) asserts, 'our ideas and experiences – both physical and cultural – remain *fundamentally patterned* by the complex material interplay of brain, body and world' (my italics). Could schematic behaviour even be *a means of activating the landscape* (Laurie

White, 2021, personal communication) so that it can do its foundational brain/body-shaping work?

Can schemas support education for sustainability?

The embodied mind is embedded both in the body and in/with the world. So I wonder whether embodied, schematic interactions with the life-world can support the growing-up experience of not feeling separate from it, but being entangled with and emplaced in it. I would like to take this combined thinking a step further into an early years pedagogy for sustainability (White, 2014), where nurturing this 'ecological' identity would, in turn, actively nurture the desire to care for our planet.

Recommended reading and viewing

Claxton, G. (2015) *Intelligence in the Flesh: Why Your Mind Needs Your Body Much More Than It Thinks*. New Haven and London: Yale University Press.

Striniste, N. (2019) *Nature Play at Home: Creating Outdoor Spaces That Connect Children with the Natural World*. Portland: Timber Press.

White, J. and Woolley, H. (2014) 'What makes a good outdoor environment for young children?' In Maynard, T. and Waters, J. (eds), *Exploring Outdoor Play in the Early Years*. Maidenhead: Open University Press.

Clips from Siren Film's Clip Library www.sirenfilms.co.uk/library/
– Tristan (trajectory), Michael (up and down), Yasmine (boundaries, transporting and grouping), Liam and Abolfazal (in and out), Skye (collecting), Bobby (edges), Erin (transferring), Jordan (rotation).

9 Bringing post-humanism and Froebel into conversation with schema play

Christina MacRae

Discovering schemas

I did a PGCE in education in 1988 in Bristol, on one of the very few courses with a dedicated Early Years focus. Since, I have worked in a variety of early years settings in various capacities, had children of my own, and currently work as a researcher. My interest in early childhood has continued. During my working life as an early years educator, I generally worked alongside children aged 3–4 years. In the last 5 years as a researcher, I have been privileged to undertake two sustained research projects in the same 2-year-old class in Martenscroft Children's Centre and Nursery School, allowing me to build relationships with parents, staff and children over time. In this role, I attended a training day on schemas, which intrigued me. Much of what I heard struck a chord for me as there was an in-depth focus on patterns of behaviour, on repetition and on affirming the intense attractions that children demonstrate towards the material world. This led me to explore the rising popularity and interest in children's schematic play, and to delve into its underpinning theories. I met Jan White at the European Early Childhood Education Conference in 2018 when I gave a paper that started to try this tease-out. She invited me to join the Schema discussion group, and I felt nervous the first time I attended because I was worried that I was coming in from the 'outside'. In contrast to the sometimes combative and theoretically partisan atmosphere of academic events, I found I was welcomed by a warm, hospitable and respectful learning circle, where people were connected by a common thread of curiosity and interest in early childhood.

Introduction

In this chapter, my aim is to explore how some dimensions of Froebel's pedagogy might contribute to theories that underpin approaches to children's

DOI: 10.4324/9781003224341-10

schematic play. The threads of Froebel's philosophy that I will pick up on are perhaps some of the wilder elements of his thinking, ones linked to his pantheistic, universalist, and holistic religiosity: ones that emphasise force, 'unfolding' and 'self-activity' and the way that children absorb the signature of things. I also hope this will allow me to see ways that Froebel's thinking might share some affinities with recent post-human approaches to early childhood. To date, most research on children's schematic play is located within cognitive and sociocultural theorising, and my aim here is to try to think about how my recent readings of Froebel, combined with slow-motion video as a research method, could expand on cognitive and sociocultural paradigms so that I can foreground the affective, sensory, and dynamic dimensions of children's spatial and material encounters. I am interested in adding to the concept of schematic play through the prism of the felt experiences of young children. Theories associated with schema play are predominantly informed by Piaget's learning theories, and I will ask how Froebel's thinking might offer different understandings to those produced by cognitive constructionist framing of schemas.

The data that I am drawing from was generated as part of the *Listening-2* project, funded by The Froebel Trust. The project explored the significance of Froebel's legacy in contributing to a pedagogy that foregrounds the material, motor, and sensory dimensions of childhood. It also explored the potential of slow-motion filming as a method of active listening to very young children. Taking place over a year in a nursery class for 2-year-olds in an inner-city UK setting, the research featured 'listening' in the name of the project to mark out a commitment to exploring how slow-motion film as a research method could generate an expanded form of attentiveness to young children. In part, this expanded use of the term 'listening' was to offer an antidote to the current national focus on words and speaking that accompanies a policy discourse around the education gap. It also signalled an attempt to frame listening as a collective and shared endeavour, where data was co-produced with parents, early years practitioners and children; some videos were made in the nursery setting, and other clips were taken by parents either at home or out and about.

Before I outline our research project, I want to briefly sketch out some of the context behind Froebel's life and the principles that characterised his thinking. As all the key theorists who have written about the schematic play of very young children use theories of learning underpinned by Piaget (1896–1980), I will also map out some aspects on commonality and of difference between these two influential figures in early childhood education. As a former forester and mineralogist, Froebel (1782–1852) was steeped in the natural sciences. He included human growth in his wider thinking about growth in animals, plants and even crystals, and from this came two of his key concepts: 'unfolding' and 'self-activity'. For Froebel, both these processes characterise the growth of all things. Like Piaget, he is interested in the process of growth, but unlike Piaget, he does not separate growth into such clear stages. He suggests that thinking in clearly demarcated stages distracts our attention from what he calls the 'permanent continuity, and the inner living essence' (2012: 27). Where Piaget emphasises a cognitively oriented mastery of the self over the external world, Froebel's idea of 'self-activity' or 'out-leading' emphasises a general life-force principle rather than something that is exclusively human.

In the *Listening-2* project, a methodology of slow-motion watching focussed our attention on the dynamics of motion itself and the responsiveness of moving bodies as they encounter matter (MacRae and MacLure, 2021). As we watched video clips of children's actions many times over in slow-motion, we became aware of how much, as Claxton says, 'the body is not a thing', but is instead 'an event', and that 'we exist by happening' (2015: 36). We also became much more aware of how the sensations that are produced inside events are a co-mingling of many senses (such as vision, touch, and proprioception), and we were forcibly struck by the way that sensation moves us, and we are moved by sensation. As researchers, we even became aware of this sense of being moved when we felt our bodies as watchers being activated as we watched animated bodies in motion. As we watched many video clips, we started to identify some recurring sensory-motor refrains, or what we started to call motifs, as this word seemed to incorporate a sense of movement (motor) and of repeated action. Examples of these include jumping, getting inside things, using string to connect, lining up objects and children responding to, or creating the conditions for, things to travel or fall through the air.

In these motifs, we recognised an affinity with Athey's (2007) work on schemas: for example, jumping could be recognised as a trajectory schema while getting inside of boxes as a containment schema. And, yet it is our caution about using the word schema that I want to explore as I write this chapter. At the same time, I want to affirm how generative the concept of schema is because of the way that it grapples with some knotty questions about transformation and growth. These questions are of interest to process philosophers such as John Dewy and William James (and of whom Piaget is sometimes included).

In this respect, like Grenier (2014), I am taking seriously the idea that it is important to examine some of the theories underpinning the term schema and the tensions that surfacing these can bring when placed alongside other learning theories. I am also keen to affirm Grenier's recognition that schematic play should be acknowledged as a deeply care(ful) and relational way of approaching early childhood. But, taking a rather different theoretical approach to Grenier, who foregrounds the sociocultural sphere, this chapter will attempt to affirm how aspects of schematic play could productively be recognised as a form of situated thought-in-action. I am also taking seriously the concern that Arnold raise when ask, 'what might be the costs of approaching schema through a purely cognitive lens?' (Arnold and the Pen Green Team 2010: 83). What is driving me is my own feeling that attending to children's schematic play recognises the animated and creative dimensions of their play and affirms children as capacious, rather than seeing them as lacking when set against a policy landscape of progression where language and rational thought are privileged.

Identifying schema – Piaget's legacy

Piaget's ideas of accommodation and assimilation are foundational in theoretically underpinning the concept of schema in Athey's ground-breaking book called *Extending Thought in Young Children* (2007). Athey defines schemas as 'patterns of repeatable actions [that] lead to early categories and then to logical thinking' (2007: 49). She also states that these patterns of behaviour and thought exist 'underneath the surface features of various contents, contexts and specific experiences' (2007: 49). This connection between action (a pattern of behaviour) and thought is productive: as adults, we are so used to thinking of thought as exclusively that which can be verbalised or represented. However, the concept of schematic play conceives a dynamic relationship between thought and action. It allows us to look at a young child's apparently idiosyncratic actions and, instead, to see them as at once creative and inherently thoughtful acts.

Another key distinction that Athey takes from Piaget's developmental map is that between *form* and *content*. So, taking the example of jumping: here, 'form' would be the concept or idea of verticality that is expressed in the trajectory of the body moving up and down, and 'content' is the water in the form of a puddle. Much of my caution about this clear separation is that these kinds of distinct categories can lead to binary thinking, something that Froebel was always at pains to challenge. For example, he rails against what he calls 'sharp limits and definite subdivisions' (2012: 27) when thinking about child development. My reasons for sounding a cautionary note about the theoretical underpinnings of schemas are threefold. Firstly, I am cautious about such a clear definition between form and content and the way that it tends to privilege form over content. Secondly, I have concerns about a division that is implied between mind and body. This Cartesian split is one that underpins Piaget's hierarchy of knowledge: so while sensory-motor learning is recognised as a form of knowledge, it is seen as more primitive and one that humans, exceptionally, are able to move away from as they are able to separate ideas from things. It is this ability to think about things in the abstract and as represented through symbolic and linguistic forms of expression that is foregrounded. Here, the driving force is an intentional mind that drives a non-thinking body. Finally, I am cautious about ways that the identification of schemas in children's play can become categorical ways for adults to comprehend children.

In this chapter, I am aiming to explore these three concerns that I have found myself worrying about. My thinking will draw both from recent post-human theories and scholarship, as well as Froebel's writings about the education for young children. In bringing post-human thinking to early years pedagogy, I am following a tradition of early years scholarship that has been evolving over the last 20 years; for example, Olsson (2009), Davies (2014) and more recently Murris (2016). These scholars have, in turn, been influenced by philosophers who include Deleuze and Guattari, Massumi, Bradotti, and Barad. Often the term 'post-human' conjures up an idea that these ideas must be fundamentally anti-human. However, rather than being anti-people, post-humanism questions much of the human exceptionalism that underpins the way that we think about the world and the place of the human in it. Much scientific study in the field of education, linguistics, and developmental psychology has a core purpose in developing a science located that specifically seeks out what it is that makes us an exceptional species. However, it is precisely through these scientifically inflected disciplines that our sense of what it is to be human is constructed. Post-human scholarship sits alongside a contemporary interest in the way that colonialism has also been implicated in how we think about what it is to be human. This starts to raise questions about how a particular idea of what it is to be human is produced, which has led in turn to studies that attempt to de-centre the human as a way of acknowledging more-than-human agency and relationality as a force that we humans are deeply implicated with. When this thinking is applied in the field of early childhood, it causes a very particular tension, as this is a field that prides itself on being 'child-centred'. Post-human approaches to early childhood likewise de-centre the child, not in an anti-child spirit, but rather to foreground the relationality between the child and the more-than-human world.

The event of puddle-jumping – separating *form* from *content*

I will turn now to the first of my worries about some theoretical assumptions that underpin thinking associated with schematic play: that of separating *form* from *content*. I will turn to one example of a jumping event, where a child jumps into a puddle. The image here (Figure 9.1) captures an instance of a child's body landing after they have launched themselves from a wooden staging post in the outdoor area of the nursery. Interpreting this play event schematically, I could recognise *form* as the trajectory pattern. As the child makes repeated leaps from a higher point into a puddle, I could read this as a sensory-motor sedimentation of the concept of verticality *(form)* as the child's body climbs up and then jumps down. I could also recognise their linear trajectory as another kind of *form*, one that is produced from the forward force of the leap that almost makes the child fly momentarily. I could recognise the water itself as *content* and as separate from the ideational quality of the more patterned and abstract idea of *form*.

In delineating form and content, there is certainly an acknowledgement that the content (the puddle) acts like a magnet to the child, and it precipitates the repetition of 'patterns of behaviour' (the schema). The child could be described, as Meade and Cubey (2008) say, as 'hooked' into this repeated behaviour. The affective aspects of this engagement (which might be the joy and excitement of jumping) could be seen in terms of how they 'help' the memory to sediment the pattern – or the form of the action – in the mind. The attraction of the water in the first place acknowledges the significant part that is played by affect

Figure 9.1 A puddle-jumping event at nursery

as it draws the child into action. The way that the memory is entangled with emotion is acknowledged by Meade and Cubey. However, they go on to say the reason why children persist in reproducing these action patterns is that 'they are trying to make sense of the abstract characteristics of particular features of their environment', in this case 'verticality', by 'fitting them into the cognitive structures they already possess' (2008: 43).

While the sensation of jumping certainly is producing an idea of verticality and the spatial awareness of up and down, I am worried that if form and content are separated, and form is privileged as abstract and something that only intentional thought can comprehend, then the singular sensation of *this* event might be overlooked as we (adults) impose our own logics and interpretations on the child's self-activity. The *this*-ness of the puddle-jump event is composed of a multitude of things, including weather atmospherics, the physical and affective capacities of the child's body at *this* moment, the height of the wooden post, the depth of the puddle, the awesome sight/sound of the corona-shaped splash that has been created (and so much more). By overlooking the *this*-ness of the jump, I wonder if we might be inclined to overlook the singular and entangled way that the child-puddle-jump event unfolds? In the singularity of the form of any jump, each one has a tone and quality that are infinitely variable and experienced in their particularity. In *this* instance of puddle-jumping, the child's body was responding to *this* body of water splashed in relation to their weight, their force and their booted feet, and to the hard/soft surface of the AstroTurf that contained the puddle. The philosophers Dewy and James remind us that 'experience is not so much a transcendent moment but a felt process of transition' (McCormack, 2013: 9). Is it possible that when *form* is privileged, the sensation produced inside the experience of puddle jumping becomes of less interest or value to me as an appropriating adult?

This makes me wonder if, by paying more attention to the attractive force of the felt sensation of setting water into motion by jumping feet, could I attend more to the intrinsic relationality that exists inside the event? And would this allow me to linger more with the aesthetics and the sensation of engaging with matter and the way that, as Froebel says, force and matter mutually condition each other? Maybe I could try to think, as Massumi does, about the ways that 'organising self-activity is a rightful expression of matter' (2002: 228). The complex physics of the surface transformations of puddle water in response to jumping feet and the experience of gravity become folded into the memory of the body as proprioception, which, in Massumi's words, translate into 'the exertions and ease of a body's encounters with objects in a muscular memory of relationality' (:39). The relationship between water as *content* and vertically as *form* goes beyond the idea that the puddle-water 'affords' the production of form. Rather, could I think of the jump event as (in)forming through impressions made on both bodies (child and water) through contact? Here I could perhaps recognise more fully the vital relationality taking place at the heart of the event, where the child *and* the water are both in a state of excitement, exchange and transformation. This would foreground a '*vital* exploration', which is a term that Atherton and Nutbrown use many times in their book about schema play (2013, my italics). Thinking about the reciprocal animation taking place between child and puddle, perhaps I even could start to understand Froebel's belief in an intuitive understanding of the self-organising principles of matter, something that he variously describes as 'premonition' or 'surmise' (Liebschner, 2001: 141).

Watching the child's body repeating a motif such as jumping, I return to Meade and Cubey's analysis that, through repetition, the child is '*trying to make sense of the abstract features of their environment*' (2008: 43). Perhaps there is a danger that the intentionality that is attributed to the body that jumps implies that concepts must be formed in the mind, driven by a brain primed to separate out *form* from *content*. This runs counter to Froebel's more holistic and unidirectional conception of how we learn the world, where he declares that 'education should not draw its inferences concerning the inner from the outer directly for it lies in the nature of things that always inferences should be drawn inversely' (:2). As Sheets-Johnstone cautions (2011b: 455), if we asked the child 'why are you jumping', they would be unlikely to reply that they are repeatedly jumping because they are cementing the concept of up and down. For Sheets-Johnstone, this is because we learn ourselves through movement: she upends Descartes's famous maxim 'I think therefore I am', to say instead, 'I move therefore I am' (2011a). She proposes that movement is closely connected with how we affectively experience and know ourselves in relation to the world. While much that is written about children's schematic play focuses on the mind, Arnold' work (2010) reminds us that even if Piaget discounted action as being truly intelligent unless it was guided by purposeful minds (Atherton and Nutbrown, 2013: 115), he did recognise the influence of affect as schemas emerge (Arnold and the Pen Green Team, 2010: 23). By foregrounding the emotional dimension of children's schematic play, Arnold' work redresses the cognitivist focus on conscious children's minds. In so doing, bring attention to the way that action as metaphor can 'give form to the inexpressable' (Lawley & Tomkins, in Arnold: 149). And again, I can see echoes with Froebel's interest in 'something [that] which remains forever beyond the reach of the human mind and beyond representation in the material world' (Lilley, 1967: 9–10).

The plastic expression of ideas – bodies that think

When Sheets-Johnstone draws attention to the absurdity of asking a question such as 'Why are you jumping in that puddle of water?', it is because she is making the case for what she calls a 'mindful body', rather than an 'embodied mind'. This seems to be a good starting point from which to explore my second concern in relation to Piaget's legacy in the conceptualisation of schema play: the mind/body split. Piaget does use the term 'prehension' (Atherton and Nutbrown, 2013: 115) in a way that can be likened to Froebel's term 'premonition' or 'surmise'. He uses the word in recognition that not all action is consciously driven by intention. However, for Piaget, this form of sensory-motor intelligence is not the true intelligence that emerges when thought replaces action (operational intelligence). For Piaget, thought arises from action. Affirming this prehensive intelligence, one that can be recognised in schematic play, Atherton and Nutbrown settle on seeing schematic play as an expression of a kind of 'becoming intelligence' and an 'intelligence in the making' (:115). However, in Froebel's more germinal philosophy, the unconscious plays a more active role, and what Piaget calls prehension (and Froebel calls premonition and surmise) is more highly valued as an intelligence that is beyond words and absorbed by an affective body. Here I am wondering if one could think, as Sheets-Johnstone does, of it as thought-*in*-action. This challenges a 'division of labour' that has tended to be 'underpinned by an implicit separation of between mind and body, with the latter serving as the acknowledged vehicle of the former' (McCormack, 2013: 11).

   Again, this reminds me of Froebel's injunctions that we should not undervalue 'the earlier stages of development in reference to the later ones' (2012: 8), nor should we neglect, as school so often does, 'the plastic expression of ideas' (2012: 37) produced when hands encounter things. When we privilege form over content and mind over matter, as adults, are we perhaps inclined to move to words too quickly as we observe and guide children as they play in our eagerness to direct children's attention to separating out pre-defined categories? And furthermore, could our 'efforts to formulate knowledge in words' run the risk of ignoring the 'value of things' (Froebel, 2012: 37)? Sometimes, words might 'destroy silent sensory pleasures of looking, feeling, smelling and listening' (Brierley in Atherton and Nutbrown, 2013: 129). When Froebel poses the question, 'How can we give language to the objects of the child's life when they are so dumb to us' (:16), he also draws our attention to the ability of children to pay attention to the 'smallest of things' (:16) and reminds us that according to his unidirectional and reciprocal principles, we should learn about how to live more fully from the actions of children.

I am not sure what to call this germinal and unfolding intelligence that Froebel seems to recognise in the self-activity of children. In this chapter, I have variously used the terms 'felt' and 'sensation' for want of a better term. These words lean toward how I understand Massumi's term 'thinking-feeling' (2017: 52), which he describes more as an intelligence that circulates through and connects bodies at pre-conscious and pre-individual levels that cannot be captured by words alone. Massumi, along with Sheets-Johnstone, emphasises how impossible it is to separate the physicality of a moving body with the affective dimension that always accompanies movement and by which we are also moved by our movement in relation to the things that we encounter.

A poetics of childhood?

> Our intention is, fundamentally, to be with childhood – to keep it with us, to hear it, to review it, to learn with it.
>
> (Leal, 2005: 120)

Finally, and by way of a conclusion, I will turn to the last of my three concerns about the possible effects of the Piagetian legacy that can arise if we become over-fixed on codifying and formalising the schemas that emerge in children's play events. I have opened this concluding section with a quote from Leal, who makes a powerful case (2005) for recognising the *potency* of childhood to revitalise a dominating conception of the child (especially in relation to the psychological and education discourses) as lacking. Her plea resonates strongly with Froebel's belief in childhood itself, and this affirmative view of the child could, I think, contribute towards opening up some current cognitivist interpretations of schema. One of the stilling effects of categorising schemas is that what was a dynamic movement becomes grammatically fixed as a noun. I worry that when we declare that a child has a 'transporting schema', or an 'enveloping schema', this runs a risk of expressing, as Ingold suggests, 'colonial imaginaries' held by adults that place the child within a general pre-defined system. This runs the risk of seeing the child's world 'spread out before it like a surface to be occupied, and whose contents are to be collected, inventoried and classified' (2011: 168).

This chapter has mused on an instant of a puddle-child-jump event where a child's body encounters a body of water contained in a small dip in the surface of some playground AstroTurf. It is easy to see that, in terms of an adult world, this kind of behaviour can be read as childish. Froebel declares that the reason we use a term like childish in a derogatory fashion is because 'the life of the child is dead to us' (2012: 15). Reading the child's puddle jumping schematically helps us to rescue the word childish, as it restores value to the self-activity of a child jumping in a puddle. And yet, I wonder if Froebel's interest in the universal growth of *all* things could help us to install even more vitality in this event. In so doing, it could foreground a relationality that he places at the heart of movement where, as Froebel says, force and matter mutually condition each other (2012: 40). This, in turn, could help to also bring the puddle itself to the fore as a lively co-participant in the event. The Froebelian belief in the manifold relations between force, life and matter is one that acknowledges that, in some respects, children are better placed to perceive their connectedness to the world around them, and in this respect, adults might learn from them. Here we could recognise the child as being more open to a state of becoming as an intrinsic worldly intelligence, rather than thinking of them on the way to 'becoming' something else (intelligent, for example). This could acknowledge a 'bodily logic of potentiality through affect, rather than imagining that all learning take[s] place through conscious thinking' (Olsson, 2009: 48). Perhaps this is akin to what Froebel calls the 'out-leading' (2012: 37) process, where adults do have a role in this unfolding, but by following closely alongside, rather than 'interfering' (2012: 6). Going back to the puddle-jumping event, it is possible to now think more productively about the sheer felt wonderment of water, ripples, splashes and the complex physics and vibrations of its corona-shaped formation impacting the water surface.

Exploring the tensions of Froebel's philosophy when set in conjunction with certain aspects of the Piagetian legacy of the theories underpinning a schematic analysis of children's play could possibly help me to reclaim the word 'developmental' from its current association with chronological time and progressive stages by rescuing some of its etymological roots that relate to unfoldment, rather than progression. They could also help me to recognise the complex way that ideas are produced and take shape, rather than such a clear division between the conceptual and the perceptual. Merleau-Ponty, who was a contemporary of Piaget, was clear that 'child development must be understood as a *dynamic* process rather than a sequential achievement at various stages'. He goes on to warn us about the dangers of what he calls a 'cutting out' aspect of a child's development when we are looking at a 'moment in a dynamic totality' (Merleau-Ponty in Welsh, 2013: 35). This way of thinking cautions against fixing schema into conceptual categories because they are always in a state of development and always in(formation) as they encounter other bodies: both human and not human. This also echoes the antipathy that Davies expresses when we explain behaviour according to pre-defined categories, as she argues that it can make it hard for us to really listen when children are engaged in play

(2014). If one of the pre-defined separations we make as adults is that mind must always be distinct from matter, then perhaps it means we are not always able to take seriously the ways that children think. And indeed, as Froebel proposes, we could learn from children that the stuff of the world cannot be so easily separated from how we know it. And if we pay attention to how we make our world through our movements in it, maybe we could understand this as more of a world-*making* rather than world-*discovering* intelligence.

For Piaget, schematic thought is an intelligence before language, but because of the way it is slotted into a progressive hierarchy of knowledge, the sensory-motor aspects of this stage are all too often overlooked because of the emphasis on the cognitive and the intentional. If we think of the plasticity of a body that thinks-in-action, this is more akin to Froebel's idea of self-activity, unfoldment and synthesis than to Piagetian ideas of assimilation and accommodation. Then schemas could be recognised less as general rules waiting to be discovered and instead as universal processes of co-formation through dynamic events animated by affective bodies and materials. When Merewether looks at a fieldnote and a photograph that are from part of a dataset from a research project in a nursery setting, she also is confronted with children encountering a puddle. In this case, the children were intently watching the puddle vanish as its contents drained through a soakaway drainage grid that piped rainwater into the ground. Merewether finds herself being struck by a sense that the children 'were somehow "with" the water; connected to it in a way that I was not' (2018: 6). When this feeling strikes her, it forces her to think more carefully about what that sense of difference in their engagement with the puddle was to hers as an observing adult. She then reflects on how her training as both a researcher and an early childhood practitioner leads her to be led by 'a gaze that sees an active subject (the children) with a passive object (the water)' (:6). This realisation leads her to reflect on how this blinds her to the manifold and complex dimensions of the movement of a body of water, such as the force of gravity pulling the water across paving stones coupled with the surface tension that made the water adhere as a puddle-body, at the same time, resisting the gravitational pull of the drain. Following this thought, she is prompted to wonder if had she been more childish, perhaps in that instant might she have even been able to 'see the tiny specks of dust as they fall into the water causing a diffraction pattern on its surface' (2018: 7).

Re-reading Mereweather as she reflects on her data and her position as an observing adult reminds me how difficult it can be, from this position, to fully engage in the fascination, wonderment and magical dimensions of these smallest of events. I am inspired by the way that her reflection on the data makes her ask difficult questions about her ways of knowing. This leads her to seek ways to approach children's encounters with the materials that allow her to share some of the enchantment that she recognises in the intensity of the children's engagement with the animated puddle water in relation with the drain. Leal identifies a strange paradox, whereby it often is precisely 'our knowledge about childhood that separates us from it' (2005: 116). I worry that if, as adults, we spend too much time trying to make sense of children's actions through too tightly prescribing a pre-defined systematising that privileges a certain kind of intelligence, there is a danger of reducing the intensity of children's materials engagements. I wonder if a Froebelian sensibility could help us to recuperate some of the animated poetics of children's schematic play: the beauty of a carefully arranged line of pebbles, the metaphorical quality of connection enacted by trailing string, the manifold complexity of a puddle that is impacted by the weight of a wellington-booted child. As Leal says, perhaps we should sometimes resist analysing what it is to be childish and instead develop ways to be alongside children that allow us to feel a little more what it is to be childish. 'Maybe we could find, in the simple poetic dimension, what deep possibility the educational act seems always to incarnate and offer' (2005: 119).

And finally, I leave the last word to Froebel:

> Let us then secure for our children that which we lack ourselves. Let is transfuse from their lives into ours that vital creative energy of child's life which we have lost. Let us learn from our children.
>
> (Froebel, in Tovey, 2017: 111)

Reflections and questions

In this chapter, I have been asking myself questions throughout. I think one of the key questions that I started with was *how can we allow ourselves to learn from children in a way that touches us, rather than simply learning about them?* This is not an easy task and raises many tensions. The inherent asymmetrical power relationships that exist between adults and children are ones that make it difficult to prevent us from observing and interpreting children from our position. Even if we try to tune in and be more present with children (with the best intentions), we also always run the risk of interfering. These can be uneasy tensions that cannot be resolved, but at the same time, I hope they can be ones that productively provoke us.

Further reading

Davies, B. (2014) *Listening to Children: Being and Becoming*. Abingdon: Routledge.
McNair, L. J. and Powell, S. (2021) 'Friedrich Froebel: A path least trodden', *Early Child Development and Care* 191(7–8), pp. 1175–1185. DOI: 10.1080/03004430.2020.1803299.

10 Children first

The relevance of schemas for children in school

Christine Parker

Co-writers: Zoë Austin and Antonio Griffiths-Murru

Discovering schemas

Reflecting back on my career of over 40 years, I acknowledge my luck in starting my teaching professional journey in Sheffield, South Yorkshire, UK. Ann Sharp was the early years advisor and had led the Structuring Play project in the 1970s with Kathleen Manning (Manning and Sharp, 1977). The notion of 'structuring play' was more constructivist than would be assumed from the title. I was teaching 6- and 7-year-olds at the time, and my understanding of children at play alongside the richness of their learning was emerging. I decided I had to go into nursery education and I accessed a 4-month long secondment to deepen my understanding of the nursery age range. The buzz that was generated when the small group of educators I belonged to visited Cathy Nutbrown's nursery class still creates a shiver down my spine. This was a moment of enlightenment. Nutbrown had studied the work of Chris Athey (2007) for her master's degree, amongst other theorists, and created a workshop environment, which she refers to as 'continuity in materials' (Nutbrown, 2011: 39). Nutbrown questioned what was then, current practice with young children, from how children engaged and were observed in play to ensuring the environment was rich with possibilities for nourishing children's schemas. Imagine my excitement when, a year later, now working in the nursery phase of education, I got to hear Chris Athey not only speak, but facilitate a day's workshop for all nursery educators across Sheffield.

The focus of this chapter

The focus of this chapter is a continuation of my schema story, be it 40 years on. Since the 1980s, I have had a rich and varied career and now find myself in the role of a teacher educator in Initial Teacher Education (ITE). What continues

DOI: 10.4324/9781003224341-11

to fascinate me is that schema theory, as interpreted in early years settings in England, could be perceived as 'dropped' for children in school and 'schooling' becomes increasingly formalised and adult-led rather than learner-led.

My intention in this chapter is to open up the dialogue about the relevance of schema theory when working with children further up the education system. Athey was keen that for children, there would be increasing 'continuity from infancy towards primary education' (Athey, 2007: 57). Athey was systematic in tracking project children and their later academic achievements following engagement in the Froebel Early Education Project (2007). Revisiting the children's academic achievements aged 7-years old, Athey concluded that they had made significant gains (2007: 219). Athey put a strong case forward for the correlation between schemas and a child's emergent mathematical and scientific conceptual development (2007), complementing Arnold's reflections on children's language acquisition (Arnold, 2018) and Nutbrown's demonstration of the relationship between stories and children's schematic interests (2011). So, it would make sense to build on this knowledge base.

As schools in England became increasingly target- and test-driven, it was perhaps understandable that dialogue about learning may have got lost within the mire of seeking to, for example, ensure children are 'school ready', to 'accelerate' children's learning and 'fill gaps' (Roberts-Holmes, 2015; Watkins, 2006). However, with a growing intent on evidence-based approaches, learning theories are coming to the fore with references to educational and academic research (DfE, 2019). The Education Endowment Foundation (EEF) (2021) published an overview of studies relating to cognitive science and its relevance to practice in school. In this report, schemas are defined as 'structures that organise knowledge in the mind' (2021: 31). This report is important for schools because it brings discussion around schema theory back into the educators' domain. My view is that making a connection with Piaget and Inhelder's theory on the contribution of concrete experiences to a child's conceptual development (1969: 128–129), alongside Athey's conclusive research on the positive impact of nourishing the youngest children's schemas (2007), would strengthen educators' insights into the child's learning processes. These thoughts prompted the question, 'What is the value and relevance of schema theory to teaching and learning in primary school and how does this benefit children?' To argue the case for including a deeper perspective of schema theory in teacher professional development, I am learning alongside educators to unravel this proposition. I have met with Antonio and Zoe via an online platform during the school year 2020–2021. This chapter is their story and that of the children they teach.

Discussing schema theory

Antonio, Zoë and I formed a schema focus group meeting throughout the school year, 2020–2021. Both Antonio and Zoë worked in reception classes, that is, classes in England for children aged 4- to 5-years old (one child was a year older). Zoë worked in a small rural primary school in the east of England, and Antonio was working in a special school situated in the Midlands. Antonio and Zoë were generous in sharing their observations, and photographs of children were consistently our starting point for dialogue. We shared our thinking about schema theory as well as other theoretical concerns.

I have been motivated to think more deeply about schema theory through my engagement in the schema focus group that has contributed to this book, as well as with the group that I initiated with newly qualified teachers. The dialogue process has informed my reading and deepened my understanding. In both groups, we have considered, 'What are we curious about?', and from this, lines of inquiry have emerged. There has been a process of what we have observed in real life, what we have thought about these observations and then dialogued.

Through our discussions, Antonio, Zoë and I identified three lines of inquiry. They were:

- How have parents been engaged in their child's learning and what difference has this made for the child?
- What is our pedagogical stance?
- How can we hold onto a cluster of theories to inform practice with all children?

These lines of inquiry shape the following discussion. Each line of inquiry will be presented in turn and illustrated with extracts from what we called our 'schema narratives' written by Antonio and Zoë. These are presented in italics. To protect the children, either they or their parents have selected pseudonyms.

How have parents been engaged in their children's learning and what difference has this made for the child?

Engagement with parents, carers and other family members was significant from the beginning of the school year, not only from an ethical perspective, but also to enable us to ascertain greater knowledge and understanding of the children involved. We had explained to parents that schema theory helped us to understand how children learn, and in this endeavour, we sought their consent to observe their child over time and to analyse these observations in order to understand better how their child was engaging in the school environment and what pedagogic strategies (Lawrence et al., 2016) supported them most effectively. The information collated was used to improve curriculum content (Athey, 2007: 56) and outcomes for each child.

In the following extracts, Antonio and Zoë write about their experiences of working with children's parents, sharing information, responding to suggestions from families and working together to support children. Three children are the focus here: Jude, Elsa and Ewan.

Extract 1 from Antonio's schema narrative

Starting school

At the beginning of the school year (2020–2021) Jude was 5 years 7 months-old. He had transferred from a mainstream school. Jude is a very

Figure 10.1 Jude's transitional object; a photograph of himself and his dad.

shy and polite boy who presents his emotional needs in ways he finds difficult to manage. Jude has a great sense of humour and he loves his friends. The first thing he did when he arrived in class was to stand at the class door and he welcomed all his friends with a big smile.

Mum and dad are separated however they tried their best to create as many opportunities as possible to do activities together and support Jude's wellbeing. Jude found separating from his dad extremely difficult. It was necessary to introduce a transitional object (home-school) to support Jude's wellbeing (Winnicott, 1971: 6). His parents were quick to provide a photograph of Jude with his dad.

I wrote at this time, 'Jude sat still for 5 minutes before creating a line with magnets. Jude could choose from triangular and square shaped magnets and he selected the square shaped magnets. Later I put some action rhymes on the classroom screen and Jude actively participated in "5 Little Ducks"'.

We pondered on the significance of Jude lining up objects, the sense of order that this may have been evoking for him. Although unplanned, did Jude's active response to '5 Little Ducks' reflect his desire for order in response to his separation from his father? Arnold reflects on her granddaughter's response to her parents' separation (2021: 104) and, revisiting Antonio's consideration of Jude's needs and his sensitive responses, I wonder what happens for a child when these adjustments are not made within the school environment.

Daily transitions in school

Daily transitions in school, including arrival and departure times; going to assembly; and moving around school, playtimes and lunchtimes, are times of unravelling moments for the child and are often conveyed to parents as times of emotional imbalance.

Extract 2 from Antonio's schema narrative

Jude and Elsa have been exploring and understanding the world around them since they started school in September using schemas as defined by Athey, 'Patterns of behaviour and thinking in children that exist underneath the surface features of various contents, contexts and specific experiences' (Athey, 2007: 5). In my observations I noticed that in their exploration and understanding there were several patterns of behaviour that were repeated over and over. These patterns or schemas made me reflect on how Jude and Elsa communicate, present their behaviour, show their emotions and deal with transitions. I used the analysis of these observations in my daily curriculum planning. Over time, I noted an improvement in the children's levels of involvement and in their wellbeing (Laevers, 1997). There was an emerging trust and planning lessons was much easier because I was using the children's patterns of actions as much as I could to create their unique context for learning. Transitions were less threatening for them both.

Searching for the relationship between 'form' and 'content' (Athey, 2007: 56)

Throughout the school year, Antonio, Zoë and I reflected on how, through observation, thoughtful curriculum planning and looking for connectivity between, what Athey calls 'cognitive form', the schemas and concepts that are important for the child, and the curriculum 'content', which Athey describes as the 'stuff of thinking' alongside our learning from the children's families (2007: 55–58). The following schema narrative extracts exemplify the strength of the relationships between educators and parents and how this has been beneficial for the children.

Extract 3 from Antonio's schema narrative

Introducing Elsa

Elsa was 4 years 10 months-old at the beginning of the school year. She has a high level of need and specifically requires additional support to be physically mobile and her speech and language are limited. Elsa is able to communicate using our school approach called Total Communication as advocated by sense (Sense: accessed 04.08.2021). In the school where I work we believe that every behaviour is communication (Boxall and Lucas, 2010) and that every child needs to have an opportunity to communicate their thoughts. We use a sign language method called signalong (Signalong: accessed 04.08.2021), communication boards, a speech output device and our own body language (Sense, 2021). Elsa was able to use communication boards, she used sign language, and she was starting to say one or two word phrases. Her speech was not always clear so it was important to have different ways to communicate reducing her feelings of frustration and to develop positive self-esteem. At school Elsa worked hard at being brave to be more independent physically. I supported her to take risks on the climbing frame to develop her confidence in her own mobility. Elsa was valiant in trying to walk unaided.

It appeared that Elsa represented her thinking symbolically through her play. I believe Elsa demonstrated her interest in containing, going through and on top of, in her play with the dolls' houses and mud kitchen. Elsa's parents shared photographs of her playing with her dolls' houses at home and cooking alongside her mother. In one photograph Elsa is placing her chosen toppings on a pizza and she uses her fingers with precision, carefully positioning the ingredients.

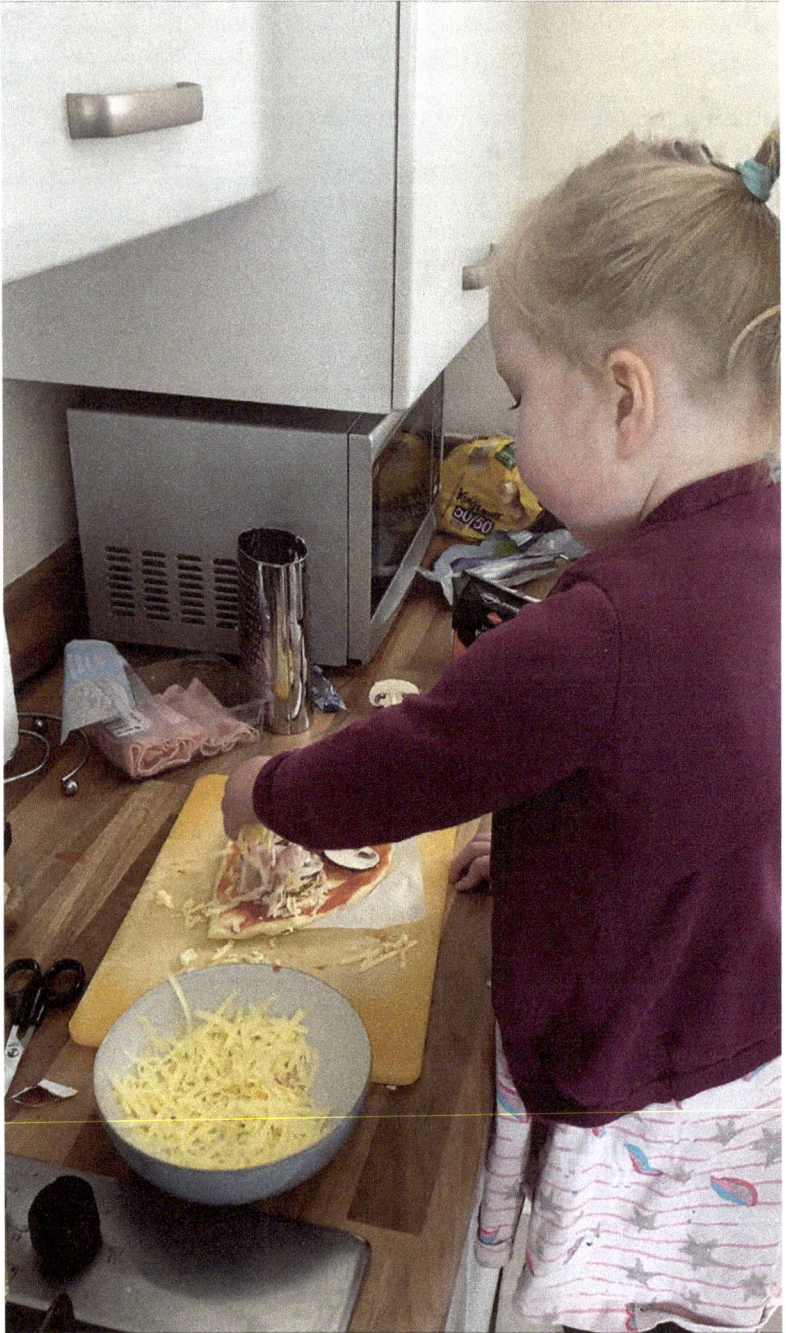

Figure 10.2 Pizza making at home

I could see the connectivity between the content of Elsa's engagement in play at home and at school (Athey, 2007: 55). I wondered how these experiences were nourishing her 'forms of thought' (2007: 55) and helping her to gain confidence in her communication with peers and adults at school.

Extract 1 from Zoë's schema narrative

This schema narrative describes Ewan's schematic interests, associated emotions and learning. Ewan is a little boy I taught in my Reception class for one year, 2020–2021. He was 4 years, 10 months old at the beginning of this time.

Ewan and his sisters live with their mum and dad on a smallholding in the local area. They have a livery and keep animals: chickens, one cat, two dogs, 2 sheep and several ponies. Ewan's parents used to grow crops such as wheat, barley, beans and potatoes. Ewan is a happy, adventurous child with a very loving nature. He is kind to other children and every day requests a hug from his teacher. Ewan's two sisters attend the same school. The oldest was, during this time, in Year 5 and his other sister was in Year 2.

Ewan's trajectory schema was so strong from the very beginning of his time in Reception. In conversation with his Mum I learned that Ewan's father had been particular about producing perfect straight lines when tending the fields and that Ewan was able, as young as two-years old, to project himself in a long, straight line whilst riding his self-propelled quad bike and, a year later, on his electric quad. She showed me a video of Ewan following behind his father who was driving a larger piece of machinery, both moving in a long, straight line.

Ewan had stayed at home with his family during the 2nd national COVID19 lockdown (HHCP, 2020). It had become apparent that Ewan did not enjoy completing any home learning tasks which required him to sit and work at a table. To help him engage in school learning, I attempted to reflect on his interest in trajectory schema. As I had observed Ewan building and playing with train tracks in school, I asked if he had a track at home. Luckily, he did, so I asked that a family member segment a consonant-vowel-consonant word, such as s-i-t, by writing each letter on a separate small piece of paper, lie these along the track at intervals, support Ewan to move a train past each sound, saying them as he went, then return to the start, then speed up the train as it passes them and blend the sounds together into the whole word. Ewan's Mum and oldest sister supported him with this activity at home and the train track proved a success. His Mum uploaded a video to Ewan's home learning profile showing him moving a train around a circular track alongside which lay pieces of paper sporting various numbers and letters: the family had taken my original idea and adapted it further! Ewan said these numbers and sounds as he pushed a toy train past them, given time by his family members to reach the correct answer as required. When he reached the last symbol, his older sister exclaimed, 'Congratulations! You have completed level one!' It was delightful that, 1) the activity had been engaging for Ewan, that he had really thought hard about what he was reading and succeeded in his task and, 2) other members of his family had gathered together to support him in this venture.

For both Zoë and Antonio, the relationships they develop with the children's parents and carers are a priority. They have a belief that these relationships can only benefit the child. I noted that they do not judge; they are respectful and listen and learn from the children's families.

What is our pedagogical stance?

I can still recall the excitement of the publication of Chris Athey's book, *Extending Thought in Young Children*, in 1990. As an educator who dared to return to primary education as a headteacher in 2008, I continued to struggle with advocating constructivist pedagogy (Athey, 2007: 44) within an educational setting that was evidently strongly behaviourist (Skinner, 1976: 21). I do understand the educators' plight from first-hand experience. I have taught classes of 30 children as the lone adult, and I have certainly used reward systems to establish some sense of order. However, through my doctoral studies (Parker, 2019), I learnt that by far, what worked best of all, was to create safe spaces for children to think deeply about what they wanted in school. Children need to be agents of their own learning and have the confidence to be advocates for themselves and others. I believe primary school–aged children have a strong sense of social justice and are more than willing to create learning community contracts which provide everyone with the safe boundaries needed to work and learn collaboratively (2019). I have observed in primary schools a combination of behaviourist (Skinner, 1976), constructivist (Lawrence et al., 2016) and didactic approaches (Roberts-Holmes, 2015: 76) to teaching and learning. As a teacher educator, I have observed trainee teachers become more confident with their practice, underpinned by strong values and beliefs as they move away from behaviourist approaches, such as reward systems and emerge as constructivists with and alongside the children. The focus becomes the children and their learning within development (Dewsbery, 2020). Children show greater interest in their learning and deeper levels of involvement (Laevers, 1997). This brings me to where Antonio, Zoe and I considered pedagogy and our line of inquiry, 'What is our pedagogical stance?'

In this third extract from Antonio's schema narrative, Antonio thinks deeply about Jude's actions. Antonio recognises that he had made assumptions and that it was better to think of lines of inquiry, talk to his colleagues and seek ways to support Jude so that he could experience success. Antonio could have taken a behaviourist approach and sought ways to change Jude's behaviour, a reluctance to speak, through rewards, but Antonio sought a constructivist approach, taking his cues from the child (Manning and Sharp, 1977: 17).

Extract 4 from Antonio's schema narrative

Jude had shown a lack of confidence in the first few days after his arrival in September and I had made the assumption that he was not able to communicate verbally. As a class team we noticed that Jude appeared to avoid asking an adult when he needed help. In fact, it was first misunderstood as a lack of interest in an activity but after some reflection and debate it was discovered to be a lack of trust in people that he did not know very well. Now, I could understand why Jude was struggling in a mainstream setting where his behaviour was misunderstood, and his wellbeing was affected.

My way forward was to play verbal games with Jude where he could alter the sound of his voice to match his emotions. So, when he struggled to say something to me or his friends, he could say something using a different voice maybe using a different tone or accent. He started to trust the adults in class and he was able to speak very clearly, in fact he had a good vocabulary to express himself. Now that our relationship was more established Jude spoke to me and all the children in class with no hesitation. Jude found that he could utilise his cross voice purposefully, demonstrating to other children if he was unhappy with their actions.

What's on top of?

Jude liked to sit on tables. I thought the quick fix was to remove the tables from the class. Then I reflected and discussed with the focus group. What does Jude need? Why is he doing this? I noticed that he liked to put objects on top of each other, and he liked to view objects from the top. I asked Jude if he wanted to sit in an adult chair, he responded saying, 'Yes!' I then created opportunities for Jude to balance on wooden steps and climb on top of an A frame every day. Jude no longer had a need to sit on tables. I could apply this knowledge of Jude's 'on top of' preference in my curriculum planning. I taught Jude to count to 20 simply using the blocks stacking them, one on top of each other.

The transformation of yoghurt

At lunch times Jude would mix a yogurt that has two containers attached to each other one with the yogurt and one with the sauce. He mixed the yogurt and the sauce from one container to the other without eating the yogurt. He made a mess every day, whilst demonstrating his fascination in the transformation of materials. I thought, 'This is not the way we eat, however what is Jude trying to tell me?' I knew he liked containers, and

I observed on more than one occasion Jude transferring objects from one container to the other. I drew Jude's attention to the containers in class and at play time to satisfy his need and over time he stopped making a mess at lunch time. I could apply my knowledge of his preference to contain by curriculum planning for his needs. Again, teaching Jude to count to 20, I provided two containers, mirroring the yoghurt pot experience. One container had 20 objects and the other was empty. Jude was able to count transferring the objects from one container to the other.

The significance of the learning environment and continuity in processes and provision (Nutbrown, 2011) has come to the fore in our discussions. Reference to schema theory enables educators to ensure that the provision is navigating a child's preferred way of learning, enabling them to challenge themselves from an intrinsically motivated viewpoint. Both Antonio and Zoë demonstrate their drive to nourish each child's learning within development (Dewsbery, 2020) by ensuring school experiences are enriched through the educators' understanding of schema theory and thus developing a constructivist pedagogy (Athey, 2007: 43).

Constructivist pedagogy nourishes Ewan's trajectory schema in action

Zoë was fascinated by Ewan's evident interest in dynamic and symbolic trajectories from the beginning of the school year.

I first noticed Ewan's interest in trajectory schema when observing his best friend. They both loved to run and shout, with Ewan often giving a loud 'Aaaaarrgh!' during boisterous play. I wondered whether the forward energy of the shout was a form of trajectory in the same way that running clearly was. Ewan speaks sometimes with unclear diction and I speculated if his happy vocal outbursts were a direct, immediate audible expression of his emotions: sent flying out into the world. Considering the running and shouting, I then recalled that both boys loved to play with long sticks in the school's nature areas: long, wooden lines, perhaps representing 'reach' and adventure? The more I pondered the connection between these actions, and the longer I spent with Ewan, the more I noticed his interest in trajectory schema in action.

Extract 2 from Zoë's schema narrative

Rocket construction

From creating single lines linking plastic cubes, Ewan's next step was to begin making 'spaceships' from plastic interlocking bricks. Initially these took on an X form and, as the year progressed, the models became more sophisticated, developing into a 'grid' formation of horizontal and vertical pieces set at right-angles to each other. One day, Ewan approached me

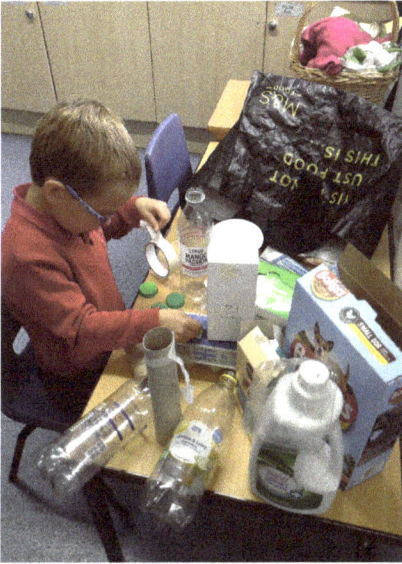

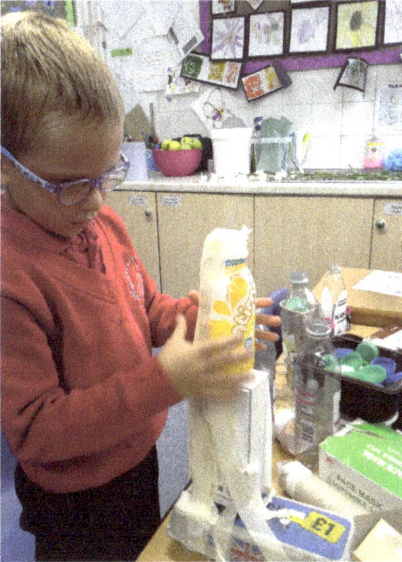

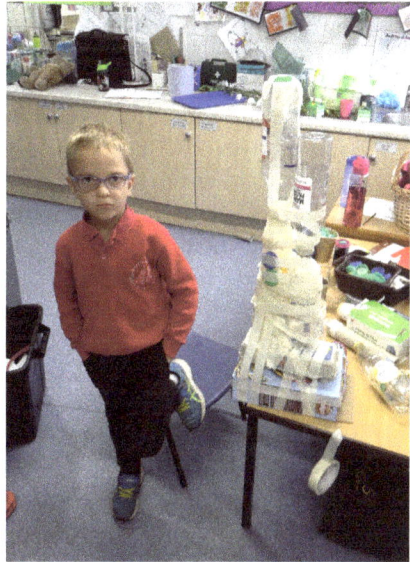

Figure 10.3 Rocket construction in progress: 28.6.21.

with one such craft and informed me that he had made it for a boy who was new to the class and who had not yet made any friends. Both boys were very happy in that moment. Over time, Ewan chose to make increasing numbers of spaceships for his friends, either from interlocking bricks or junk modelling.

Early one school morning in June, I noticed that Ewan was sitting alone at a table, surrounded by junk modelling items. I asked him what he was doing and he said he was making a rocket. Ewan had torn off a piece of masking tape which had then become tangled and he was trying to get it to attach two boxes together (Figure 10.3A).

I asked Ewan if I could help him and he said 'Yes'. I tore off a long strip of masking tape, attached it to the top box and showed him how I smoothed it down so it stuck to both boxes, saying to him, 'You've got to smooth it down. Smooooth it down' – running my hand down the length of the tape as I did so. This was deliberate. I hoped that by moving my hand along the length of the structure, Ewan, with his understanding of lines and long structures would quickly grasp what I was showing him (Arnold, 2018). And he did!

We continued to build the rocket together: I would ask Ewan which piece he wanted to attach next and where he wanted it to go. I tore off pieces of tape, he held the top of the tape in position or I stuck a small bit of it down so it was attached to the structure, then he ran his hand down the tape, repeating, 'Smooooth it down. Smooooth'. We then progressed to me handing him lengths of tape and him completing the sticking process independently. When he had attached several pieces together, Ewan looked up at the overall structure, smiled and clapped his hands (Figure 10.3B). Over time Ewan became more independent in using the masking tape successfully (Figure 10.3C).

Ewan and I were making the rocket whilst his best friend was completing a writing task at another table. Ewan informed me that the rocket was for this friend as a gift. When the friend finished his work, he approached the table and asked Ewan what he was making. Ewan told him that it was a rocket. The other boy walked to the drawers containing junk modelling materials and returned with a bag of plastic milk bottle tops. He took two out and told Ewan that they were 'the windows' of the rocket. He then left to play elsewhere in the classroom.

Later in the morning, when the class returned from a walk around the village, Ewan was keen to return to his rocket-building and asked me if I would help again. The plastic bottle tops were still on the table, unused. Ewan clearly remembered his friend's suggestion that they become windows, because immediately he returned to the rocket, he picked one up, held it to the side of the rocket and said to me, 'Want to stick it there'. I attached the bottle top, during which time he held another to a different spot on the rocket.

We continued to add further sections to the structure and at one point, when I was too hasty in my taping, Ewan told me, 'You forgot to smooth it down'. I was pleased that he used the word we had been employing earlier in the day – a word now associated for him with the skill of smoothing lengths of tape onto junk model sculptures in order to best allow the component parts to stick together.

Each time we completed adding a new segment, I asked Ewan, 'Do you want to add some more?' Eventually, when I asked this question, he shook his head. I wanted to make sure he had completed his task: 'Is that enough? Have you finished?' He nodded his head to indicate 'yes'. I was conscious of ensuring Ewan had sufficient time, the time he needed to create a sense of satisfaction at the completion of a self-initiated task (Figure 10.3D).

Ewan said, 'Me and my friend made it!' This intrigued me: although the other boy had had minimal involvement in creating the rocket and even though I had assisted him greatly in its creation, he saw his friend as being its co-constructor. He later went on to gift the rocket to this friend as he originally intended: its significance was now more than structural or imaginative: it was also social and relational.

Ewan has helped me to understand some of the potential for children's schemas to enable their understanding of the world. In his case, not just (as I originally imagined) in terms of comprehending shape, space and distance but also as a means to engage in shared activities in school and at home, to imaginatively create new things which can be given as gifts and to feel great pride in one's achievements. He has also helped me to understand the obligation for adults to support children's schematic experiences in an appropriately scaffolded manner. Had I taken over the construction of the rocket rather than taught Ewan the skill of smoothing, he may not have felt as proud of the completed piece nor have been able to maintain his sense of having made it with his friend.

Revisiting Zoë's schema narrative, I cannot help but be drawn to the emotional aspects that underpin Ewan's experiences during his first year at school (Arnold and the Pen Green Team, 2010). From my perspective, because of Zoë's keen interest in schema theory, she was able to recognise those significant emotional moments for Ewan; for example, when Ewan decides to gift his models to friends, some of whom he perceives to be feeling upset.

How can we hold onto a cluster of theories to inform practice with all children?

In spite of the turbulent sea of educational change currently experienced in schools, I remain heartened by the expectation that, within teacher education, there has to be an evidence-based approach, an understanding of learning, cognitive and relational theories (UCET, 2020). So, what does this mean for the position of schema theory within the primary school context? It is my hope that there will be space and time to consider its relevance but not as a lone theory to be upheld in isolation, but one of a 'cluster of theories' that inform educators about children, the child's communications with adults and peers and their patterns of actions and conceptual development and understanding.

Throughout our focus group conversations, Antonio was a keen advocate for unpicking the interconnectivity between learning theories. He maintained a powerful stance, stating that educators have to consider and engage in a 'cluster of theories' which he termed 'a pot of theories'. By articulating their connectivity, Antonio was able to assimilate and accommodate new theoretical knowledge and understanding. This, in turn, had impact on Antonio's practice and how he viewed each child in his class.

Extract 5 from Antonio's schema narrative

Starting my career at a Special School has opened my mind to so much more in terms of how to support children with special educational needs and disabilities in ways that are effective and meeting the needs of each individual. This year I attended a course called 'Intensive Interaction' (Hewitt, 2012) that on reflection I realised has a strong connection with schema theory because it uses the children's patterns of behaviour and communication to create a connection and dialogue with the children that are unable to use the school's communication systems of interaction. Hewitt explains that 'the greater component of a communication exchange is not speech, it is non-verbal by far'. (Hewitt, 2012: 5–6). He acknowledges that every person using this way to interact develops their observational skills, learning with practice, how to read 'the significance, the profundity and the complexity of non-verbal [language by observing] of faces, eyes and body language'. (Hewitt, 2012: 5–6).

After I had attended the course I decided to implement this technique with the children who have profound and multiple learning difficulties.

It was another busy afternoon when I noticed a child, who has profound and multiple learning difficulties, doing a sequence of movements with their hands. The child was tapping on the tray attached to their wheelchair and then making verbal sounds with exclamations like 'Oooooh! And Oooh!' It was as if they were surprising themselves with the sounds they produced on the tray. I decided after five minutes to implement 'intensive interaction'. I started to tap out the same sequence on the child's wheelchair and we took it in turns to tap. For the first five minutes the child led the interaction. Then I decided to change the sequence to see if the child was able to mirror my tapping. The child started to copy my sequence of tapping on the wheelchair tray. They continued to make similar exclamations as before using their voice. I decided to try out new noises, so I produced a dinosaur roar and immediately the child copied me. This was a great opportunity of connection between us and from that moment the dinosaur roar became our way of saying 'Hello!' to each other when we met.

The emphasis on learning as a process and not as a predicted outcome was an important focus of our debates. To be able to create time to look through a schema lens has meant we have been able to see the correlation between the child's independent play and their conceptual developmental journey. From this, we have been able to further enrich provision to nourish the child's engagement with schema and have seen that their learning within development is deepened further. The role of the practitioner is to support the child to make the connection between concrete experiences and explore further through co-construction, especially when it is evident that a child is representing an idea symbolically and then noting when the child makes the connection through abstract thought. Zoë has exemplified this viewpoint with her schema narrative, unpicking through a schema lens Ewan at play.

What next?

This chapter is about the value of dialogue between educators within the school sector in England and how time and space needs to be made for theoretical discourse as a reflection of practice with children. I believe Zoë, Antonio and I should continue to meet as a schema focus group to consider further how we might think more deeply about the children, what difference is being made when schema theory informs curriculum plans and see if we can widen the scope of the group to educators in Key Stage One, and possibly Key Stage Two (DfE, 2013). We need to continue to communicate what we are doing and find out within the organisations we work in, as well as further afield (Griffiths-Murru and Parker, 2021). We acknowledged that we need to substantiate our case for a constructivist pedagogy, including schema theory, as defined by early years theorists. Supporting children to be autonomous in their learning, including bringing their own ideas and initiatives into the school's learning space, gives children a chance to show that they are intrinsically motivated to learn (Rogers and Wyse, 2015). Opportunities to co-construct with peers and interested adults secures an educational environment that is inviting, stimulating and aspirational for students and educators alike.

There is a correlation between children's deep learning through their schema engagement and later academic achievement, but there needs to be more research to demonstrate this hypothesis. The dilemma of work-life balance for educators means that making long observations, or even a series of short observations, is not necessarily considered desirable (DfE, 2021). Therefore, it is important for those involved in teacher and early years practitioner education to support educators to be able to articulate their understanding and knowledge of children. I would suggest that having the vocabulary around schemas is a useful tool to accurately describe what is happening for each child, even if these insights are not always formally documented. Timely use of video and sharing with the child is a form of documentation but does not involve the educator spending hours creating a text to go alongside it.

Finally, from my experience as a teacher educator, it remains my considered view that all educators of children and young people need to acquire and develop keen observational skills. Learning to observe children has to be there in initial teacher and early years practitioner education. At this point in an educator's professional journey, these observations do need to be carefully recorded, including film and photography and always shared with parents and carers. Arnold's case studies provide an ideal methodology for this observational approach (Arnold, 2015a, 2021). Observations need to be analysed, applying relevant theories including the emotional and relational aspects of learning, play, and conceptual development. Observations need to be peer and tutor reviewed. How exciting, to be watching, thinking and sharing theoretical stances to attempt to understand a child. This is a privilege for adults, and the time needs to be allocated for the process to be both meaningful and a rich learning experience for all involved. Athey's words are as relevant today as they were when she wrote them in 1990 to be revisited in 2007, 'Professional advancement necessarily requires the development of a well-thought out peda-gogy. Pedagogy is for the teacher what medical knowledge is for the doctor' (2007: 27).

Reflections and questions

Through these processes of observation, consideration, dialogue, com-paring ideas and notes and co-construction, we conclude the following:

- Educators benefit when they have a focus group to go to, to reflect on their observations of children and the children's actions, ways of communication and developing relationships. They can think more deeply about their pedagogy aligned to their cluster of theories, including schema theory.
- Educators who understand the value of a respectful relationship with the children's parents and carers learn from families as well as share their knowledge and understanding of the children they are respon-sible for. The children become the primary beneficiaries of these relationships.
- Educators benefit from considering the emotional and relational aspects of teaching and learning in primary schools. Educators who believe in and value children's intrinsic motivation to learn within development, move away from behaviourist adult pedagogic strate-gies towards constructivist ways of thinking and learning.
- Ask yourself, 'What is my pedagogical stance? Where does it come from? Is my pedagogical stance underpinned by theory and what I experience with and understand about children?'

Recommended reading

Arnold, C. (2021) *Observing Gabby: Child Development and Learning, 0–7 Years.* Berkshire: Open University Press.

Athey, C. (2007) *Extending Thought in Young Children: A Parent-Teacher Partnership.* 2nd edn. London: Paul Chapman Publishing Ltd.

Concluding thoughts

Jan White and Cath Arnold

Firstly, we are overwhelmed by what this group of authors have provided. Our intention was to demonstrate 'uncertainty and not knowing and, like young children, to be comfortable with these states of mind and to enjoy them'. Within education today, there may be a tendency to try to 'pin things down' and to reach preset goals. We hope this book is an antidote to that way of thinking. We got together in the first place because we wanted to know more. It would be too easy to have some sort of fixed thinking about schemas; however, what we have tried to do, individually, and, as a group, is to learn from children, from each encounter with each child without imposing our ideas on them. We want to challenge each other respectfully. We hope readers enjoy the challenge.

Each chapter begins with how the author(s) came across schemas in the first place and each story is individual. Each chapter ends with 'Reflections and questions', opening things up for the reader to investigate or ponder.

The language used respects children and their emerging learning. In Chapter 1, Julie describes herself as 'not an expert' (on the brain) and she introduces some detailed information on the importance of movement. Her observations of a very young child show his 'persistence and determination'. Julie does a lot of 'pondering' on what is happening based on her close observations. In Chapter 2, Colette offers 'some thoughts' but is always tentative and attempts to 'wonder creatively' about the repeated actions of her grandson. She highlights the importance of reflecting *with* children on what is to come and what has happened. In Chapter 3, Amanda observes Lewis in school and takes on the enjoyable task of introducing schemas to educators for the first time. Amanda offers 'thoughts' on what might be happening. In Chapter 4, Emma takes up the interesting challenge of considering 'schemas and language'. Emma studies four children and thinks schemas may be an 'alternative form of communication for pre-verbal children'. Chapter 5 picks up on the link between 'schemas and metaphor'. Sue, as a therapist, and Cath, as an educator, offer different perspectives on observations of three young children. Again, their thoughts are tentative, and parents offer their reflections. Kate, in Chapter 6, is fascinated by boys' play and wants to know 'Why do they do that?' Her focus is on 'schemas and gender'. Her observations of the four boys include the thoughts of their four mothers. Kate is very aware that her knowledge is partial. Chapter 7 offers two perspectives on 'schemas and autism'. Tamsin presents observations of her three daughters, with insights gained as their mother

DOI: 10.4324/9781003224341-12

and an early years specialist. Sue offers reflections as a therapist. They helpfully include the 'role of the adult'. In Chapter 8, Jan asks 'Why do they do it?' and widens the remit to include an ecological perspective in trying to understand the link between schemas and landscape. She poses several questions, one being 'Do schemas invite the world to build the child?' Christina, in Chapter 9, is interested in 'the felt experiences of children' and uses slow-motion video to look very closely. She talks about 'allowing ourselves to learn from children in a way that touches us', drawing on Froebelian theory. Finally, in Chapter 10, Christine and two teacher colleagues consider the influence of schemas on children in school. They 'ponder' on their observations and consider the children's 'lines of inquiry' (a term frequently used by Menna Godfrey in our face to face discussions) and conclude that they want the children to be 'agents of their own learning'.

We all started with a question and ended up with more questions – just as children do (and which is exciting!) We were learning *from* children and also learning *in* the curious, open, uncertain and even intuitive ways of childhood, whilst also seeking to harness the rigour of a more 'scientific' approach: learning from how children learn.

Writing and compiling this book has caused us – and reading it might cause readers – to think further about what this powerful idea can help us do in attempting to really see children and how they go about making their world in collaboration with their environment and the others within it.

Finally, the last word goes to Chris Athey, who inspired all of us to seek more knowledge about schemas: 'early enrichment has a cumulative effect in that subsequent experiences are amplified by enriched minds' (1990: 205).

Figure 11.1

References

Abramov, I., Gordon, J., Feldman, O., and Chavarga, A. (2012) 'Sex & vision I: Spatio-temporal resolution', *Biology of Sex Differences* 3, p. 20. https://doi.org/10.1186/2042-6410-3-20

Alexander, C., Ishikawa, S. and Silverstein, M. (1977) *A Pattern Language: Towns, Buildings, Construction*. New York: Oxford University Press.

Appleton, J. (1975) *The Experience of Landscape*. New York: John Wiley & Sons.

Arnold, C. (1999) *Child Development and Learning 2–5 years: Georgia's Story*. London: Paul Chapman Publishing.

Arnold, C. (2003) *Observing Harry: Child Development and Learning 0-5*. Berkshire: Open University Press.

Arnold, C. (2005) Article in *Nursery World* about 'Chris Athey as a Pioneer'.

Arnold, C. (2007) *Young children's representations of emotions and attachment in their spontaneous patterns of behavior: An exploration of a researcher's understanding*. PhD study. Coventry University.

Arnold, C. (2013) 'Drawing our learning together from the case studies'. In Mairs, K. and the Pen Green Team (eds.), *Young Children Learning Through Schemas*. Oxon: Routledge.

Arnold, C. (2015a) *Doing Your Child Observation Case Study. A Step-By-Step Guide*. Berkshire, England: Open University Press.

Arnold, C. (2015b) 'Schemas: A way into a child's world', *Early Childhood Development and Care* 185(5), pp. 727–741.

Arnold, C. (2018) 'How action schemas are reflected in young children's emerging language', *Early Child Development and Care* 189(12), pp. 1–13.

Arnold, C. (2021) *Observing Gabby. Child Development and Learning, 0–7 Years*. Berkshire, England: Open University Press.

Arnold, C. and the Pen Green Team. (2010) *Understanding Schemas and Emotions in Early Childhood*. London: Sage.

Atherton, F. and Nutbrown, C. (2013) *Understanding Schemas and Young Children From Birth to Three*. London: Sage.

Atherton, F. and Nutbrown, C. (2016) 'Schematic pedagogy: supporting one child's learning at home and in a group', *International Journal of Early Years Education* 24(1), pp. 63–79.

Athey, C. (1990) *Extending Thought in Young Children: A Parent-teacher Partnership*. London: Paul Chapman Publishing.

Athey, C. (2007) *Extending Thought in Young Children: A Parent-teacher Partnership*. 2nd edn. London: Sage.

Athey, C. (2010) Personal correspondence.

Athey, C. (2013) 'Beginning with the theory about schemas'. In Mairs, K. and Arnold, C. (eds.), *Young Children Learning through Schemas*. London: Routledge.

Autism Research Institute (undated) *Diagnostic Checklist Form E2*. Available at: https://www.autism.org/diagnostics-checklist/ (Accessed on 11/09/2021).

Bandura, A. (2006) 'Toward a psychology of human agency', *Perspectives on Psychological Science* 1(2), pp. 164–180. Available at: http://www.jstor.org/stable/40212163 (Accessed on 20/20/2011).

Bauer, K. and Dettore, E. (1997) 'Superhero play: What's a teacher to do?', *Early Childhood Education Journal* 25(1), pp. 17–21.

Bayley, R. and Broadbent, L. (2013) 'Child-initiated learning and developing children's talk'. In Featherstone, S. (ed.), *Supporting Child-Initiated Learning: Like Bees, not Butterflies*. London: Bloomsbury Publishing.

Bion, W. (1962) *Learning from Experience*. London: Heinemann.

Blurton Jones, N. (1974) 'Categories of child-child interaction'. In Blurton Jones, N. (ed.), *Ethological Studies of Child Behaviour* (pp. 97–127). Cambridge: Cambridge University Press.

Bochner, S. and Jones, J. (2003) *Child Language Development: Learning to Talk*. 2nd edn. London: Whurr Publishers Ltd.

Boulton, M. and Smith, P. (1992) 'The social nature of play fighting and play chasing: Mechanisms and strategies underlying cooperation and compromise'. In Barkow, J., Cosmides, L. and Tooby, J. (eds.), *The Adapted Mind: Evolutionary Psychology and the Generation of Culture* (pp. 429–444). New York: Oxford University Press.

Bowlby, J. (1997) *Attachment and Loss Volume 1*. London: Pimlico.

Bowlby, J. (1998) *Attachment and Loss Volume 2*. London: Pimlico.

Boxall, M. and Lucas, S. (2010) *Nurture Groups in School: Principles and Practice*. 2nd edn. London: Sage Publications Ltd.

Brierley, J. and Nutbrown, C. (2017) *Understanding Schematic Learning at Two*. London: Bloomsbury.

Britannica Encyclopaedia. (2020) https://www.britannica.com/science/Newtons-laws-of-motion

Brock, A. and Rankin, C. (2008) *Communication, Language and Literacy from Birth to Five*. London: Sage.

Browne, N. (2004) *Gender Equity in the Early Years*. Maidenhead: Oxford University Press.

Bruce, T. (2005) *Early Childhood Education*. 3rd edn. London: Hodder Arnold.

Bruce, T. (2011) *Early Childhood Education*. 4th edn. London: Hodder Education.

Bruce, T. (2015) *Early Childhood Education*. 5th edn. Oxon: Hodder Education.

Bruner, J. (1966) 'On cognitive growth'. In Bruner, J., Oliver, R. and Greenfield, P. (eds.), *Studies in Cognitive Growth*. London: John Wiley & Sons.

Bryman, A. (2012) *Social Research Methods*. Oxford: Oxford University Press.

Campbell, R. (2010) Dear Zoo. London: Macmillan Children's Books.

Campbell, A., Shirley, L., Heywood, C. and Crook, C. (2000) ' "Infants" visual preference for sex-congruent babies, children, toys and activities: A longitudinal study', *British Journal of Developmental Psychology* 18, pp. 479–498.

Carofiglio, G. (2020) *A Festive Thought. Visual Metaphor in Children's Learning Processes*. Reggio Children. Available at: https://www.reggiochildren.it/en/exhibitions/un-pensiero-in-festa-le-metafore-visive-nei-processi-di-apprendimento-dei-bambini-en/ (Accesssed on 20/11/2020).

Carpenter, B., Happé, F. and Egerton, J. (2019) *Girls and Autism: Educational, Family and Personal Perspectives*. London: Routledge.

Carr, M., Smith, A. B., Duncan, J., Jones, C., Lee, W. and Marshall, K. (2010) *Learning in the Making: Disposition and Design in Early Education*. Rotterdam: Sense Publishers.

Cashin, A. and Barker, P. (2009) 'The triad of impairment in autism revisited', *Journal of Child and Adolescent Psychiatric Nursing* 22(4), pp. 189–193.

Cattanach, A. (1997) *Children's Stories in Play Therapy*. London: Jessica Kingsley Publishers.

Chomsky, N. (1986) *Knowledge of Language: It's Nature, Origin and Use*. New York: Praeger.

Claxton, G. (2015) *Intelligence in the Flesh: Why Your Mind Needs Your Body Much More Than It Thinks*. New Haven and London: Yale University Press.

Cole, M. and Cole, S. (2001) *The Development of Children*. 4th edn. New York: Worth Publishers.

Cottle, M. (2016) *Involving Children in Ethnographic Research Using Photographs: Reflecting on the Development of Participatory Visual Research Methods in an English Primary School*. London: SAGE. Available at: http://methods.sagepub.com.ergo.southwales.ac.uk/base/download/Case/children-ethnographic-photographs-participatory-visual-primary-school (Accessed 3/11/2020).

Cox, S. (2005) 'Intention and meaning in young children's drawings', *International Journal of Art and Design Education* 24(2), pp. 115–125.

Crowe, B. (1983) *Play is a Feeling*. London: Unwin Paperbacks.

Csikszentmihalyi, M. (1990) *Flow: The Psychology of Optimal Experience*. New York: Harper and Row.

Cupit, C. (1996) 'Superhero play and very human children', *Early Years* 16(2), pp. 22–25.

Daly, M., Byers, E. and Taylor, W. (2004) *Early Years Management in Practice*. Oxford: Heinemann.

Dannenmaier, M. (1998) *A Child's Garden: 60 Ideas to Make Any Garden Come Alive for Children*. Portland OR: Timber Press.

Davies, B. (2014) *Listening to Children: Being and Becoming*. London: Routledge, Taylor & Francis Group.

Deci, E. L. and Ryan, R. M. (2000) 'The "what" and "why" of goal pursuits: Human needs and the self-determination of behavior', *Psychological Inquiry* 11, pp. 227–268.

Deguara, J. and Nutbrown, C. (2018) 'Signs, symbols and schemas: Understanding meaning in a child's drawings', *International Journal of Early Years Education* 26(1), pp. 4–23. Taylor and Francis [Online]. Available at: https://www.tandfonline.com/action/showCitFormats?doi=10.1080%2F09669760.2017.1369398. DOI: 10.1080/09669760.2017.1369398

Dent, B. and the Spatial Reasoning Study Group (2015) *Spatial Reasoning in the Early Years: Principles, Assertions and Speculations*. Abingdon: Routledge.

Department for Children, Schools and Families (DCSF) (2008) *The Bercow Report: A Review of Services for Children and Young People (0-19) with Speech, Language and Communication Needs*. Available at: https://dera.ioe.ac.uk/8405/7/7771-dcsf-bercow_Redacted.pdf (Accessed on 31/12/2018).

Department for Education (DfE) (2013) *The National Curriculum in England. Key Stages 1 and 2 Framework Document*. Available at: https://assets.publishing.service.gov.uk/government/uploads/system/uploads/attachment_data/file/425601/PRIMARY_national_curriculum.pdf

Department for Education (DfE) (2018) *Improving the Home Learning Environment: A Behaviour Change Approach*. Available at: https://assets.publishing.service.gov.uk/government/uploads/system/uploads/attachment_data/file/756020/Improving_the_home_learning_environment.pdf (Accessed on 03/01/2019).

Department for Education (DfE) (2019) *ITT Core Content Framework*. Available online at: ITT_core_content_framework_

Department for Education (DfE) (2021) *Help for Early Years Providers: Reducing Paperwork*. Available at: https://help-for-early-years-providers.education.gov.uk/get-help-to-improve-your-practice/reducing-paperwork

Dewsbery, F. (2020) *How psychoanalytic observation could support early years practitioners to understand children's spontaneous play, and how this might contribute to learning within their development and support practitioners to reflect on their interactions with the children?* MA Dissertation, University of Essex.

Dixon, J. and Day, S. (2004) 'Secret places: "You're too big to come in here!"'. In Cooper, H. (ed.), *Exploring Time and Place Through Play* (pp. 92–108). London: David Fulton Publishers.

Donaldson, G. (2015) *Successful Futures*. Available at: https://dera.ioe.ac.uk/22165/2/150225-successful-futures-en_Redacted.pdf (Accessed 3/11/2020).

Duckett, R. and Drummond, M. J. (2014) *Learning to Learn in Nature*. Newcastle: Sightlines Initiative.

Duncombe, R. and Preedy, P. (2020) 'Physical development in the early years: Exploring its importance and the adequacy of current provision in the United Kingdom', *Education 3–13* 49(8), pp. 920–934. DOI: 10.1080/03004279.2020.1817963

Dweck, C. (1999) *Self-Theories: Their Role in Motivation, Personality, and Development*. Abingdon: Taylor and Francis Group.

Eagleman, D. (2021) *Livewired: The Inside Story of the Ever-changing Brain*. Edinburgh: Canongate Books.

Eaton, O. and Keats, J. (1982) 'Peer presence, stress, and sex differences in the motor activity levels of preschoolers', *Developmental Psychology* 18(4), pp. 534–540.

Education Endowment Foundation (EEF) (2021) *Cognitive Science Approaches in the Classroom: A Review of Evidence*. Available at: https://educationendowmentfoundation.org.uk/public/files/Publications/Cognitive_science_approaches_in_the_classroom_-_A_review_of_the_evidence.pdf (Accessed on 20/07/2021).

Elfer, P., Goldschmied, E. and Selleck, D. (2012) *Key Persons in the Early Years: Building Relationships for Quality Provision in Early Years Settings and Primary Schools*. 2nd edn. Oxon: Routledge.

Ephgrave, A. (2018) *Planning in the Moment with Young Children: A Practical Guide for Early Years Practitioners and Parents*. London: Routledge.

Fine, C. (2010) *Delusions of Gender: The Real Science Behind Sex Differences*. London: Icon Books.

Fisher, J. (2016) *Interacting or Interfering? Improving Interactions in the Early Years*. Maidenhead: Open University Press.

Fjortoft, I. (2004) 'Landscape as playscape: The effects of natural environments on children's play and motor development', *Children, Youth and Environments* 14(2), pp. 21–44.

Fletcher, C. (2014) 'Preface: A review of the Pen Green research paradigm'. In McKinnon, E. (ed.), *Using Evidence for Advocacy and Resistance in Early Years Services: Exploring the Pen Green Research Approach*. Oxon: Routledge.

Fletcher-Watson, S. and Happé, F. (2019) *Autism: A New Introduction to Psychological Theory and Current Debates*. London: Routledge.

Follett, M. (2017) *Creating Excellence in Primary School Playtimes*. London: Jessica Kingsley Publishers.

Freud, S. (1915) *General Psychological Theory*. New York: Collier Books.

Froebel, F. (2012). *The Education of Man*. Memphis: General book.

Fry, D. (2005) 'Rough-and-tumble social play in humans'. In Pellegrini, A. and Smith, P. (eds.), *The Nature of Play: Great Apes and Humans* (pp. 54–85). New York: The Guilford Press.

Garnett, M. and Attwood, A. (undated) *Australian Scale Questionnaire*. Available at: https://www.aspennj.org/pdf/information/articles/australian-scale-for-asperger-syndrome.pdf (Accessed on 11/09/2021).

Gascoyne, S. (2012) *Treasure Baskets and Beyond – Realizing the Potential of Sensory-rich Play*. Maidenhead: Open University Press.

Gascoyne, S. (2019) *Messy Play in the Early Years*. London: David Fulton.

Gascoyne, S. (2020) Information Sheet: A Parent's Guide to Providing a Sense of Safety & Structure. *Training handout*. Available at https://playtoz.co.uk/training/ (Accessed on 19/04/2022).

Gibbs, R. W. Jr. (Ed). (2008) *The Cambridge Handbook of Metaphor and Thought*. Cambridge: Cambridge University Press.

Gibson, J. J. (1986) *The Ecological Approach to Visual Perception*. Hove: Psychology Press.

Goddard Blythe, S. (2005) *The Well Balanced Child; Movement and Early Learning.* 2nd edn. Gloucestershire: Hawthorn Press.

Goldberg, S. and Lewis, M. (1969) 'Play behaviour in the year-old infant: Early sex differences', *Child Development* 40(1), pp. 21–31.

Goldschmied, E. (1987) *Infants at Work* (Video). London: National Children's Bureau.

Goldschmied, E. and Jackson, S. (2004) *People Under Three: Children in Daycare.* London: Psychology Press.

Goldstein, J. (1995) 'Aggressive toy play'. In Pellegrini, A. (ed.), *The Future of Play Theory: A Multidisciplinary Inquiry into the Contributions of Brian Sutton-Smith* (pp. 127–147). Albany: State of New York Press.

Goleman, D. (2004) *Emotional Intelligence & Working With Emotional Intelligence.* London: Bloomsbury.

Grant, I. (2008) *Growing Great Boys.* United Kingdom: Vermillion.

Gray, C. (2015) *The New Social Story Book, 15th anniversary edn.* Arlington, TX: Future Horizons Firm.

Greenland, P. (2000) *Hopping Home Backwards: Body Intelligence and Movement Play.* Leeds: Jabadao Publication.

Grenier, J. (2014). 'Understanding schemas and young children from birth to three and young children learning through schemas: Deepening the dialogue about learning in the home and in the nursery', *Early Years* 34(4), pp. 437–439.

Griffiths-Murru, A. and Parker, C. (2021) 'Investigating young children's learning through a schema lens: How can schema theory inform practice in an Early Years class in a special school?', *Impact: Journal of the Chartered College of Teaching* I(12, Summer), pp. 48–50.

Grimmer, T. (2017) *Observing and Developing Schematic Behaviour in Young Children: A Professional Guide for Supporting Children's Learning, Play and Development.* London: Jessica Kingsley Publishers.

Grimmer, T. (2020) *Calling all Superheroes: Supporting and Developing Superhero Play in the Early Years.* London: Routledge.

Grimmer, T. (2022) *Supporting Behaviour and Emotions: Enabling Children to Communicate Their Feelings Through Positive Behaviour.* London: Routledge.

Gross, J. (2013) *Time to Talk: Implementing Outstanding Practice in Speech, Language and Communication.* London: Routledge.

Haas, R., Watson, J., Buonasera, T., Southon, J., Chen, J. C., Noe, S., Smith, K., Llave, C. V., Eerkens, J., and Parker, G. (2020) 'Female hunters of the early Americas', *Science Advances* 6, eabd0310. https://doi.org/ 10.1126/sciadv.abd0310

Hannaford, C. (2005) *Smart Moves: Why Learning is Not All in Your Head.* 2nd edn. Utah: Great River Books.

Harding, S. (2005) 'Outdoor play and the pedagogic garden'. In Moyles, J. (ed.), *The Excellence of Play (2nd edn.)* (pp. 138–153). Maidenhead: Open University Press.

Hart, B. and Risley, T. (1995) *Meaningful Differences in the Everyday Experience of Young American Children.* Baltimore: Paul H. Brookes Publishing.

Hartley, L. (2005) *Seeking a Sense of Self.* Available at: www.lindahartley.co.uk/index_ files?page323.htm (Accessed on 24/03/2021).

Hayes, C. (2016) *Language, Literacy & Communication in the Early Years: A Critical Foundation.* Northwich: Critical Publishing.

Hayward, G. (1993) *Garden Paths: Inspiring Designs and Practical Projects.* Charlotte, Vermont: Camden House Publishing.

Heft, H. (1988) 'Affordances of children's environments: A functional approach to environmental description', *Children's Environments Quarterly* 5(3), pp. 29–37.

Helen Hamlyn Centre for Pedagogy (HHCP) (0–11 years) (2020) *The impact of COVID-19 on education and children's services*. Written evidence submitted by the Helen Hamlyn Centre for Pedagogy (0-11 years), Department of Learning and Leadership, UCL Institute of Education to the House of Commons Education Committee Inquiry.

Herrington, S. and Lesmeister, C. (2006) 'The design of landscapes at child-care centres: Seven Cs', *Landscape Research* 31(1), pp. 63–82.

Hewitt, D. (2012) *Intensive Interaction. Theoretical Perspectives*. London: SAGE Publications Ltd.

Hildebrand, G. (1999) *Origins of Architectural Pleasure*. Berkeley: University of California Press.

Holland, P. (2007) *We Don't Play with Guns Here: War, Weapon and Superhero Play in the Early Years*. Maidenhead: Oxford University Press.

Hollich, G., Hirsh-Pasek, K. and Golinkoff, R. M. (2003) 'What does it take to learn a word?', *Monographs of the Society for Research in Child Development* 65(3), pp. 1–16.

ICAN and Royal College of Speech and Language Therapists (RCSLT) (2018) *Bercow: Ten Years On: An Independent Review of Provision for Children and Young People with Speech, Language and Communication Needs in England*. Available at: https://www.bercow10yearson.com/wp-content/uploads/2018/03/337644-ICAN-Bercow-Report-WEB.pdf (Accessed on 31/12/2018).

Ingold, T. (2007) *Lines: A Brief History*. Abingdon: Routledge.

Ingold, T. (2011) *Being Alive: Essays on Movement, Knowledge and Description*. London: Routledge.

Ingold, T. (2015) *The Life of Lines*. Abingdon: Routledge.

Isaacs, S. (1930) *Intellectual Growth in Young Children*. London: Routledge and Kegan Paul.

Isaacs, S. (1933/1967) *Social Development in Young Children*. London: Routledge & Kegan Paul (first published 1933).

Isaacs, S. (1952) 'The nature and function of phantasy'. In Riviere, J. (Ed.), *Developments in Psychoanalysis*. London: Hogarth Press.

Jennings, S. (1990) *Dramatherapy with Families, Groups and Individuals*. London: Jessica Kingsley.

Johnson, E. J. (2015) 'Debunking the "language gap"', *Journal for Multicultural Education* 9(1), pp. 42–50.

Johnson, M. (2007) *The Meaning of the Body: Aesthetics of Human Understanding*. Chicago: University of Chicago Press.

Jung, C. G. (1946) *Psychology of the Unconscious*. London: Kegan Paul.

Kalff, D. (2003) *Sandplay – A Psychotherapeutic Approach to the Psyche*. Palm Desert: Temenos Press.

Kalliala, M. (2006) *Play Culture in a Changing World*. Maidenhead: Oxford University Press.

Keeler, R. (2008) *Natural Playscapes: Creating Outdoor Play Environments for the Soul*. Redmond: Exchange Press.

Kirkby, M. (1989) 'Nature as refuge in children's environments', *Children's Environments Quarterly* 6(1), pp. 7–12.

Laevers, F. (1997) *A Process-oriented Child Follow Up System for Young Children*. Leuven: Centre for Experiential Education.

Laevers, F. (2000) 'Forward to basics!' Deep-Level-Learning and the Experiential Approach,' *Early Years* 20(2), pp. 20–29.

Laevers, F. (2003) *Intensive Seminar on Experiential Education*. Ilminster, Devon.

Laevers, F. (2005) *Well-being and Involvement in Care Settings. A Process-oriented Self-evaluation Instrument*. Leuven: Kind & Gezin and Research Centre for Experiential Education.

Lakoff, G. and Johnson, M. (1981) *Metaphors We Live By*. London: The University of Chicago Press.

Landreth, G. L. (2002) *Play Therapy: The Art of the Relationship*. London: Routledge.

Lawrence, P., Gallagher, T. and the Pen Green Team (2016) 'Pedagogic strategies': A conceptual framework for effective parent and practitioner strategies when working with children under five', *Early Child Development and Care* 185(11–12), pp. 1978–1994. DOI: 10.1080/03004430.2015.1028390

Leal, B. (2005). 'Childhood between literature and philosophy. Readings of childhood in Manoel de Barros' poetry', *Childhood and Philosophy* 1(1).

Levin, D. and Carlsson-Paige, N. (2006) *The War Play Dilemma: What Every Parent and Teacher Needs to Know*. 2nd edn. New York: Teachers College Press.

Liebschner, J. (2001). *A Child's Work. Freedom and Play in Froebel's Educational Theory and Practice*. Cambridge: The Lutterworth Press.

Lilley, I. (1967). *Friedrich Froebel. A Selection from his Writings*. Cambridge: Cambridge University Press.

Lindsey, E. W. and Mize, J. (2001) 'Contextual differences in parent–child play: Implications for children's gender role development', *Sex Roles* 44, pp. 155–176. https://doi.org/10.1023/A:1010950919451

Maccoby, E. (2002) 'Gender and group process: A developmental perspective', *Current Directions in Psychological Science* 11(2), pp. 54–58.

Macleod-Brudenell, I. and Kay, J. (Eds.) (2008) *Advanced Early Years For Foundation Degrees & Levels 4/5*. Essex: Heinemann.

MacRae, C. and MacLure, M. (2021) 'Watching two-year-olds jump: Video method becomes "haptic"', *Ethnography and Education* 16(3), pp. 263–278. DOI: 10.1080/17457823.2021.1917439

Mairs, K. and the Pen Green Team. (2013) *Young Children Learning Through Schemas*. In Cath Arnold (ed.). London: Routledge.

Manning, K. and Sharp, A. (1977) *Structuring Play in the Early Years at School*. London: Ward Lock Educational Co. Ltd.

Manor-Binyamini, I. and Schreiber-Divon, M. (2019) 'Repetitive behaviors: Listening to the voice of people with high-functioning autism spectrum disorder', *Research in Autism Spectrum Disorder*, 64, pp. 23–30.

Martin, J. (2007) 'Children's attitudes toward superheroes as a potential indicator of their moral understanding', *Journal of Moral Education* 36(2), pp. 239–250.

Martin, C. and Fabes, R. (2001) 'The stability and consequences of young children's same-sex peer interactions', *Developmental Psychology* 37(3), pp. 431–446.

Massumi, B. (2002) *Parables for the Virtual: Movement, Affect, Sensation*. Durham: Duke University Press.

Massumi, B. (2017) *The Principle of Unrest. Activist Philosophy in the Expanded Field*. London: Open Humanities Press.

Mathieson, K. (2015) *Understanding Behaviour in the Early Years*. London: MA Education.

Matthews, J. (2003) *Drawing and Painting Children and Visual Representation*. 2nd edn. London: Paul Chapman.

Maude, P. (2001) *Physical Children, Active Teaching: Investigating Physical Literacy*. Maidenhead: Open University Press.

Maynard, T., Taylor, C., Waldron, S., Rhys, M., Smith, R., Power, S. and Clement, J. (2012) *Evaluating the Foundation Phase: Policy Logic Model and Programme Theory*. Cardiff: WISERD Cardiff University, Welsh Government. Social Research Number: 37/2012. Available at: http://wales.gov.uk/docs/caecd/research/130318-evaluating-foundationphase-policy-logic-model-programme-theory-en.pdf (Accessed 3/11/2020).

McBratney, S. and Jeram, A. (2007) *Guess How Much I Love You*. London: Walker Books.

McCormack, D. (2013) *Refrains for Moving Bodies: Experience and Experiment in Affective Spaces*. Durham: Duke University Press.

McMillan, M. (1919/1930) *The Nursery School*. London: Dent.

McNiff, J. and Whitehead, J. (2011) *All You Need to Know About Action Research*. 2nd edn. London: Sage.

Meade, A. and Cubey, P. (2008) *Thinking Children, Learning About Schemas*. Berkshire: Open University.

Mercer, N. (2004) 'Development through dialogue'. In Grainger, T. (ed.), *The Routledge Falmer Reader in Language and Literacy*. London: Routledge Falmer.

Merewether, J. (2018) 'New materialisms and children's outdoor environments: Murmurative diffractions', *Children's Geographies* 17(1), pp. 105–117.

Modell, A. H. (2009) 'Metaphor – the bridge between feelings and knowledge', *Psychoanalytic Inquiry* 29, pp. 6–11.

Money, D. and Thurman, S. (1994) 'Talkabout Communication', *Bulletin of the College of Speech and Language Therapists* 504, pp. 12–13.

Moore, R. C. (2018) *Childhood's Domain: Play and Place in Child Development*. Abingdon: Routledge.

Mukherji, P. and Albon, D. (2015) *Research Methods in Early Childhood: An Introductory Guide*. 2nd edn. London: Sage.

Murris, K. (2016). *The Posthuman Child: Educational Transformation Through Philosophy With Picturebooks*. New York: Routledge.

Music, G. (2011) *Nurturing Natures: Attachment and Children's Emotional, Sociocultural and Brain Development*. Hove: Psychology Press.

Nakamura, K. (2001) 'Gender and language in Japanese preschool children', *Research on Language and Social Interaction* 34(1), pp. 15–43.

National Autistic Society (2021) *What is Autism?* Available at: https://www.autism.org.uk/advice-and-guidance/what-is-autism (Accessed on 15/06/2021).

National Health Service (NHS) (2018) *Communication Pyramid*. Available at: http://www.cht.nhs.uk/services/clinical-services/childrens-therapy-services/childrens-speech-and-language-therapy/ (Accessed on 25/10/2018)

National Ocean Service (2020) *What is an Eddy?* Available at: https://oceanservice.noaa.gov/facts/eddy.html (Accessed on 17/11/2020).

Neisser, U. (1976) *Cognition and Reality Principles and Implications of Cognitive Psychology*. San Francisco: Freeman and Company.

Nutbrown, C. (1994) *Threads of Thinking: Young Children Learning and the Role of Education*. London: Paul Chapman Publishing.

Nutbrown, C. (2008) *Threads of Thinking: Young Children Learning and the Role of Early Education*. 3rd edn. London: Sage Publications.

Nutbrown, C. (2011) *Threads of Thinking: Schemas and Young Children's Learning*. 4th edn. London: Sage.

O'Connor, A. (2012) *Understanding Transitions in the Early Years: Supporting Change Through Attachment and Resilience*. Oxon: Routledge.

Olds, A. (1987) 'Designing settings for infants and toddlers'. In Weinstein, C. S. and Thomas, G. D. (eds.), *Spaces for Children: The Built Environment and Child Development* (pp. 117–138). New York: Plenum.

Olds, A. R. (2000) *Child Care Design Guide*. London: McGraw-Hill.

Olsson, L. (2009) *Movement and Experimentation in Young Children's Learning: Deleuze and Guattarri in Early Childhood Education*. London: Routledge.

Paley, V. (1986) *Boys & Girls: Superheroes in the Doll Corner*. Chicago & London: University of Chicago Press.

References 199

Paley, V. (1991) *Bad Guys Don't Have Birthdays: Fantasy Play at Four*. Chicago & London: University of Chicago Press.
Parker, C. (2019) 'We all have the potential to lead because we all have responsibilities'. In Whalley, M., John, K., Whitaker, P., Klavins, E., Parker, C. and Vaggers, J. (eds.), *Democratising Leadership in the Early Years: A Systemic Approach*. London: Routledge.
Payne, G. and Isaacs, L. (2008) *Human Motor Development: A Lifespan Approach*. 7th edn. New York: McGraw-Hill.
Pellegrini, A. (1995) 'Boys' rough-and-tumble play and social competence: Contemporaneous and longitudinal relations'. In Pellegrini, A. (ed.), *The Future of Play Theory: A Multidisciplinary Inquiry into the Contributions of Brian Sutton-Smith* (pp. 107–126). Albany: State of New York Press.
Pellegrini, A. and Gustafson, K. (2005) 'Boys' and girls' uses of objects for exploration, play and tools in early childhood'. In Pellegrini, A. and Smith, P. (eds.), *The Nature of Play: Great Apes and Humans* (pp. 113–135). New York: The Guilford Press.
Pellegrini, A. and Smith, P. (1998) 'Physical activity play: The nature and function of a neglected aspect of play', *Child Development* 69(3), pp. 577–598.
Pellis, S. and Pellis, V. (2017) *The Playful Brain: Venturing to the Limits of Neuroscience*. London: Oneworld Publications.
Piaget, J. (1936/1953) *Origins of Intelligence in the Child*. London: Routledge and Kegan Paul.
Piaget, J. (1951) *Play, Dreams and Imitation in Childhood*. London: William Heinemann.
Piaget, J. (1954) 'The child's conception of number', *Journal of Consulting Psychology* 18(1), p. 76.
Piaget, J. (1962) *Play, Dreams and Imitation in Childhood*. London: Routledge and Kegan Paul.
Piaget, J. (1969) *The Mechanisms of Perception*. London: Routledge and Kegan Paul.
Piaget, J. (2001) *The Psychology of Intelligence*. London: Routledge.
Piaget, J. and Inhelder, B. (1956) *The Child's Conception of Space*. London: Routledge & Kegan Paul.
Piaget, J. and Inhelder, B. (1969) (English Ed.) *The Psychology of the Child*. London: Routledge and Kegan Paul.
Piaget, J. and Inhelder, B. (1973) *Memory and Intelligence*. London: Routledge and Kegan Paul.
Reggio Exhibition. (2018) Visit to the exhibition.
Roberts-Holmes, G. (2015) 'High stakes assessment, teachers and children'. In Wyse, D., Davis, R., Jones, P. and Rogers, S. (eds.), *Exploring Education and Childhood: From Current Certainties to New Visions*. London: Routledge.
Robinson, S. (2011) *Nesting: Body, Dwelling, Mind*. Richmond: William Stout Publishers.
Rogers, S. and Wyse, D. (2015) 'Agency, pedagogy and the curriculum'. In Wyse, D., Davis, R., Jones, P. and Rogers, S. (eds.), *Exploring Education and Childhood: From Current Certainties to New Visions*. London: Routledge.
Ronnberg, A. and Martin, K. (2021) *The Book of Symbols – Reflections of Archetypal Symbols*. Cologne: Taschen.
Rosen, M. and Oxenbury, H. (1989) *We're Going on a Bear Hunt*. London: Walker Books Ltd.
Rubin, K., Fein, G. and Vandenberg, B. (1983) 'Play'. In Hetherington, E. (ed.), *Handbook of Child Psychology: Volume 4, Socialization, Personality and Social Development* (pp. 693–773). New York: Wiley.
Schema Toolkit (2020) Available at: https://hwb.gov.wales/search?query=schemas&strict=true&popupUri=%2FResource%2Fe0ef76fe-334f-45ae-a6c8-7aa630e64310
Schön, D. (1983) *The Reflective Practitioner*. London: Temple Smith.
Schwandt, T. (1998) 'Constructivist, interpretivist approaches to human inquiry'. In Denzin, N. and Lincoln, Y. (eds.), *The Landscape of Qualitative Research: Theories and Issue* (pp. 221–259). Thousand Oaks: SAGE.

Sense (The National Deafblind and Rubella Association) (2021) *Total Communication*. Available at: https://www.sense.org.uk/get-support/information-and-advice/communication/total-communication/?gclid=CjwKCAjw9aiIBhA1EiwAJ_GTSjFRcGKBW_AjY9y-7NbEaLknBi6z3lUDQyR1lCXj_ho-x7GjWIWinBoCRG4QAvD_BwE (Accessed on 04/08/2021).

Shaw, J. (2019) 'A psychoanalytic framework for interpreting young child observations that integrates emotional and cognitive development', *Early Childhood Development and Care*, 191(4), DOI: 1080/03004430.2019.1698560

Shaw, L. G. (1987) 'Designing playgrounds for able and disabled children'. In Weinstein, C. S. and Thomas, G. D. (eds.), *Spaces for Children: The Built Environment and Child Development* (pp. 187–213). New York: Plenum.

Sheets-Johnstone, M. (2011a). *The Primacy of Movement*. Philadelphia: John Benjamins.

Sheets-Johnstone, M. (2011b). 'Embodied minds or mindful bodies? A question of fundamental, inherently inter-related aspects of animation', *Subjectivity* 4(4), pp. 451–466.

Shore, S. (2018) *Leading Perspectives on Disability: A Q&A with Dr. Stephen Shore*. Available at: https://www.limeconnect.com/opportunities_news/detail/leading-perspectives-on-disability-a-qa-with-dr-stephen-shore (Accessed on 26/09/2021).

Siegel, D. (2017) *Dr Dan Siegel's Hand Model of the Brain*. Available at: https://www.youtube.com/watch?v=f-m2YcdMdFw (Accessed on 20/11/2020).

Signalong. Available at: https://signalong.org.uk/ (Accessed on 04/08/2021).

Siren Films (2010a) *Babies Outdoors*. DVD Newcastle: Siren Films.

Siren Films (2010b) *Toddlers Outdoors*. DVD Newcastle: Siren Films.

Skinner, B. F. (1976) *About Behaviorism*. New York: Vintage Books.

Smith, P. (2005) 'Social and pretend play in Children'. In Pellegrini, A. and Smith, P. (eds.), *The Nature of Play: Great Apes and Humans* (pp. 173–209). New York: The Guilford Press.

Smith, P. and Lewis, K. (1985) 'Rough-and-tumble play, fighting, and chasing in nursery school children', *Ethology and Sociobiology* 6(3), pp. 175–181.

Smith, P. and Pellegrini, A. (2005) Play in great apes and humans: Reflections on continuities and discontinuities. In Pellegrini, A. and Smith, P. (eds.), *The Nature of Play: Great Apes and Humans* (pp. 285–298). New York: The Guilford Press.

Sobel, D. (1998) *Mapmaking With Children: Sense of Place Education for the Elementary Years*. Portsmouth: Heinemann.

Sobel, D. (2002) *Children's Special Places: Exploring the Role of Forts, Dens and Bush Houses in Middle Childhood*. Detroit: Wayne State University Press.

Sobel, D. (2008) *Childhood and Nature: Design Principles for Educators*. Portland Maine: Stenhouse Publishers.

Stewart, N. (2011) *How Children Learn: The Characteristics of Effective Early Learning*. London: The British Association for Early Childhood Education.

Striniste, N. (2019) *Nature Play at Home: Creating Outdoor Spaces That Connect Children With the Natural World*. Portland: Timber Press.

Sutton-Smith, B., Gerstmyer, J. and Meckley, A. (1988) 'Playfighting as folkplay amongst preschool children', *Western Folklore* 4(3), pp. 161–176.

Tait, C. (2004) *Chuffedness*, EECERA Presentation, Malta.

Thibodeau, P. H., Hendricks, R. K. and Boroditsky, L. (In Press) 'How linguistic metaphor scaffolds reasoning', *Cognitive Science*. Available at: nmckenna.me/papers/metaphor-scaffolding.pdf.

Thomas, A. (2018) *Exploring the role of schemas within the Welsh Foundation Phase curriculum*. Unpublished PhD thesis. University of South Wales.

Thomas, A. (2020) 'Exploring schemas in the Welsh curriculum – *A coming to know* for educators and children', *Early Childhood Research* 19(1), pp. 98–112. Available at: https://doi.org/10.1177%2F1476718X20969750 (Accessed 12/04/2021).

Thomas, G. (2016) *How To Do Your Case study*. 2nd edn. London: Sage.

Thomas, A. and Lewis, A. (2016) *An Introduction to the Foundation Phase*. London: Bloomsbury.

Tomassello, M. (2009) 'The usage-based theory of language acquisition'. In Bavin, E. L. (ed.), *The Cambridge Handbook of Child Language*. Cambridge: Cambridge University Press.

Tovey, H. (2017). *Bringing the Froebel Approach to your Early Years Practice*. Routledge: Oxon.

Trevarthen, C. (2002) 'Learning in companionship', *Education in the North: The Journal of Scottish Education*, New Series Number 10 (Session 2002–2003), pp. 16–25.

Turner, M. (1996) *The Literary Mind: The Origins of Thought and Language*. Oxford: Oxford University Press.

Unicef (1989) *United Nations Convention on the Rights of the Child*. Available at: https://www.unicef.org.uk/what-we-do/un-convention-child-rights/ (Accessed on 15/06/2021).

Universities' Council for the Education of Teachers (UCET) (September 2020) *ITT core content framework exemplification resources*. Available at: https://www.ucet.ac.uk/12124/itt-core-content-framework-exemplification-resource-sept-2020

Vygotsky, L. S. (1978) *Mind in Society*. London: Harvard.

Vygotsky, L. (1986) *Thought and Language*. Cambridge, MA: The MIT Press.

Wall, K. (2010) *Autism and Early Years Practice*. London: Sage.

Watkins, C. (2006) 'When teachers reclaim learning', *FORUM* 148(2). DOI: 10.2304/forum.2006.48.2.121

Watson, M. and Peng, Y. (1992) 'The relation between toy gun play and children's aggressive behaviour', *Early Education & Development* 3(4), pp. 370–389.

Welsh Assembly Government (2008) *Learning and Teaching Pedagogy*. Cardiff: WAG.

Welsh Government (2015) *Revised Framework for Children's Learning in the Foundation Phase Aged 3–7 Years*. Cardiff: WG.

Welsh, Talia (2013). *The Child as Natural Phenomenologist: Primal and Primary Experience in Merleau-Ponty's Psychology*. Evanston, Illinois: Northwestern University Press.

Werner, H. (1948) *Comparative Psychology of Mental Development* (Revised Edition), New York: International University Press.

Whalley, M. (2001) *Involving Parents in Their Children's Learning*. London: Paul Chapman Publishing.

Whalley, M. and the Pen Green Team. (2017) *Involving Parents in their Children's Learning: A Knowledge-sharing Approach*. 3rd edn. London: Sage.

White, J. (2010) *Babies Outdoors Notes Accompanying the DVD*. Newcastle: Siren Films.

White, J. (2011) 'Capturing the difference: The special nature of the outdoors'. In White, J. (ed.), *Outdoor Provision in the Early Years* (pp. 45–56). London: Sage.

White, J. (2014) 'Ecological identity: Values, principles and practice'. In Duckett, R. and Drummond, M. J. (eds.), *Learning to Learn in Nature* (pp. 234–245). Newcastle: Sightlines Initiative.

White, J. (2015) *Every Child a Mover: A Practical Guide to Providing Young Children with the Physical Opportunities They Need*. London: Early Education.

White, J. and Woolley, H. (2014) 'What makes a good outdoor environment for young children?'. In Maynard, T. and Waters, J. (eds.), *Exploring Outdoor Play in the Early Years*. Maidenhead: Open University Press.

Whitehead, M. (2001) *Supporting Language and Literacy Development in the Early Years*. Buckingham: Open University Press.

Wilenski, D. and Wending, C. (2013) *Ways into Hinchingbrook Country Park*. Cambridge: Cambridge Curiosity and Imagination.

Wing, L. and Potter, D. (2002) 'The epidemiology of autistic spectrum disorders: Is the prevalence rising?', *Mental Retardation and Developmental Disabilities Research Reviews* 8, pp. 151–161.

Winnicott, D. W. (1965/2006) *The Family and Individual Development*. London: Routledge Classic.

Winnicott, D. W. (1971) *Playing and Reality*. London: Routledge.

Wood, D. (1993) 'Ground to stand on: Some notes on kid's dirt play', *Children's Environments* 10(1), pp. 3–18.

Wood, E. (2007) 'New directions in play: Consensus or collision?', *Education 3-13* 35(4), pp. 309–320.

Yuejuan, P. (2004) *Preliminary research on schemas of young children in China*. Conference on Schema at Pen Green Research Base, UK.

Index

For Product Safety Concerns and Information please contact our EU
representative GPSR@taylorandfrancis.com
Taylor & Francis Verlag GmbH, Kaufingerstraße 24, 80331 München, Germany

www.ingramcontent.com/pod-product-compliance
Lightning Source LLC
Chambersburg PA
CBHW050647280326
41932CB00015B/2809

9 7 8 1 0 3 2 1 2 3 9 6 7